The Next
Billion Users

PAYAL ARORA

The Next
Billion Users

Digital Life Beyond the West

 Harvard University Press

Cambridge, Massachusetts, and London, England   2019

Library of Congress Cataloging-in-Publication Data

Names: Arora, Payal, author.
Title: The next billion users : digital life beyond the West / Payal Arora.
Description: Cambridge, Massachusetts : Harvard University Press, 2019. | Includes bibliographical references and index.
Identifiers: LCCN 2018038724 | ISBN 9780674983786 (alk. paper)
Subjects: LCSH: Internet users—Developing countries. | Internet and the poor—Developing countries. | Internet—Social aspects—Developing countries. | Computer security—Developing countries.
Classification: LCC HM851 .A744 2019 | DDC 302.23/1—dc23
LC record available at https://lccn.loc.gov/2018038724

To René

Contents

The Next
Billion Users

Prologue

THREE BILLION PEOPLE, almost half the world's population, live on two dollars a day. Most are young, live outside the West, and have been acquiring and using mobile phones at a rapid pace over the last decade. In fact, there are just as many mobile phone subscriptions in Nigeria and South Africa as there are in the United States. In China, there are more cell phones than people. India has the most Facebook users; Brazil ranks third.[1]

Obviously, this has excited development agencies, which see in this digital network new opportunities to tackle poverty in these regions. Agencies have called upon Silicon Valley to produce applications that will offer or improve access to jobs, health care, education, and other public services for those three billion. Their work is driven by the assumption that the poor will budget scarce digital resources and limited time online for seeking this information rather than for entertainment. Their attitude is fueled by a deep-seated worldview of the poor as utility-driven beings.

Given the high stakes involved, it is worth asking what has led to this perception of the global poor, especially as this view goes against the vast evidence on internet users in general. Statistics on browsing patterns confirm that the sites most frequented online, whether in a suburb in Ohio or a favela in Brazil, are social networking sites, pornography sites, romance sites, and gaming sites.[2] People enjoy entertainment, romance, gaming, and sex, regardless of their economic status. Thus, it is no wonder that pleasure is at the forefront of digital life. Although this is a readily accepted fact of contemporary digital life in the West, many still cling to the belief that the global poor are inherently different from typical users. Poverty, many assume, is a compelling enough reason for the poor to choose work over play when they go online.

I have been examining computer and internet usage outside the West for almost two decades. The first development project I participated in was launched in a small rural town in the south of India. It was an ambitious project. The goal was to infuse this town with new digital technologies to help the poorer members of the community leapfrog their way out of poverty. We set up computer kiosks everywhere to provide internet access. We envisioned women seeking health information, farmers checking crop prices, and children teaching themselves English through these kiosks. We sent vans with computers to remote villages to build awareness of the potential of the internet. We hoped the villagers would become inspired to adopt these new technologies and would mobilize themselves toward a better future. We funded cybercafés for more tedious tasks, like downloading government forms and searching for jobs.

Months went by and rumors about the project filtered in. People really liked the computer kiosks, vans, and cybercafés, but not for the reasons we imagined. The kiosks had become gaming stations. Children were spending much of their time after school playing Pac-Man. The vans came to be known as "movie vans"; we showed free movies to draw villagers to the computers. Cybercafés became "friendship cafés." Many of the café owners swore by social networking sites like Orkut, the Facebook of the day, which kept their businesses alive. Many of the technology development projects I have worked with since have yielded similar results. Play dominates work, and leisure overtakes labor, defying the productivity goals set by the development organizations.

In the face of this evidence, I wondered why there is a pervasive belief that the global poor are more likely than the wealthy to use the internet for practical purposes. Why does the idea of poverty sitting side-by-side with leisure create such discomfort? Does play seem threatening when in the hands of the poor? This question has led me to examine how the global poor have been framed over decades, and who benefits from this kind of framing. I ask what constitutes play and how play relates to labor and productivity. I consider it essential to move away from assumptions and hype to root this discussion in evidence. We need a new narrative that authentically represents online behavior of the global poor, who are rapidly becoming a center of interest in the growing digital economy.

Some recent books have celebrated the empowerment provided by cheap mobile phones. This book instead reveals inherent tensions in global development and new forms of pathology seen through the lens of a powerful triumvirate—poverty, technology, and play. It embarks on intersecting the serious business of poverty and the sacred notion of technology with the supposed frivolousness of leisure time. Through this venture, I confront one of the notable fictions of the digital age—the idea that low-income people will always express preferences that wealthier people assume will improve their economic conditions.

Why should it even be a question, whether people who are poor should enjoy themselves? Why do some people begrudge others who are struggling when they seek an occasional indulgence?[3] Aren't we all entitled to moments of pleasure and joy? Does poverty have to be miserable? Is productivity a moral requirement of poverty? In the twenty years that I have spent studying the lives of impoverished people outside the West, I have found it common for many in the West to assume that the worldviews of rich and poor are as dissimilar as their lives. "People are products of their environments" is the general Western view. Surely, in conditions of scarcity, people will act in a desperate manner. Civility and dignity are luxuries. Humanity is an act of cultivation made available through wealth.

This attitude may be adjusted only through experience. When I was a teen growing up in Bangalore, India, construction sites surrounded my home. Every day on my way to school I would pass a mother and her teenage daughter who worked at the construction site. I decided to do something good. I gathered some old clothes from my closet, and the next time I passed by, I handed them the package. To my astonishment, they did not want the clothes. I was befuddled and angry at their ingratitude. Why would they reject aid? Their actions seemed irrational. It had not crossed my mind, seeing their state of adversity, that they could be too proud to accept the clothes.

Years later I confronted my assumptions again, this time in a village in the south of India. I was there in a professional capacity, and poverty was now my area of expertise. A health-care worker invited me to stay in his family's hut, where they fed me a meat-based meal that must have cost them a week's wage. The family of four insisted on giving me the hut to sleep in while they slept out in the field. Their hospitality and generosity astonished me.

New technology platforms provide an opportunity to discard clichés about the global poor outside the West. A boy in an Indian slum may choose to spend his hard-earned money on mobile credit to chat up a girl. A family in rural Ethiopia may decide to pay a hefty fee to a professional photographer for a top-notch Facebook profile photo. Paraguayan children living in poverty might watch pornography through government-gifted laptops and delete their homework to create space for their favorite music downloads. Amid privacy debates today, a vast, disenfranchised people may take to Facebook with gusto, sharing their lives online in spite of intense state, corporate, and interpersonal surveillance.

These are just a few of the numerous stories that contradict preconceived notions of digital lives beyond the West. Although the dominant narrative suggests that low-income people in developing countries are using the internet and mobile phones to search for jobs, check on their health, educate themselves, and conduct business, such use is barely a fraction of what people do when they go online. For the most part, the poor explore new technologies through games and entertainment and invest much of their energy and scarce income toward what makes them happy. Sometimes play teaches them to bend the rules for survival. Their entrepreneurship may come in the form of strategies to maximize their data bundles for love or may border on the illicit through the building of media piracy empires.

Clearly, this does not fit the picture of what development agencies believe the poor should do with the internet. Many of these agencies see technology as the answer to the intractable poverty plaguing the marginalized majority. How, such agencies ask, could they be frivolous with what could be a tool for their salvation? For postcolonial nations, it is their government's ticket to national respect on a global stage. When low-income citizens choose entertainment over education through these expensive digital resources, they are perceived as failing the state. When farmers choose to browse for porn on their mobiles instead of checking for information on crop prices, aid agencies are at a loss to justify further funding to mitigate the digital divide. Leisure sabotages the development agencies' grand plans for global social mobility.

This book explores such expectations of how the global poor should interact with technology, in tandem with the history of institutional and financial arrangements that have made this technology accessible. This history reveals the multitude of demands placed on the poor who play with these new tools. In spite of significant obstacles, the poor continue to play. By clarifying the actual behaviors, practices, and perceptions of those at the margins, I expose why and how fictions and falsehoods are perpetuated regarding the online behaviors of the global poor.

1

The Leisure Divide

THE NAMIBIAN VILLAGE of Onamafila is one of the hundreds of villages celebrated for their arrival into the information age. Mobile phones have become ubiquitous in this region. As early as 2012, Joël Kaapanda, then Minister of Information and Communication Technology, announced proudly at the Telecom Namibia summit that there were "more cellphones than people in Namibia."[1] With 2.35 million active customers, the market penetration rate for mobile phones had surpassed 110 percent. What is more, in 2016 a teenage boy from Namibia's Ohagwena Region invented a "SIM-less" mobile that does not require airtime to make calls.[2] Using spare parts from old televisions and phones lying around, Simon Petrus created a device that leveraged radio frequency to provide better internet speed for the region. Traditional media are paving the way for new media.

In the throes of such excitement, it is easy to forget that for decades—with visions driven by a potent mix of arrogance and idealism—governments, international agencies, and libertarians have viewed internet access as a great leveler. Making new technology ubiquitous would create a digital utopia, bringing those at the margins into an inclusive and global digital life, greatly reducing the widening chasm between the haves and the have-nots. New media platforms would alleviate social and economic inequality.

The mission appeared simple at first: Give every person access to a computer or cell phone and the internet, and the poor could make their way out of poverty. Numerous governmental and private-sector projects came to fruition to make this dream a reality. Many developing countries declared their state of "e-readiness"—the capacity and preparedness of their citizens to compete in this information economy.

It soon came to light, though, that providing everyone with internet service and devices with which to access the internet would be just a small part of reducing the digital divide. The real challenges lay in the messy realities of social life, such as the reality that many children who were given access to computers did not know how to read and write, and many girls who received a mobile phone were permitted to use it only for making emergency calls. This called for a two-tier approach, the first to invest in equitable access to bridge the "first digital divide" and the second to support diverse and meaningful usage to tackle the "second digital divide."[3]

There are still many obstacles to access and usage, but people worldwide have a drive to be connected. The struggle to achieve global digital access is worth the effort, though not for the reasons envisioned by governments and aid agencies. Namibia, for example, is a young democratic country that in 2015 celebrated its first twenty-five years as an independent nation.[4] Many would expect Namibian youth in low-income and rural regions to use their newfound connectivity to access social services and educational sites. However, my colleague Sadrag Shihomeka and I discovered that these young people instead use most of their scarce online minutes to listen to music, watch entertainment videos, and share jokes.[5] They use Facebook in the same way as most other users: they post about their private lives—what they ate, what they did that day, photos from wedding parties, and so on—and wait for the comments to come in. Leisure, we discovered, is playing an essential role in motivating these youngsters to use the internet. As this book will illustrate, these Namibian youth are not the exceptions in this.

To make sense of this trend, I propose a "third digital divide": differences in the access, intent, and use of digital leisure time as the dominant paradigm shaping global internet usage. The leisure economy needs a new description in terms of digital life today, especially among those at the margins in the Global South (Africa, Latin America, and much of Asia, including the Middle East). Framing tensions in terms of the leisure divide brings attention to how and why digital leisure manifests differently among low-income youth outside the West. Limitations in their internet access tends to limit the set of online sites that people at the margins can use for their leisure pursuits. The focus on leisure enables us to detach from claims that mitigating the digital divide leads to the lessening of poverty, a myth perpetuated by corporations in order to scale their new technologies across nations and markets. This third digital divide marked by leisure signals the popularization of the internet in daily life, including that of the global poor.

It is a centuries-old hypocrisy that leisure is the prerogative of the elites while labor is the fate of the masses.[6] Bringing to light the divide in access to digital leisure challenges the sacred tenet on which the global digital project has been built upon over decades—the belief that a good digital life for the poor would be based in work and inherently utilitarian. Underlying this belief is the expectation that the internet should be used by the disenfranchised for nonfrivolous purposes. When it becomes clear that leisure pursuits are what motivate people at the margins to embrace new media tools, will development agencies and grant organizations lose their own motivation to provide universal internet access in the Global South? In other words, how will the mission of the digital divide reconcile with the leisure divide?

Divides of All Kinds Flock Together

There is another side to the Onamafila story. Like the other villages in Namibia, it has an acute shortage of electricity. Mobile phone users can go days without being able to recharge their phones, and often someone must take the phones into town to recharge them. Going into town is itself quite a feat. It's a walk of about fifty kilometers to the nearest gravel or tarred road, and if they miss their bus, they are stuck at the station overnight. A few houses in the village have solar panels that can charge these phones, but the owners charge five Namibian dollars per charge. This is a hefty sum for these youth, for whom regular income may be scarce.

Simply connecting to the internet is also difficult there. Lleka, a twenty-four-year-old young man, explains that being able to connect is a matter of timing:

> During the day, the network is very weak . . . so you will find some people waiting until midnight to go and look for a specific point where they normally access the network. But this is better than during that time when there were no mobile phones in the village.[7]

Krista, also in her twenties, notes that finding the right timing and location to get the best connectivity carries some risk:

> Even if you have a mobile phone you can stay even for a week or two without using it as there is no network coverage . . . we sometimes get the network at one spot in the neighbor's field but that one you have to go there around 12h00 o'clock midnight . . . it is very risky as we have wild animals too here.[8]

Those whose phones are charged become village messengers, walking vast distances to communicate the news to others. Even listening to the radio depends on finding the right locations. Youth in this village have already figured out which trees to climb to get the best radio frequencies to catch the news or their favorite entertainment programs.

The villagers can listen to popular radio stations, such as NBC Oshiwambo and Omulunga, without needing credit or a connection to the internet because most of their phones, both smart and non-smart, come with built-in radio tuners—so the trick is simply to find a signal. Still, several of the youth in this rural region complain that they frequently miss their radio programs because they are broadcast at times when they need to take the animals to a water source. Downloading programs to listen to them later at leisure generally is not an option, as most of their mobiles do not have that much data capacity, making them in this sense as immobile as traditional mass media such as television and radio.

In the last few decades the drive to eliminate the digital divide by providing all people with access to the internet, computers, and mobile phones has highlighted numerous other divides, underlining the complexity of access and the nature of usage. In the case of the Namibian village, we cannot have an honest conversation about the digital divide without looking at the gaps between the rural and the urban, the young and the elderly, and those with high and low incomes.

Adding to these layers is the fact that, contrary to expectations, the old mass media, such as newspaper, radio, and television, have not been made redundant. These traditional tools have found their way into the world of digital media, challenging the neat categorization of old and new. Because newspapers are unavailable in many villages in Namibia's Ohagwena Region, mobile users circulate clips of newspaper articles on WhatsApp. Only 12 percent of the people in this region own a television, so those with this access often share entertaining and newsworthy videos from TV programs on Facebook. Traditional media have melded into new media in ways that defy the momentum to leave the past behind. Old technology seems to reinvent itself, offering new channels for expression and communication.

On the surface it seems that addressing the first divide, access, would pave the way for addressing the second, usage. However, access is never quite resolved because with every new technology the digital divide starts to widen again. In other words, inequality is in a state of constant flux. Take national bandwidth: A study of domestic bandwidths in 172 countries from 1986 to 2014 showed that bandwidth is closely linked to national income.[9] This reinforces the divide between developed nations and developing nations. Tracking the progress among nations across these years revealed that the bandwidth divide between low- and high-income countries did not begin to decrease until 2012.

There has been one major change in this power dynamic. In 2011 China replaced the United States as the new global leader in bandwidth concentration and distribution. But three countries (China, the United States, and Japan) still host 50 percent of the globally installed bandwidth potential, creating a significant power imbalance. Although 2G and 2.5G phones and now smart phones are becoming more accessible in the Global South, fixed-line broadband continues to dominate in many low-income regions. As users become more data hungry and consume more visual and video material than text, access to bandwidth undoubtedly affects the quality of digital life.

Regarding the second digital divide, the original goals for expanded access, which were economic, have been broadened. Success in bridging the digital divide is now also measured by criteria of gender empowerment, child autonomy in learning, and government transparency. New declarations have surfaced. The African Union designated 2010–2020 as the African Women's Decade and spotlighted the gender divide as one of the major obstacles to African women's progress.[10] This is a bold goal, given the strong patriarchal culture prevalent in many of Africa's societies, where it has been primarily men who have been able to access and use new technologies while women have been forced to the sidelines as spectators and peripheral consumers.

Preventing women from having a digital life is an extension of the long deprivation of access to public space that women have struggled with for centuries. Turning this around is tantamount to addressing discriminatory institutional and legal policies and cultural norms, which is no small challenge. It will take time to provide everyone with access to new technologies, but encouraging a shift in attitudes and social practices is an even more daunting task. The communications scholar Sreela Sarkar examined a group of Muslim women trained as "computer girls" at a cybercafé in a low-income neighborhood in New Delhi.[11] She found that even though the cybercafé empowered these young women with these new positions, their upgraded status was confined to their workspace. Outside of work these Muslim women must conform to their inherited status within India's rigid boundaries of caste and class, where people are trained to "know their place."

The gender divide can explain to some extent the persistent participation divide in low-income and conservative communities, where boys are more likely to produce online content and girls are more likely to consume content.[12] However, with equal time and training, this gender disparity disappears. In fact, given that women and girls in developing countries constitute the bulk of the world's poor, focusing on the gender divide can be the most effective way to eradicate the gap between the digital haves and have-nots.[13]

While social and economic factors play an important part in this persistent divide, a lack of interest also plays a role. Contrary to expectations, low-income individuals in developing countries were not flocking to computers and the internet to rescue themselves from poverty. In the early years they were largely indifferent to these technologies because they did not see their usefulness to their lives.[14] The ability to gain access to information on crop prices, health information, and such was not compelling motivation for them. But cell phones and social media have been critical game-changers. People do not need much convincing to use these tools. Everyone hungers to socialize and be entertained, and demand drives the momentum and spread of these new media.

International youth surveys on internet usage found that young people were more likely to use the internet for entertainment and social networking than for pedagogic activities. A South African student put it, "I enjoy it [the internet] not for learning as it is complicated and boring, but for socializing with friends, being updated with the latest sports news and viewing the latest pictures of items and video clips of them."[15] This is clearly problematic for agencies that have sold the mission of mitigating the digital divide as a way to help reduce the education divide. The international development researcher Kentaro Toyama proposes the "law of amplification" to comprehend this conundrum.[16] He argues that technology's primary effect is "to amplify human forces" and that even though the internet is a vast and unlimited learning resource, it amplifies youths' tendency to choose entertainment over education.

Leisure is, however, deeply gendered. Children from rural villages in India were studied to see how they used mobile phones when unsupervised.[17] It was found that the girls used mobile phones far less often than the boys did. When asked why, the girls explained that their brothers monopolized the mobile phone. Also, as girls, and unlike their brothers, they had to do housework and had far less uninterrupted leisure time to play games on the mobiles. In my own fieldwork in rural and urban India, it was a constant struggle to get a balance between the voices of boys and girls, because of the priority boys had when it came to using, and having the leisure time to use, the mobile for gaming, chatting, and listening to music. One can even argue that women's and girls' labor enables the leisure of the young males in the society.

Girls were also afraid of ruining their reputation by going into cybercafés, which were marked as male spaces, and they had to be far more wary of their posts on Facebook or their friending practices because their digital engagements represented, not themselves, but their family honor, female virtue, and national pride. A similar divide was found in remote aboriginal communities in Australia, where men reported spending much of their time online playing games and watching videos but women used the internet for task-driven purposes, efficiently shopping for domestic goods and managing household finances online, and searching for information to enhance their children's education.[18]

My colleague Sadrag Shihomeka spent seven months investigating how youth groups from the Ohangwena Regional Youth Forum in rural Namibia used mobile social media to participate in regional and local politics. He found a thriving forum where the youth and the political leaders, primarily males, used their leisure time, after working hours and during weekends, to post, comment, share videos, and check on likes on these platforms. Sometimes moderators had to remove pornographic videos shared on these political forums and block crude remarks that made these spaces more unsavory for young women.

This feeds into the general distrust of technologies that have been usurped by leisure, such as the television. A common cultural belief prevalent in this Namibian region is that television encourages immoral activities. Moses, a twenty-one-year-old unemployed young male, says there are "myths about TV as the main spread of all evils."[19] Pam, a young woman, expresses a distrust of mobile phones, especially unregistered phones, because they can be used for "corrupt" purposes such as gossip and planning crimes.[20]

That said, leisure continues to be a central motivating force behind low-income communities' adoption and use of digital media. Scholars studying internet usage in 2016 in Nanjing, an eastern province in China, compared usage by a low-income community on the urban fringes to that of a high-income group.[21] What they found was that, by far, the low-income individuals spent a majority of their time shopping online and hanging out on social networking sites. In contrast, the wealthier group with a higher education level directed more of their energy toward activities that helped them in their professional lives. A similar study of the Dutch population in 2014 found that people with low income used the internet largely for entertainment, whereas the more privileged were found to be more productive online.[22]

This is remarkable, as it turns the leisure economy on its head.[23] The idea that the global poor would use their limited resources for entertainment instead of productive tasks is not good news for development agencies and governments. This supposedly irrational choice defies the poverty alleviation agenda. Admittedly, this is no new revelation. As early as in 1899, the Norwegian-American economist Thorstein Veblen argued that social classes, contrary to expectations, did not behave rationally according to their status. For instance, he found that the working class disproportionately spent their scarce resources on luxury goods, or "conspicuous leisure," as they yearned for a higher status. Participating in the leisure economy designed for the upper class enhanced their reputation within their community. In my fieldwork in rural India, I often witnessed lavish weddings and festivals that were well beyond the family's means.

My proposition of the third digital divide, regarding leisure, can guide an understanding of the current dynamics shaping global digital life. As we have seen with the first and the second digital divides, they are not necessarily progressive. The second divide is not contingent on the resolution of the first divide. These divides emphasize what a society marks as the core values of connectivity: capacity to access, and the skills and opportunities to use new media. The third digital divide draws much-needed attention to motivation, driven by pleasure, sociality, and entertainment. This recognizes happiness as part of the equation of a good life, online and offline.

This proposition disrupts popular beliefs that the global poor move in a linear trajectory. The deeply gendered dimension of this divide reveals the globalization of young male practices and the systemic exclusion of the vast majority of disadvantaged females. The leisure divide is about understanding what the global poor want from their digital life and why it matters to them. It reminds us that fulfillment is not necessarily a matter of efficiency or economic benefit but can involve a more elusive, personal, and emotive drive.

As the Global South has increasingly gained access to leisure, a moral panic has arisen among governments and aid agencies. Considerable funds are being invested to help bring low-income persons into the global digital public sphere, but this is regarded as problematic when those living in poverty choose to use their internet access for entertainment instead of for education and economic advancement. Governmental and aid agencies then reform their mission as one of resocializing the poor so they can reap the benefits of the internet instead of wasting its potential by whiling away their time in frivolity. After all, the seriousness of poverty is yet to be tackled. Paternalism kicks in. Surely, the global poor do not know what is good for them. To understand why the desire for digital leisure is anathema to those who lead the digital divide mission, we need to confront the historic tensions between work and play in the struggle for social equality.

Work and Play

For centuries in the West there has been a double standard regarding leisure and class.[24] In the industrial era, leisure was a sign of culture in the upper class. "Man of leisure" and "woman of leisure" were titles most aspired to. However, for those less well off to have leisure was viewed as a source of trouble and inherently immoral. Mottoes such as the Puritans' "An idle mind is the devil's workshop" were hammered into the lower classes so they would accept a life of labor with little respite. The rich invoked religious gospels to convince manual workers that honest toil would pave them an easier pathway to heaven. While the rich deliberately cultivated leisure as part of their status, they simultaneously preached the dignity of labor for the masses.

It was an uphill battle for the lower classes to earn the right to a weekend or even access to the public park. The historian Roy Rosenzweig paints a vivid picture of the labor movement for an eight-hour workday.[25] Workers fought hard to earn the right to leisure. In 1889 hundreds of trade unionists took to the streets of Worcester, England, holding a banner that read "Eight Hours for Work, Eight Hours for Rest, Eight Hours for What We Will." It took numerous protest marches until this became a topic of discussion at a United States Senate committee, where one senator remarked in defense of laborers that "a workingman wants something besides food and clothes in this country... he wants recreation. Why should not a workingman have it as well as other people?"[26] This was a moving speech, but weekends off became law only when the industrialists realized that productivity increased when their workers enjoyed some leisure.

In the nineteenth century, in Bournville, England, Britain's Cadbury Brothers set up factory pleasure gardens as leisure spaces for their workers to use for their enjoyment and relaxation during breaks.[27] The National Cash Register Company in Dayton, Ohio, soon followed suit with its own corporate park for its laborers. These companies recognized that workers desired leisure, and that leisure enhanced their workers' competency and drive for work. Small promenades were built around the factories where the workers could take a stroll during breaks, or picnic and socialize.

For thousands of years leisure was defined in the West as the antithesis of work, or as the result of it. They were two sides of the same coin, but opposite forces. Aristotle remarked, "We labor in order to have leisure."[28] Leisure was positioned as a luxury, whereas work was seen as a necessity of everyday life. Today, in contrast, many societies have come to see leisure as being essential to human well-being.[29] Many younger people nowadays seek work in professions that provide them with personal satisfaction and pleasurable social lives. This is still a class issue, though, because these expectations tend to be applied to the well-off and not to those who are poor.

Technology was to play an important role in creating a balance between labor and leisure. It was meant to liberate its users from work. Instead, it freed them up for more labor. The sociologist Judy Wajcman argues that new technologies have had an adverse effect on leisure time, as people tend to be in a constant state of busyness with their mobile devices. In the developed world today, busyness is commonly conceptualized as a sign of high social status.[30] From the industrial era to the digital era, many have believed that people would labor less as they became wealthier. Yet the evidence points to the contrary.

White-collar workers can be trapped in a 24/7 world of labor if they are unable to switch off their digital devices. The "crackberry" generation—addicts hooked on their Blackberries—gave way to "sheeple" (people who behave like sheep), people who are addicted to their smartphones and for whom digital life means constantly refreshing pages to stay up to date.[31] In contrast, people who have fewer resources, who often have unsteady, badly paid, or no employment, seek ways to cope with their vast amount of free time—and mobile phones give them this, primarily by providing them with entertainment.

In developing nations there is a complex relationship between idleness and busyness. With unemployment rife in low-income communities, young males spend much of their day in cybercafés or on their cell phones.[32] With slow bandwidth, they learn to juggle multiple errands while waiting for a song to download. Sometimes busyness is a by-product of the institutional bureaucracies that engulf the lives of many in the Global South. Lines abound for government forms, ration cards, and licenses. "Killing time" becomes a large part of daily life, being neither purely productive nor leisure oriented. Facebook comes to the rescue as low-income youth pass their time checking status updates and liking new posts while waiting in line.

In many developing nations, wealthier individuals pay poorer individuals to stand in line for them. In India, technology entrepreneurs have capitalized on this national queueing malady through startups such as BookMyChotu and DoneThing, where one can hire another person to hold one's place in line for 90 to 150 rupees (US$1–2).[33] Idleness has become a commodity as well as an opportunity for leisure. In emerging economies, from Egypt to South Africa, sometimes one-quarter or even half of the youth lack steady employment.

In the Ohangwena Region in Namibia in 2017, the unemployment rate for village youth was an astounding 43 percent. World Bank surveys recently found that 262 million young people in developing countries—equivalent to four-fifths of the population of the United States—are economically inactive.[34] The work that is available to these youth is often repetitive, mundane, and unstimulating. Mobile phones and the internet have carved a space into these moments of idle laboring, complicating what constitutes labor and leisure.

Digital Labor for Another's Leisure

For the longest time, the leisure of the rich has been enabled by the labor of others. This old-style feudalism has gained a new life in the contemporary leisure economy. Ill-paid workers in factories of the Global South, including young children toiling in the factories of Bangladesh, produce toys for the children of the world's wealthy. What is less understood is the vast amount of digital labor involved in providing leisure services for the wealthy. Labor appears to morph into a blurring of work and play.

A current example is the rise of "gold farming"—the practice of selling in-game currency to players, based primarily in the West, for real money, usually through online intermediaries like eBay.[35] The sellers—the "gold farmers"—spend many hours playing online, acquiring these in-game currencies. The buyers who want to progress fast in the game are willing to pay substantial sums to take this shortcut. The sellers are usually low-income players from developing nations who get onto these platforms to earn their living by making these in-game trades. This became a burgeoning gray market in the world of gaming beginning in the 1990s.

Gamers in general condemn the practice of buying in-game currency as cheating. However, such cheating occupies a gray area in gaming. It is rationalized as an enabling tool for players who are stuck in the game, helping them move on instead of quitting when it gets hard. The relativity of this moral stance benefits the game industry and the players simultaneously.[36] While there is much room built in to humanize the player, there is a collective effort among gamers in the West to dehumanize the sellers. They are tagged with the derogatory label "gold farmers," implying that they are "gold diggers" of virtual value with little concern for the interests of the group. This often takes on a racialized aspect. Many players believe the gold farmers are Chinese who invade and violate the sanctity of the game space—unwanted virtual migrants plaguing the players' home turf. This has created a polarized gaming environment between the so-called authentic virtual property buyers who are from the West and the digital laborers who are considered to be Asian.

Morality has become the justification for racism toward these digital laborers. Much resentment toward gold farmers has built up among gamers in the West, reflected in racial online content. "Chinese gold farmers must die" and "Chinese farmer extermination" are just some titles of YouTube videos circulating on game trailers.[37] Jingles such as "Where did all the doggies and kitty cats go, since the gold farmers started to show, don't want to know what's in the egg roll," continue to circulate.[38] Appearing to be Asian can automatically get one typecast on a game as a gold farmer. In spite of the anonymity of gaming platforms, all it takes is an Asian-looking avatar or broken English to get this label.

However, gold farmers are far from rolling in gold coins, as commonly envisioned. Many are low-income youth in developing countries clocking in for twelve to fourteen hours at a stretch in game factories across Asia. They sleep in massive sweatshops, on mattresses next to their computers, and then get back online to continue their labor for other people's online leisure. They have to remain in character for hours on end, staring at the computer screen. In this multimillion-dollar industry of gold farming, few laborers get to enjoy the fruits of their own labor. While the products are digital and coded, the labor is very much embodied and visceral, and hardly different from factory work. Far from the blurring of labor and leisure, of work and play, to these people this is very much work and nothing else. There is no fun in this survival game.

In fact, it can be downright exploitative. In 2011 *Forbes* published a story of how Chinese prisoners were forced to work as gold farmers.[39] Online gaming was yielding more profits for the prison guards than the manual labor of the inmates. Of course, none of the profits went to these digital laborers. The *New York Times* reported on the arrest of people in South Korea who were accused of organizing a gold-farming operation for the North Korean regime.[40] This operation is estimated to have made US$6 million in just two years.

The dehumanization of low-income workers and the demonization of their labor in the world of play is enhanced by the blurring of the human and the robotic. It seems that automation could replace most forms of low-end human labor—the redundant, simple, and repetitive tasks performed by persons of the lowest and most uneducated ranks of society. Yet when we look closely at the digital economy, automating is far from easy.

Bots, for instance, are web robots in the form of automated scripts that perform repetitive actions on the internet. They are constantly at work synthesizing, compiling, sorting, and analyzing users' data. However, this artificial intelligence, while undoubtedly impressive, cannot easily compute culture in its rich diversity. Navigating through people's data from their day-to-day life requires not just technical but cultural competency, which is hard to code. In the world of gaming, this sometimes translates to gold farmers creating bots that can automate some parts of the game while the other parts are done manually.[41] However, these bots are in need of constant supervision. The digital laborers need to continuously monitor their computers and debug and update software programs, at times modifying them to fit to the evolving tasks. While players are well aware that bots are at play in the game, it is veritably impossible to differentiate a bot from the gold farmer.

Sometimes algorithms get the credit for the manual labor of these digital workers. For instance, keeping Facebook clean of "dick pics," beheadings, and other disturbing and offensive content requires a team of digital laborers going through this mountain of data for hours on end. Facebook's sanitation takes place outside the West—for instance, in small towns in the Philippines.[42] These laborers go through all kinds of disturbing content, from child pornography to gruesome Russian highway accidents, deleting them to create a family-friendly social networking site. These digital workers become inadvertently the moral police of users in the West, enabling a wholesome leisure activity of browsing on Facebook. This invisible labor deletes the signs of the dregs of society, portraying a much more palatable humanity for Facebook users. These laborers sign strict nondisclosure agreements, so they do not reveal the actual content that comes through to them on a daily basis. They soak up vast amounts of psychological horror so that Facebook users can keep their ideal vision of the internet as a space of leisure.

Clearly, digital laborers play a complex role in developing countries. They are vilified as gold farmers, ruining the democratic ethos in gaming where play is meant to be fair. They are blamed for rigging the game, favoring those who can afford to buy virtual currency over those who cannot. Today, as social inequality widens, games are even more valued as an escape mechanism where true justice can prevail. Regardless of race, sex, or class, anyone can succeed in the game world, ideally. However, the gold-farming economy fosters a game environment that is more like real life, favoring the wealthy over the underprivileged as the rich succeed with the help of purchased virtual goods. On the flip side, it is hard not to recognize that in developing countries, entrepreneurship carves out novel opportunities for a living based on the Western players' need to succeed at any cost. They build their capital on a mundane human vice—cheating. Even though cheating falls low on the moral curve for users in the West, the level of hatred toward these laborers who make it possible is disproportionately high. Such are the double standards held by players.

In recent years game developers have been cracking down on such practices. Companies like Blizzard and ArenaNet decided to combat such illicit trading by instituting real money transactions within the games. Mobile applications create strong walled gardens that do not easily allow third parties to infiltrate the games. As it becomes harder for gold farmers to produce and sell in-game virtual goods and services, more opportunities expand in the spam-blocking world, where digital laborers are needed more than ever to keep the internet "clean." They are the silent heroes and quiet vigilantes of the internet. Their labor keeps our leisure "pure." Yet they do not enjoy the media limelight as morally upright workers because they are rendered invisible by strict company contracts of social networking sites such as Facebook.

Perhaps the most hypocritical aspect here is that digital labor in developing countries is framed as criminal and immoral but digital labor in the West is framed as entrepreneurial and innovative. For instance, take the popular application Pokémon Go, a free location-based augmented-reality game developed by Niantic. The goal of the game is simple. Players use their mobile phones' GPS to locate, capture, and control virtual creatures called Pokémon, who become visible on the screen if they are situated in the same real-world location as the player. The intention is that players will walk around and hunt for these creatures, but a potential economy has emerged for those who want to skip the legwork. PokeWalk, a company based in Silicon Valley with US$4 million in backing, offers a new vision for players:

> Imagine a world where you had the flexibility to do what you wanted to do like watch tv, sit on a stationary bike, stand on a skateboard, and not have to move to collect Pokémon. We want the millions of Pokémon Go players to have the freedom to do what they want without the pressure of walking.[43]

This application clearly enables cheating, but the idea has aroused little moral condemnation or indignation compared to the wrath directed at gold-farming companies in developing countries. On the contrary, in the West, mobile applications by potential startups such as PokeWalk are largely viewed as pathways to innovation and digital entrepreneurship. Why, then, does the West tend to debase the digital labor of workers in the Global South? The essential issue seems to be that labor that supports the existing power structures of Western capitalism is acceptable to the West. Labor, such as gold farming, that creates parallel and contesting markets that threaten the current Western multinational structures tend to alarm Western capitalists. The language of morality is the contemporary weapon of choice against this disruption of the world order.

Like much of their digital labor, the leisure of the lower classes—and their hunger for romance, sex, and entertainment—can instill a moral panic in persons who are better off, including the government agencies and aid foundations that seek to reduce the digital divides. Never mind the fact that leisure is the key gateway to the internet for most of the world's youth who happen to be low-income and in the Global South. Never mind the fact that what constitutes a good life is hardly a matter of utilitarian and pragmatic ends. Although Maslow's hierarchy-of-needs theory from the 1940s, which states that the poor can focus on leisure only after they have met their basic needs, has been debunked, governments and some economists continue to be influenced by the assumption that the poor should do productive work instead of leisure.

While there is much talk about the blurring of digital labor and leisure, the lived realities of these laborers tell a story that is more black and white, of gaming as laborious and repetitive work within the sweatshops of virtual leisure. Inventive practice from below that does not feed into the current institutional structures of power is framed as immoral and deviant. Such deviance is thoroughly discouraged through technological crackdowns on digital labor and the criminalization of the poor. The privileged across the leisure divide do not necessarily experience more leisure as society morphs in complicated and diverse directions. A mix of status, opportunity, societal bias, and other factors influence the nature of digital leisure on both sides of the divide.

Bridging the Leisure Divide

Much has transpired since Joël Kaapanda, then Minister of Information and Communication Technology of Namibia, enthusiastically shared the news of his country's uptake of mobile phones in 2012. Namibia has found its place in the "Africa rising" discourse, where progress is equated with economic mobility, including the embrace of new technologies.[44] The Namibian mobile network operator Mobile Telecommunications Limited (MTC) plans to invest N$1.1 billion to expand its network capacity by 2020.[45] Given the abysmal state of the telecom infrastructure and bandwidth in the Namibian villages, it is promising to see that this grand plan includes a specific commitment to target these regions. More than 400 new cell towers will be erected in rural areas compared to 88 in urban areas. 3G will be rolled out in many of Namibia's rural regions, which have been stuck so far with the 2G network.

Telecom innovations in India offer a promising future for digital connectivity in the Global South, especially as they spread beyond Asia and into Africa. On September 5, 2016, upheaval struck the Indian telecom sector. Mukesh Ambani, India's richest man and the head of Reliance Industries, did the unthinkable. He launched Jio, a 4G-telecom plan that allows consumers for just US$2.20 a month to access as much internet as they want at a speed that had been available primarily to consumers in wealthy nations.[46] To sweeten the deal, consumers are allowed to access Bollywood songs and movies free for a limited time through their data plans. This was motivated by the "ABCD principle" dictating the online market in India—based on the fact that most Indian consumers use most of their data to access content on the Astrology, Bollywood, Cricket, and Devotion sites.[47] This launch shook the telecom sector to the core, compelling it to drop rates significantly and offer attractive data packages that are affordable even for people with very little income. This news promises a more even playing field between those with wealth and those without as they surf online, for work and play.

Facebook has joined this pursuit to bridge the first digital divide with its Free Basics initiative. Launched in 2013 in partnership with locally operated telecom companies, this mobile phone application enables people to access a limited set of sites, including Facebook, without incurring data charges. By the end of 2016, forty million people were using this service.[48] This initiative of framing digital connectivity as a human right has aroused considerable controversy, and some countries, including India, have banned it. The core criticism of this initiative is that it violates net neutrality by favoring certain sites to be accessed over others.

Global Voices, a citizens' media and activist group, has accused Facebook of false marketing because what its Free Basics application provides access to is not an open internet but instead a walled garden of limited services—including, of course, Facebook.[49] Users must pay to step outside these select sites. For instance, if a young man in a Namibian village clicks on an article on Facebook, a pop-up appears telling him to pay for it or sign up for a data plan. Given their limited resources, many low-income youth can access only peripheral areas of the internet and end up consuming headlines without delving deeper into the content. Global Voices sees this as a commercial trap to convert the global poor into new customers to increase Facebook's market share in these emerging economies, calling it an act of "digital colonialism."[50]

The political scientist Darrell West argues that Facebook's initiative has improved access for the vast disenfranchised and has stimulated competition in developing and innovating applications for the world's poor.[51] He cites Africa as an example of the success of Free Basics. There was a reported 114 percent increase in Facebook users in Africa after the launch of this application. He argues that the digital divide can be bridged only by fueling the demand for such services, which will instigate other companies to develop local content to serve this vast disenfranchised demographic.

This debate will continue, but we cannot ignore the deliberate choice of platforms to stimulate the bridging of the first digital divide. From Jio to Facebook, these initiatives have at least one thing in common: they promote leisure usage to motivate people to adopt these new technologies. This third digital divide, the leisure divide, is a turning point as usage becomes increasingly driven by the need to chat with strangers, to watch cat videos, or share feel-good stories online. Some are disturbed by this drive toward leisure usage. Ramesh Srinivasan, a scholar of media, shares his concern about amusement taking over the internet. He worries that the internet is devolving into a space that offers superficial content, sacrificing its true potential. The power of entertainment is so overwhelming that he questions if "this should really anchor what makes the Internet go around."[52]

Srinivasan's reservations are rooted in the history of technology, where the virtue of the machine lay in whether or not it advanced social equality.[53] In the Industrial Revolution, the machine was meant not just to uplift the downtrodden working class but also to strengthen the nation. In the early twentieth century, the virtue of technology was judged by its ability to advance productivity and efficiency.

The notion of the digital divide naturalized the link between technology and poverty. In the early 1990s, technology access came to mean more than just availability and affordability. It was the pathway to social mobility. Politicians and technology companies joined hands to create a new vision for poverty alleviation—one that weaponized the internet as a tool against hunger, violence, and unemployment. This brought "information poverty" to the forefront of the battle. Bridging the digital divide became synonymous with bridging social inequality.

The adoption of new technologies was intended to upgrade the human potential to face the new realities that came with the digital economy. In the United States, the Clinton administration spearheaded a digital divide project that channeled poverty funding toward new technology.[54] This allowed the US government to retract resources earmarked for welfare and appropriate them toward developing the digital skills of the working class. To be poor was to be deficient in the information required to escape poverty traps, and new technology offered a way out. This rhetoric was adopted readily by development agencies, which promoted internet access as a solution to poverty worldwide. Technology policy became poverty policy.

Over the decades, vast evidence on the causal relationship between connectivity and social inequality suggests that, far from reducing poverty, these new tools may in fact widen the divide.[55] Access without opportunity or ability can have a negative result. The wealthy are more likely to use these new tools to advance themselves and consolidate their position in the economic hierarchy, leaving the poor even further behind. The same holds true for nations. Advanced nations, with their more stable political and market institutions, are better able to leverage internet technologies. Less advanced nations do not share the same benefit, as they struggle to reduce poverty in spite of their commitment to spread technologies even to their most rural constituencies.

The fallacy that the digital gap could be eliminated gave rise to some delusions about ending poverty. Given the bottomless pit of technology consumption, the digital divide mission is a guarantee of endless consumerism of new media tools subsidized by the state. Here the user is not a citizen but a consumer, and the vision of digital innovation is limited to that which is market friendly. This is not entirely a bad thing. In economically advanced countries, consumers come with rights: the right to privacy, the right to safety, the right to choose, the right to be informed, the right to be heard. Their empowerment is strengthened as weaknesses in the digital realm are recognized and eliminated. However, many developing countries come with weak states, and weaker rights, with few consumer protection laws. This aggravates existing conditions of poverty, adding digital vulnerabilities to the mix.

Leisure clearly falls between the cracks. Technocrats have long been confounded by the boundlessness of leisure activities that have no obvious instrumental value to society. To assume that everyone will use their internet access with productive intent is to assume that human beings are geared to pursue a Western notion of social progress. These fabrications can do more harm than good when plans rest on utopian expectations. In the twenty-first century, these sentiments still prevail, except among the technology companies. Leisure is their friend—it attracts new consumers to their platforms. The internet is ruled by a few multinational technology conglomerates that are committed to studying the digital lives of people at the margins in order to expand their market base.

If governments and aid agencies continue to focus on the utilitarian aspects of the internet and neglect the rise of this third digital divide, they will be inadvertently handing over the internet to corporate market researchers. We are already seeing patterns of stratification among those who live in poverty, be it along the lines of gender or their peripheral usage of Free Basics instead of unlimited data plans. We are seeing new forms of leisure and labor manifest through the rise of phenomena like gold farming and digital busyness that require us to reflect upon digital life beyond the parameters of a company's bottom line. The construct of the "divide" serves to stratify digital leisure practice and recognize how unique forms of play are formulated within entrapped digital and social environments reproduced over time. For example, many low-income people share a number of constraints that are social, cultural, and infrastructural. These constraints can influence them to behave similarly online.

Leisure is something we do, and not what we have. Leisure is a complicated business. It is hard play. It is menial labor. It is play for survival. It defies any clear moralistic stance. Yet leisure has the potential to help cultivate humanity. To deprive anyone of leisure is to deprive them of the opportunity to experience the best that humanity has to offer. To ignore the fact that people at the margins entertain themselves online is equivalent to creating a fictional global audience. Nowadays many people would find it difficult to picture their lives without Facebook, Twitter, Google, and the numerous other applications that have become part of modern life for vast numbers of people. Few would argue that these digital resources are solely sources of good, yet many would vehemently defend a person's right to access these new media technologies.

The good life is not necessarily a high moral life. Therefore, let us look at the gap in digital leisure, not from an instrumental and moralistic stance, but in the direction of desire. In doing so, let us shelve the fairy tales of the digital divide project as we explore the digital realities of a complex and much overlooked global populace.

2

Deviant by Design

GETTING TO ALMORA, a rural town in the Himalayas, involves a long journey: an eight-hour overnight train from Delhi to Kathgodam station, then a mesmerizing, occasionally nauseating three-hour jeep ride up winding mountain roads. As you near the main square, you pass fruit and vegetable stalls, chai shops, billboards, and numerous cybercafés with signs promising competency in "English, Arabic, or Computers in 30 days only." For decades, subsistence agriculture and spiritual pilgrimages were the core economy in this Himalayan region. With the coming of broadband in 2008, cybercafés became the new hubs of enterprise.

In my eight-month stay in this remote town, I came to recognize the tremendous entrepreneurship that drove these cybercafés. Sensing an opportunity, many locals—retired army officers, restaurant owners, mobile phone dealers—launched small, one-room computer centers offering a spectrum of services. Positioned as multipurpose portals, the café owners helped pensioners fill out online forms, assisted students with Wikipedia for their homework, and helped local nongovernmental organizations design and print out their proposals using Photoshop.

The cybercafés' main revenue, though, came from Orkut, a social networking site. Thanks to that online site, the cybercafés transformed quickly into recreational hubs. Govind Bhisht, a café owner, expressed his gratitude for Orkut:

> Honestly, it's the students that keep this place going. It's changed so much. They sit all day doing these friendship sites like Orkut. Day in and day out . . . if it wasn't for Orkut, my computers would not be used much.[1]

Five years later, a number of things have changed. Facebook has overtaken Orkut as the young people's primary addiction, and cell phones have replaced cybercafés as the powerful portals of popular culture. But just as they did with the computers in the cybercafés, the young people use their cell phones for entertainment and pleasure, demonstrating again that they are not just productive but also passionate and emotive beings.

In these rural areas, where income may be scarce, the youth show great ingenuity in getting online and using social media sites. But little research has been done to reveal the details of their online activities. How do they construct their digital selves online? Do they hide their poverty or reveal it to bond with their newfound networks? What kinds of posts go viral? Westerners have tended to exoticize the internet use of persons in the Global South, so it will be useful to explore the details of their actual digital lives. Obstacles to their use of the internet can include high costs, poor digital infrastructure, and gender bias, but these do not deter these young people as they go about passionately participating in the online world of leisure.

Recreational Hubs for the Poor

In communities where income and resources are scarce, a risk culture is pervasive—not because residents of those communities are necessarily braver, more creative, or more entrepreneurial than other people, but because without available alternatives, people with scarce resources are compelled to invent opportunities. Survival economies become a way of life, and risk is an intrinsic part of such informal systems. But it should not be assumed that the needs driving the poor to take risks are mainly instrumental. In the last decade, field studies have found that risk taking in the Global South is driven more by aspiration than by utilitarianism. The internet is the poor person's leisure economy.

Take the mobile phone. There has been an exponential rise in the demand for cell phones among people with scarce resources, making mobiles one of their most prized assets. They do use their phones for utilitarian purposes, such as transferring money, texting with clients and business partners, and checking health information, but they mostly use them for leisure.[2] A majority of these users are young and curious, and access to the internet by way of cell phones gives them a powerful way to explore not only a wider world but also their own identity and self-expression.

Any young person yearning for perpetual connectivity to digital worlds would feel frustrated by limited data plans and nonsmart basic phones, and by the inadequate technological, infrastructural, and economic resources common to rural areas of the Global South. For persons living in areas of scarcity, such limitations can create a high incentive to come up with strategies to increase their internet access. For example, in Côte d'Ivoire there was a tremendous increase in cell phone usage starting the mid-1990s. But internet service for mobiles was slow, so there was a surge in illegal "mobile booths" that provided Wi-Fi that was faster and enabled users to surf, download, upload, text, and make new online friends without having to use their own, slow mobile service. These Wi-Fi booths not only provided better access than the slow mobile infrastructure, but they also obviously vastly outperformed the old-fashioned traditional public phone booths run by the only legal operator in that region, Télécom, which in spite of its resources and established networks could not compete with the scale and diversity of the illicit Wi-Fi market.[3]

In industrialized countries, the common model is usually a fixed monthly fee for a mobile package that allows calling and internet access. In all areas of the world, though, people for whom resources are scarce tend to use prepaid SIM cards. The sharing economy is essential in communities at the margins. In Rwanda, multiple family members and close friends often share a single handset, swapping out SIM cards. Limited funds also lead to creative communication strategies, such as "beeping"—where the caller hangs up before the recipient answers, thereby conveying, with the beep, a prearranged message without incurring calling costs.[4]

With the rise of cell phones, the cybercafés in the Himalayas, where we began this chapter, have had a reduced role as recreational hubs. Yet they still serve a purpose. For data-intensive activities like downloading music and movie files and gaming, computers are more capable than phones. And the computers give the young men access to Photoshop, which they use to combine images of themselves with images with popular film stars, such as Angelina Jolie and Bollywood star Aishwarya Rai, in romantic scenarios. They also love to portray themselves as action heroes, inserting their head shots into scenes from *The Matrix, Die Hard,* and the Bollywood blockbuster movie *Dhoom.* These young male cybercafé customers use these doctored photos to portray themselves as "cool" and "masculine" on social networking sites. Villages like Almora don't provide many places where the young can conduct romance, consume diverse media, and hang out with friends, so cybercafés also serve these purposes for their customers.

The Indian government has played a critical role in establishing rural cybercafés to reduce the digital divide and foster community development through these public access centers. It subsidized the setting up of "community information centers" in each of the 600,000 villages across the country. In the late 2000s the government of Brazil subsidized similar cybercafés known as "LAN houses," local area network venues. These became a common sight in low-income neighborhoods, making internet access cheaper and readily available to the public. Within a short period, LAN houses made internet access available to more than 60 percent of low-income Brazilian communities. With the burgeoning of LAN centers to number almost 90,000, this came to be known as the "LAN House Revolution."[5]

People did use these spaces to develop their computer skills, search for jobs, and print documents, but in Brazil, as in India, they primarily used them for leisure. LAN houses became synonymous with gaming centers, much to the chagrin of the government. According to Ronaldo Lemos, director of the Institute of Technology and Society in Rio de Janeiro, LAN houses are "places of intense sociability, and are occupying an important place in the life of the favelas."[6]

This kind of digital inclusion was not what the governments in India and Brazil had in mind. It is hard for the state to translate Orkuting and gaming into instruments for creating good citizens. The government's purpose in these efforts was to socialize people living in poor communities to be productive. To make matters worse, more than 85 percent of the Brazilian LAN houses are unlicensed. This is not unique to Brazil or India. In China, government cybercafés are highly regulated and expensive. This has led to a massive gray economy of private cafés that allow users to browse anonymously and cheaply. They capture more than 90 percent of this market, making them the norm in China.[7]

In recent years these internet cafés have sometimes come into the limelight in ways that have triggered some moral panic in the middle-class population. In Brazil, one customer used a LAN center to distribute pornographic pictures of children on the internet. His arrest caught the attention of the media, and LAN centers ended up being labeled as pedophile meeting points. Rafael Maurício da Costa, then director of the Brazilian Association of Digital Inclusion Centers, feared that the resultant stringent new regulations would lead to many of the LAN houses being shut down.

In China in 2004, the government's fear that the illicit internet cafés could breed antistate activity and consumption of pornography by underage users led to a national campaign against unlicensed centers that resulted in the closing of 70,000 internet cafés. In 2014 alone, the Chinese government invested 20 billion yuan (US$3.1 billion) in the crackdown.[8] The internet cafés that were allowed to remain open have a long list of regulations to abide by. Persons younger than eighteen are not allowed in. Supposedly to track deviancy, cafés must register their customers with their real names, which is a strong deterrent for users and seriously reduces business for the cafés. Mandatory tracking online and the use of licensed Microsoft software are other strategies deployed to tighten the reins on these telecenters.

The media continue to demonize these centers, highlighting episodes of café-associated murder or depravity. A few such episodes have led to the sweeping generalization that these hubs are depraved spaces. Wang Dapeng, city manager of the Wang Yu Wang Ka internet café chain, says that to survive, the industry needs to rebrand itself as a wholesome upper-market public space. Wang acknowledges that the internet can cause much harm, which he sees as being even more reason for places like his to serve as a space that is different—"happy and regulated."

> When the government first saw our presence, they felt a boost because we are different from others. Years ago "internet café" was a synonym for being full of minors, dirty, messy and with people smoking and drinking in them. We are doing our part to save the industry.[9]

Be it Brazil, India, or China, as the government starts to monitor these cybercafés and engulf them in regulations, many cafés are shifting their focus from a low-income to a more middle-class consumer base. This is ironic, given that the original purpose of these telecenters was to provide internet access to marginalized communities and reduce the alarming gap between the digital haves and have-nots. Hubs that continue to serve such users have little choice but to go deeper into the shadow economy to survive.

From the fact that these markets, from Côte d'Ivoire's mobile booths to Brazil's unlicensed LAN houses, do not have official status, it does not follow that the entrepreneurs and their low-income users are not moral. Instead, the crippling regulations speak more to the government's paternalism and low expectations for the online behavior of low-income internet users. Such regulations make it difficult for local businesses to offer services to a more inclusive public; instead they force the businesses to collaborate with the government to suppress enterprises the government deems threatening to the status quo.

Friending, Frolic, and Fantasy

Youth tend to arouse some moral anxiety in elders. Young people are more likely to challenge the status quo, question the system, and push back against the society's dominant rules of conduct. "Hooliganism" and "delinquency" are the usual labels given to the more visible episodes of this kind of discord. Low-income young males are often portrayed by the media as the biggest threat.[10] Their social affiliations—which in some areas include caste, tribal affiliation, or religion—can increase the anxiety some people feel about their behavior, and news stories often create unjust caricatures that sometimes become the basis of laws to contain such youngsters.

Technology continues to play a role in this mediated imagination. The news media have often claimed that for many young people, crime is inspired by violence viewed on television and in video games—and, today, on cell phones. In India, as cell phones become an essential and common tool for its vast numbers of low-income youth, the media began to run stories about the dangers lurking in this uncontrolled instrument. The Tamil press, for instance, ran sensational headlines such as "Cell Phone Revolution: Satan in Palm," "Tragedy Caused by Cell Phone: College Student Arrested for Killing Co-Student," and "Seller of Cell Phone Memory Cards with Obscene Pictures Arrested."[11]

Recent studies have emerged on how young people in developing countries use cell phones and computers, offering an alternative narrative. Far from being sensational, these stories are profoundly mundane. Their utterly commonplace observations indicate that a user's age—being a teenager or a young adult—is far more useful than poverty as a lens through which to view online behaviors. Take Facebook, the current obsession among most youth in low-income communities. As one young adult from a slum in Hyderabad, India, puts it, he "cannot live without Facebook."[12] He is hardly alone in his passion for this social media platform.

Friending is a big part of the lure. There is much excitement and interest in connecting with strangers. Contrary to usage patterns in the West, where young people rarely friend strangers due to issues of trust and privacy, in many marginalized communities strangers make up the bulk of online friends. Teens who have grown up in a slum surrounded by their family, relatives, and neighbors, in highly constrained settings, are attracted to befriending people from another city or, better yet, someone who is foreign, not only because it widens their horizons but because it can enhance their social status among their friends. One Indian male teen put it, "I will look for and friend certain names . . . like Jack or John for instance."[13] It is common and unsurprising to find that teens aspire to connect with their favorite film stars, sport personalities, bodybuilders, beautiful women, and rich tycoons in their society. If a celebrity like Bill Gates has a Facebook presence, rest assured these teens have already sent him a friend request.

To maximize data usage, Nimbuzz, a popular app, offers short-term and unlimited data plans. Through this app, users can chat on Facebook while staying within Nimbuzz. Youth can indulge themselves in perpetual contact through voice and chat messages. Nimbuzz's "favorites" feature is popular among the youth as it helps nurture new relationships with strangers and acquaintances, particularly people they might be interested in dating. Take Kulbeer, a sixteen-year-old Sikh boy living in an Indian slum.[14] His father is a truck driver and his mother is a servant in a wealthy household. Kulbeer discovered the mobile internet through a friend and since then has become addicted to it. He worked all summer at a pharmacy and with his savings chose one out of the twelve telecom plans offered by service providers in his slum. In the evenings, he meets up with friends and discusses new ways to customize their internet plans, phone features, and the best sites for movie and music downloads.

Kulbeer desperately wants to connect with girls—especially someone with a higher social status, because such cross-status connections are forbidden. He posts a sleeping ginger-colored puppy as his Facebook profile photo to attract girls. It is unusual for young men in slums to speak to girls openly. Another young man, Mohan, explains, "In the 10th and 12th [grades] I never used to talk to girls . . . even now I don't." However, Facebook has somewhat changed his romantic prospects.

On FB, one can talk freely without having any fear. That girl asks me "come on FB." She cannot ask me like that to come outside. . . . She also uses informal vocabulary. She may not talk outside at all . . . it is easier to talk with a girl on Facebook than in person. . . . Face to face, we cannot really talk anything.[15]

Romance is a strong incentive to build digital literacy. Sanjay, a male teen in a Delhi slum, gets some advice.[16] His friends tell him that Indian girls are fussy about adding boys as friends. However, there is a country called Brazil. Brazilians are friendly and the girls will more likely accept his request. Sanjay tries his hand, sending out requests. To his delight, a Brazilian girl accepts his friendship.

There is a small problem, though. She does not understand Hindi, Sanjay's native language, and he does not understand Portuguese. But "where there is a will, there is a way." He discovers Google Translate. Many teens who live at the margins dream that some of these strangers, even if in Brazil, will one day become friends in real life. Anecdotal stories circulate, fueling this dream. When I was doing fieldwork in India, the local newspaper ran a story of a local Indian artist meeting a Swedish nurse on the beach. The headline read "Local Boy Marries White Woman." Neither one knew the other's native language, but they formed a bond and eventually married. She went back to Sweden and arranged for papers to have him join her there.

Fantasy and social status often go hand in hand. In Viwandani, a slum in Nairobi, a young man by the name of Dida accumulated 500 friends on Facebook.[17] Most of the people on his Friends network are from outside the settlement he lives in; they include some researchers from the United States and a few people from nonprofit organizations and religious organizations. He shows off some photos of him and his foreign friends on Facebook. It is an interesting twist on how Dida is harnessing development workers for his benefit.

In rural Kenya, foreign networks can be a matter of survival. A foreigner can be an insurance policy against the hardships of life.[18] Rural youth eventually send requests to their foreign friends, asking for money, hoping that one of them will come through. Some rural communities also have vast diasporic networks abroad that extend their insurance against the unpredictability of their daily life. Facebook helps them to search for their distant relatives living abroad so they can connect and sustain a relationship with them and perhaps receive money or other forms of assistance.

Cultivating friends on Facebook is a lot of work. Tremendous effort goes into the building of profiles and crafting posts to appear cool, connected, and creative. Teens from industrial China to rural Kenya all share the common need to express their aspirations and build their identity online in ways that are meaningful and representative of their self and their culture.

The anthropologist Daniel Miller and his team spent fifteen months in nine communities in different parts of the world, from rural China to northern Chile, capturing some fascinating internet interactions. A dominant theme of the collective digital practice they observed was people's playful nature. Take the classic selfie, for instance. In the West, selfies might be regarded as narcissistic, but in northern Chile selfies are a social performance, a way people can visually display their social ties. Chilean teens have a unique genre called "footies"—photos of their feet taken in mundane moments, like when watching television or sitting on a balcony. Time off is time displayed. Leisure feeds teens' social status. Memes are also popular, and these often address social disadvantages with satire. For example, this meme about Adam and Eve in the Garden of Eden:

> Eve asks, "Adam, where do you think we are?" Adam responds, "We are in Chile, Eve. Don't you see that we are without clothing, without food, without a house, without education, and without hospitals? And they still tell us we're in paradise!"[19]

Publicly acknowledging their marginalization makes them feel more authentic and differentiates them from the elites in cities like Santiago.

Similarly, youth from "ghetto" neighborhoods in Buenos Aires did not shy away from their status online.[20] These adolescents came from Lugano, a low-income neighborhood in the South Zone of the city where many do not have access to clean running water or gas in their homes. Despite all their difficulties as they struggled to work and study, they passed their time in the evenings chatting on WhatsApp, watching videos on "Play," and discussing the latest gossip on Facebook.

They were well aware of the stigma that came from being "villero"— people from the ghettos—and yet they vehemently tied their identity to their neighborhood. Their nicknames on Facebook included a reference to their locality. For instance, teenagers from Lugano put an abbreviation of their neighborhood name, "Lgn," right after their first names, displaying where they came from and anchoring their identity openly for all to see. The teens claimed certain values that emanated from their neighborhood culture, including loyalty, perseverance, and resistance.[21] Far from shaming them, their poverty was a marker of their identity that reflected their resilience as people and as a community.

Self-branding and self-management online is a constant preoccupation. It is a vital driver for sharing memes, jokes, photos, and inspirational sayings. These form personalized repositories, carefully shaping the Facebook self. For many teens it is important to appear cosmopolitan, global, urban, and fun. In rural China, young women use special apps to add cartoon effects to their selfies such as stars, flowers, and even mustaches. They have entered the "cuteness" race. Males also are concerned about their appearance, especially their height, and might choose hairstyles that make them look taller.

In many of these low-income contexts, religion plays a strong part in the shaping of identity. Social media accentuates people's beliefs by enabling them to share spiritual sayings with their friends online. It is common for the youth in rural India to share photos of gods on their walls. Not all gods are equally popular. Of some thousand deities, Krishna and Ganesh are shared the most. Youth in a Nairobi slum often share Bible verses to keep everyone's spirits up.[22] In Saudi Arabia, some of the most popular Twitter accounts belong to Muslim preachers who have mastered the art of combining religion with entertainment for this young populace. Seventy-five percent of Saudis are under thirty years of age, and Saudi youth are obsessed with social media.[23] Pop music and rock concerts, cinema, and theaters were banned for many years in Saudi Arabia, so YouTube, Twitter, and Facebook become the prime hangouts for fun.

The running thread to build a profile, create social bonding, and have fun in these online spaces is the dominance of visual imagery. Videos and photos make up the bulk of what is shared. This is not just a visual economy but also a data economy. Given that visual material requires much more data than text does, it is a major investment for youth who have few resources at their disposal. It is costly for them to make a Facebook profile photo. Some will take a photo of themselves to a local computer professional who can use Photoshop to transform it and make them look worldly and well-to-do. Uploading photos costs both money and time, because available internet service is often slow. But for teens it is all worth the time and the cost.

Clearly, young people, regardless of their income or the region they live in, place high value on visual images. Visuals always attract more likes, the fuel for further social bonding. They are confidence builders, and they work particularly well for the vast number of semiliterate youth—enabling them to comfortably participate in this online world by sharing posts and expressing themselves in spite of their limited literacy. This is a key reason Facebook Zero, the text-only mobile version of Facebook that was launched for the global poor, struggled to gain traction in low-income communities.

It follows that teens value having a cell phone that has a camera. One study documented the many creative ways people use camera phones in rural South Africa.[24] Most of the cell phones available to people with scarce resources do not connect to the internet automatically. But camera phones create images without accessing the internet, and the imagery can be shared by passing the phone around. A popular feature is the video function used to record conversations with their friends, children singing and dancing, and images of their family and community events. Unlike in the West, where popular media production tends to be casual and haphazard, the people of rural South Africa take media production seriously. They dress up, they pose, and they need to look their best. With low amounts of data storage on their phones and a few backup devices like home computers, most of this material eventually has to be deleted. So it is a competition to get the perfect photo or video worth saving. Photographs of wives are of particular importance, as husbands in these low-income communities often have to travel far in search of work, carrying the photos with them. Voice recordings of live community music events at churches are also important, as people listen to them frequently for a morale boost. These gospel recordings inspire them and help them in their singing practice. The recordings also bring positive energy and serve as a reminder of good times.

Perpetual connectivity does not necessarily mean connecting to people. From rural India to Kenya and Brazil, one thing that people feel the need to be constantly connected to is music. The radio plays in the background throughout the day, as long as the phone's battery lasts—and this is another reason mobile phone providers were quick to notice the importance of providing phones with long-lasting batteries.

Through cute and crafted profile photos, humorous memes, selfies and footies, gospel voice recordings, and family videos, utilitarianism is moved to the backseat by the more emotional and sentimental drives that glue societies together. Pleasure and play are at the forefront of social interaction. These new technologies extend and enrich social capital. Foreign friend networks offer a promise of social mobility, even if only "virtual." A romance, one of the strongest motivations to adopt social media, can escape the prying eyes of the community when conducted online. Young people in conservative communities can discover the forbidden art of flirting when they go online. When incentives are strong, so is the passion to learn new ways to maximize these new tools. Google Translate, data sharing via memory cards and USB sticks, and using the Nimbuzz app and other access-enabling strategies go viral with young people, who have a voracious hunger to penetrate these new worlds.

Facebook plays a special role in the lives of young people who are living at the margins, most of whom have never traveled outside their own communities, Facebook gives them a universal passport to travel the web, and thereby the world. They can feel part of a global citizenry and a cosmopolitan public by friending pop stars like Justin Bieber and posting on their wall Photoshop images of themselves next to movie stars like Angelina Jolie. In fact, a 2016 BBC World Service poll on global citizenship revealed that outside the West, more people identified themselves as international citizens than as national citizens.[25] Interviews with more than 20,000 people in eighteen countries worldwide showed that as industrialized countries are reverting to more local and nationalist orientations, emerging economies are moving in the opposite direction. In countries such as Nigeria, China, Peru, and India, more than 70 percent of the population described themselves as global citizens, in contrast to Germany, where fewer than 30 percent described themselves in that way.[26]

However, this red carpet offered by Facebook is also a pathway to envy and frustrated aspirations. As people in these low-income communities manipulate their online profiles to create their perfect fictions, they inevitably create for themselves dreams that will go unfulfilled. Recent studies on the Facebook behavior of Western users reveal that spending too much time on this platform can lower users' self-esteem and decrease their life satisfaction.[27] Passively viewing Facebook pages can exacerbate loneliness. The jury is still out on whether the youth of low-income communities in the Global South, with their tight social bonds, will face the same fate as youth in the West as they struggle to cope with these "perfected" realities masterfully paraded on Facebook.

Clearly, people who live in areas with limited resources feel the full spectrum of human aspirations, desires, and fantasies—including, of course, sexuality—and these drive their quests for self-fulfillment. They are proud, passionate, emotional, and expressive beings. But the development agencies and grant organizations that fund projects to reduce the digital divides tend to present a tidied-up and "purified" portrayal of people of the Global South who are living with scarce resources, expunging from the narrative such "problematic" aspects as their sexuality. Development agencies traditionally moralize about, condemn, and problematize the intimacy and eroticism in the lives of the people whom the agencies' work is meant to benefit.

Media scholar Indira Maya Ganesh discusses the recurrent sidelining of sexuality by development agencies. She was involved in a mobile development project meant to empower farmers via text messages with information to support their agricultural practices. When it came time to analyze the usage of mobile data, the organization found that farmers used most of their data to surf for pornography.[28]

When agencies are seeking funding for future projects, it would be difficult for them to convince potential funders that the use of cell phones to access erotica is an effective pathway for social development. So, in their project reports, the aid agencies feel compelled to either suppress information about how users of the funded technology are actually using the technology or else reduce such data to anecdote, further mystifying and fictionalizing people who are poor as being asexual, virtuous subjects.

However, these "anecdotes" tell a fascinating story. A group of boys shared their strategy for accessing English-language pornography films—what they call "Blue Films"—despite constant surveillance from villagers and their family members. One of their tricks was to tamper with the television antennae during family time in the night. This cuts the reception for the family's favorite television program and gives the boys a good excuse to leave the house, saying they do not have the patience to wait around for the signal to come back. The boys can then gather to watch the film in the house of the boy who has private access to a videocassette recorder.

This strong motivation to pursue the consumption of sex content is deeply concerning for government agencies and aid foundations. They worry about teens' safety, protection, and potential addiction to these "deviant" acts. For these aid providers, welfare of the young people of the Global South translates into protecting them from themselves and such content. The erotic economy and the moral economy clash with each new entrepreneurial venture these young people create with the technology the agencies make available for them.

The demonization of adolescent sexuality is not completely without basis. All it takes is a few incidents to create some moral panic. Viral videos of teenagers having sex on multimedia messaging services make the headlines. The recurrent obscenities and sex solicitations on sites like Facebook and WhatsApp further this narrative. Captured sexual content used for blackmail can devastate the girls involved. The circulation of images in which local girls' faces have been photoshopped onto other women's naked bodies can ruin the girl's reputations and worse.

Even famous film actresses are not exempt from this online sexual tyranny. Jyothi Krishna, an actress from Kerala in the south of India, confronted this behavior. When she discovered that the internet was swarming with fake photos that were supposed to be her naked body, she appealed to her 1.5 million followers on Facebook to speak up against such online harassment, urging them to "bring culprits in front of the law."[29]

In a deeply suppressed culture like India's, sexuality has few outlets. In the state of Kerala, the situation is far worse than usual. Catalyzed by Kerala's deadly combination of high literacy, mobile access, and conservative cultural norms, a quarter of all pornography produced in India is created in this state. In such repressive contexts, the outlet for sexual exploration is often through these creative "collages" of fantasy. Such activity can fuel vulnerability, particularly in the current climate of rape and sexual harassment in India.

India has one of the world's highest rates of internet pornography consumption, mostly streamed through mobile devices.[30] In 2016 porn consumption in India, mostly in tier-2 and 3 towns, rose by 75 percent when mobile data rates dropped.[31] When pornography sites such as Pornhub are data-mined, researchers discover some of these pornography consumers' sexual preferences, habits, and changes in browsing behavior. For instance, Sunny Leone, a Canadian of Indian origin, is by far young Indian males' favorite porn star. The most popular search terms include Indian terms for "wife" and the term "bhabhi" (older brother's wife), particularly in North India. India ranks third, after the United States and the United Kingdom, as Pornhub's most loyal customer base, primarily via Android phones.

The search for gay and lesbian pornography jumped by 213 percent when in 2015 the Indian Supreme Court reinstated the law against sodomy, a legacy from the British colonial era, and females constitute more than one-fourth of the pornography consumers in India.[32] These revelations have triggered an intensification of social restrictions. Asserting its role as a moral authority, the state now censors content deemed even remotely offensive.

Iran is another example of a country undergoing such social upheaval. Young Iranian girls, for instance, flock to Instagram to post photos of themselves without headscarves. This has caught the attention of the Iranian moral police. Since 1979 it has been illegal for women to expose their hair in public. In 2016 the police arrested eight people involved in these photo productions for being "un-Islamic."[33] Javad Babaei, the court prosecutor, explained during a state television broadcast that these digital images are "threats to morality and the foundation of family."[34] Iranian authorities are also cracking down on other emerging uses of the new technologies, of course, and created the Iranian Centre for Surveying and Combating Organized Cyber Crimes to combat hackers engaged in financial crimes and crimes against morality.

Digital leisure spans the spectrum of activity from the quaint, cute, creative, and mundane to insidious uses that can cause harm to others. Users who engage in these activities include persons from all classes and all levels of income, including persons who are poor. The very fact that people with scarce resources engage in the same sorts of leisure activities as people who are much better off tells us, quite simply, that this very ordinariness can provide better insight into the day-to-day motivations of people who are poor.

When I volunteered at the cybercafé in Almora as part of my research, I arrived with several assumptions. I assumed that because broadband had entered this rural town only a few months earlier, the youth would be desperate to learn about the world around them. They would use this opportunity to run internet searches on matters that affected their communities and their families—such as water scarcity, soil erosion, deforestation, and politics in the Himalayan region. After all, theirs was primarily a subsistence agricultural economy with a deep and proud history and a legacy of environmental movements that have resulted in many environmental protection laws in India.

What I encountered over the months I spent there was far from my starting point. I had forgotten that, first and foremost, they were teenagers with teen desires. Given the dearth of opportunities for boys and girls to meet in public, the cybercafé became the dating café. Boys and girls would sit behind the computers while chatting with each other online, occasionally stealing glances at one another. Their friends would stay right outside, serving as their escorts and guardians lest these interactions strayed into inappropriate advances or undesirable behaviors. In my enthusiasm for their local culture and history, I had inadvertently expected a layer of exoticism in their digital life.

It is safe to say that the more the development agencies and grant organizations exoticize people who are poor—portray them as different from everyone else in the world—the more likely it is that the people they intend to benefit will violate the beautiful fictions created about them, resulting in the failures of projects that were meant to improve their lives. Agencies and foundations that want to benefit them need to pay attention to the fact that people who live in circumstances of scarce resources are, in the most fundamental ways, just like everyone else. They are proud. They are sexual beings. They look for love. They use humor as a powerful coping mechanism, as can readily be seen in their daily online posts. They hunger for entertainment. Moreover, they do not sit and wait for the market to recognize them as legitimate consumers of leisure. Instead they creatively forge ahead, using whatever technology is available to them to pioneer novel—and, yes, often illegal—ways to gain access to the online hubs of happiness.

3

Media Bandits

THE ENTERTAINMENT DEMANDS of people who live in poverty in the Global South often go unmet by the media conglomerates. There are few movie theaters in rural Ethiopia or in the slums of the Philippines. Buying a DVD or a music CD could cost low-income youth a week's wages. These young people are not viable consumers for the likes of Time Warner (now Spectrum), Disney, or Netflix.

It is no wonder that there has arisen a vast and thriving illegal media economy that caters to this marginalized majority. This economy thrives despite the fact that wealthy nations have crafted global copyright laws to penalize it. Western media industries aggressively pressure countries in the Global South to control piracy, and developing countries comply with raids and crackdowns in order to secure their membership in the World Trade Organization and win the approval of its neoliberal leaders.

It takes great ingenuity to design entire systems of media production and distribution and keep them below the radar of the state and the entertainment companies. Media pirates play creatively with the rules of the game and develop new guidelines for building parallel local media empires. The majority of low-income people in the Global South persist in consuming pirated media. Given this enduring fact, perhaps it is time for the global media conglomerates to reform their business models to make their media available to people with scarce resources, instead of continuing to tighten the noose in enforcing regulations that make a majority of the world's people unable to access their products by legal means.

Media Piracy and Morality

There is a war out there on media piracy. In September 2016, Karen Bradley, Secretary of State for Culture, Media, and Sport for the United Kingdom, equated media pirates to burglars, promising tough action against them: "Burglars can be sentenced to ten years in prison, but the criminal gangs that are making vast sums of money through exploiting the online creations of others only face a two-year sentence. We will increase this to ten."[1] Apparently the world has an "epidemic" of piracy. Pirates are being declared "leeches," "parasites," "criminals," and downright "terrorists."[2]

As early as 2009 a RAND report circulated an unsubstantiated claim that DVD piracy has a higher profit margin than the sale of illicit narcotics, which escalated the media conglomerates' antagonism toward piracy.[3] The music industry rode this wave of paranoia by releasing its own report, claiming a connection between piracy and people trafficking, money laundering, violence, drug smuggling, and terrorism.[4]

The public discussion of piracy tends to consist of moralizing instead of debating corporate profiteering and a model of media distribution and pricing that prevents half the world's population from being able to enjoy popular entertainment media legally. Regarding piracy of entertainment media, passions run high in Western news media, which tend to publish extreme claims with little verification. Who are the real victims of piracy? Who are the world's media pirates? How disruptive are their practices to the Western media industries?

How enormous are the profits of the global media conglomerates, and how much profit do they extract from the poor in the Global South despite piracy? What are the repercussions on criminalizing piracy, especially in the Global South? What kind of enforcement efforts are out there to tackle this "crime," and do they have an impact? These questions matter, particularly as we focus on how the poor access and consume digital media to enhance their overall well-being, happiness, and contentment as they struggle to eke out a living in conditions of scarce resources.

Since the 1980s the moguls of the entertainment media have funded research against piracy to support their cause. Their commissioned reports have spurred mainstream news media to push a rhetoric of fear. The fact is that legal media goods are a luxury for most of the world's population. High rates of piracy drive the media markets of most emerging economies. According to the entertainment industries, pirated media goods constitute about 82 percent of the music market in Mexico and 90 percent of the movie market in India, and their war on piracy is focused on the Global South.[5] The global entertainment media conglomerates are based primarily in the West and wage their war against so-called criminals residing outside the West. Given this situation, a group of independent researchers came together to look at this issue objectively, beyond the interests of US and other Western corporations.

The Media Piracy Project was launched in 2007 to investigate piracy in Brazil, India, Russia, and South Africa. The final report revealed an underrepresented, countering voice to the mainstream debate.[6] Its ultimate conclusion was that piracy is not a problem, not a crime, but instead a problem of pricing: what has made piracy ubiquitous is, quite simply, the media industry's refusal to lower prices and its continuous neglect of the billions of low-income consumers in countries of the Global South, who simply want to be able to experience the pleasures provided by entertainment media that are so easily accessible for wealthier people. This is the simple reason for the fact that, in the last decade, increased access through cheap mobile phones, broadband, and the entrepreneurship of media pirates has made illicit consumption the norm outside the West.

Media piracy has risen because Western economic regulations continue to privilege the interests of the haves over those of the have-nots. Legitimizing the ingenuity of the poor in creating a marketplace for digital leisure through pirated goods comes at the cost of disrupting the core business model of the Western media industries. Western governments have refused to institute legal reform of intellectual property rights to make digital media affordable for all, and Western media conglomerates have chosen to consolidate their position on the criminalization of media piracy. They deny the global poor the dignity of a formal system that enables them to legally access sources of entertainment available to the rest of the world, and they justify their actions with hypocritical moralizing.

The Colonial Legacy of Entertainment Deprivation

Criminalization is legitimate only when there is genuine choice. In South Africa, the legacy of apartheid has deprived most of the population of legal access to digital media. One-third of the people of South Africa live on less than one dollar a day, so it is impossible for them to purchase unrealistically priced DVDs, music CDs, and streaming services. Most movie theaters are located in the elite areas of the cities; the first multiplex in a black township did not open until 2007. During the apartheid era, the government imposed restrictions on media content in the townships (segregated areas inhabited by nonwhites), fueling the practice of piracy. In the postapartheid era, with few legal and price-customized distribution channels available in the townships, the pirate market is the only affordable market for the vast majority of low-income South Africans.

Colonial communication policies deeply shaped Africa's networks for media consumption and distribution. The media were used as tools for colonial propaganda. With a clear goal of "civilizing the natives" in the image of Western modernity, the mass media (television, radio, and so on) were used to "educate" rather than to entertain—to instruct or indoctrinate rather than make the pleasures of entertainment available to everyone. This colonial perspective continues to influence policies and practices across Africa.

For instance, relatively few people in Africa are able to go to the movies.[7] For those Africans who have been able to enjoy this simple pleasure, the cinemas primarily show movies from America and Hong Kong. The African film critic Emmanuel Sama has argued that African films have long been "foreigners in their own countries."[8] Even in the 1990s, African films accounted for less than 0.1 percent of all movies screened on the continent.[9] In Malawi, for instance, there is not much of a domestic film or television production industry, so very few of the movies and television programs shown there have a Malawian audience in mind.[10] In such cases, it can be argued that illegal copying and distributing of media are acts of rightful defiance. In addition, where the legal entertainment media are not affordable, there is no competition with, and thus no loss of sales for, the global media conglomerates. Corporations cannot lose sales that they would never have made. In other words, piracy is the genuine, legitimate market in most of the Global South.

Instead of overhauling their business models, Western film and music corporations have chosen to pressure governments worldwide to take punitive action against piracy. This powerful copyright industry has channeled hundreds of millions of dollars toward local anti-piracy campaigns in developing countries, including the funding of media campaigns that portray piracy as immoral and police efforts to prevent viewers from filming new-release movies showing in the cinemas.

In Brazil, for instance, Western media corporations offer gifts— printer cartridges, refrigerators, new offices, buildings, cars, and so on— to the resource-hungry police and government agencies to encourage them to prioritize piracy enforcement. They have even attempted to influence judges in regional court systems, to "sensitize" them to their interests, resulting in complaints of foreign interference in the domestic rule of law.

This is reminiscent of the classic colonial divide-and-rule practices. Foreign powers were enabled to implement rules and laws in their colonies by creating a privileged minority among the colonized to control the locals. But times have changed, and attempts to police public media consumption are unpopular, with little reward for local government.

Some scholars blame the ongoing media piracy on "culture"—the "collectivist" nature of developing countries that inherently opposes Western individualism.[11] They argue, in other words, that in tightly knit traditional communities, sharing is part of the cultural values—and this, not their economic situation, is why people in the Global South enthusiastically share digital media. But the inherent message of this view is that traditional cultures are primitive—valuing gratification (a primitive pursuit) above ethics (a hallmark of modernity). Cultural difference thus is taken to be evidence of moral laxity. These theorists advise policymakers and marketers to help socialize these populations into so-called Western values, which is essentially the rhetoric of colonial days—the social values of the colonizers versus the colonized. Foreign powers justified their interference in foreign lands by declaring a need to "civilize the natives"—and it appears that this is continuing today in the name of globalization.

To blame piracy on culture is to limit the conversation to the realm of morality, with the West claiming the high moral ground. If we are to understand why implementation of intellectual property rights has failed in many developing countries, we need to go beyond the dichotomies of good and bad, and legal and illegal. Guatemala is a case in point. Anthropologist Kedron Thomas reminds us that context influences our outlook on legality.[12] Her ethnographic work in this region reveals how Guatemala's bloody history has shaped Guatemalans' view of the law as a weapon wielded by elite groups in power. After the genocide in the 1980s, which left more than 200,000 dead, the vast number of displaced Guatemalans saw the perpetrators of the massacres given a free pass by the amnesty laws. Today Guatemala continues to have a high homicide rate and few convictions, and the law is continuing to fail these people. It is no wonder that, within such a climate, Guatemalans who are not wealthy view anti-piracy laws as a mockery of justice.

Through interviews with street vendors, Thomas learned how piracy crackdowns reinforced the local perception of anti-piracy laws. According to the vendors, the underpaid police used raids as a way to line their pockets. The fact that most vendors were poor and indigenous fed into the prevailing stereotypes of indigenous communities as delinquent and morally corrupt. The divide between the Latinos, people with Spanish heritage from colonial times, and the Mayans, indigenous to this region, persists and overlaps with the poverty divide.

On the flip side, the indigenous believe that wealthy Guatemalans have accumulated their wealth through illegal means. Historically, peasants in Latin American have held the belief that accumulation by the few comes at the price of deprivation of the many.[13] In other words, it is a zero-sum game. So as the indigenous poor take it upon themselves to try to build a fairer society, one small part of that is to make copies of what are considered finite and scarce goods—expensive digital media products. It is possible to understand notions like authenticity, ownership, and originality as having more to do with a product's symbolic role for social equality than with the Western obsession over brands and trademark laws.

Piracy as Development

Local raids have become commonplace as developing countries are being absorbed into a global neoliberal market dominated by the West. But the raids result in few convictions. Raids can cost low-income media entrepreneurs their livelihood. The risk is particularly high for women and children. The reality is far from the image of media pirates as being similar to narcotics dealers. In media piracy, there are distinct roles for each member of the family. The women mind the shop, the children do the math on the payments, and the men move the boxes.

Quiapo in Manila is a good example.[14] This thriving media piracy mecca is run primarily by Muslim Filipino women. There are large emporiums with hundreds of retail stores selling pirated foreign and domestic movies. Raids on these emporiums are commonplace. Enforcers come to the stalls to check on the media and confiscate as much material as possible. To avoid this, vendors have set up an alert system to quickly move their merchandise to hidden warehouses and nearby vans. Elena, one of the women at a retail shop, exclaims how farcical this process is: "It's all a joke! They do this, we come back, they return, we run again; waste of time."[15] In this ritual cat-and-mouse game, the police seize even the legitimate media goods. It is hard for the police to differentiate between the fake and the real. Sometimes they take months to go through this material, forcing these families to find alternative means to survive.

Even when pirate media entrepreneurs want to go legal as the domestic market becomes more inclusive and competitive, as is happening in India, it is hard to compete against the new technologies in everyone's hands. A shopkeeper in an Indian village explains his frustration with memory cards, Bluetooth, and cell phones. Music and movies go viral in a flash as memory cards with downloaded media move from one mobile phone to another.[16] Bluetooth allows music to be transferred seamlessly. This trend seems unstoppable and has stimulated a new profession—the download entrepreneurs, who help users download music from computers to memory cards. These downloaders operate in a gray market; although the downloading itself is illegal in many places, the entrepreneurs usually offer it alongside legal activities such as selling mobile phone plans.

Not all developing countries are moving in a linear fashion from street vendors to digital pirates. This is contingent on each government's approach to policing these sites. Brazil is relatively lax in cracking down on these forms of informal enterprise, but China has been far more effective. Since China joined the World Trade Organization in 2001, it has been under tremendous pressure to liberalize its economy, including its media industries. When China agreed to honor international copyright laws, this made the many peer-to-peer video-sharing sites in China illegal.[17] The government has shut down enormously popular sites, like Bit Torrent, pushing the media fans back to the street vendors.

However, there are new legitimate business models emerging among video-sharing sites, once deemed illegal. For instance, Xunlei is a popular site for downloading television programs and films at high speeds. In the early 2000s it had almost 80 percent of market share in China, staying within the gray economy. In recent years, however, it initiated a service called "claim copyrights" that enables copyright holders to claim their content on Xunlei's platform. The company is moving farther into the formal economy by promising to take down unauthorized content following notification. Another strategy is to stream licensed content, which saves money for the copyright holder because it reduces the amount of physical storage of media goods. Because East Asian media have far more affordable copyright licenses than Western media, this site has become a critical conduit for spreading popular culture from these regions, compared to products from the United States, which in comparison are immensely expensive.

The Chinese media industry has been maturing, but for decades its development model for improving production quality and globalizing its goods has been based on imitation.[18] Copying other countries' media products built China's media production and distribution channels and enabled it to become a major player in the global marketplace. Since the 1980s, China has been a powerful source of media commodities for low-income populations in developing countries. The Chinese state viewed this as a prime driver for national development.

Anthropologist Rosana Pinheiro-Machado conducted fieldwork among employees and entrepreneurs dealing in pirated media goods in Shenzhen. In response to her question on piracy, what she commonly heard was a famous quote from Deng Xiaoping: "It doesn't matter if the cat is white or black, so long as its catches rats."[19] The end justifies the means. Speed was essential—China was striving to catch up with the West. Another common argument she heard was that if the media product was made in China, then it's not a fake, it's a national product. One vendor put it:

> Western people think this Rolex [he pointed at his wrist] is not a Rolex because it is a replica. For us, this is a Rolex, a real one. The difference is the origin, because this was made in China, and for us, it's better to help our national industry.[20]

It is hard to blame low-income nations for building their economies by disregarding international laws. Historically, this has been a common practice in nation-building. The imposed laws were often foreign and biased toward those already in power. Take the British colonization of the eastern coast of North America. Numerous laws, such as the Navigation Acts, were imposed to suppress industry within the colonies and to favor Great Britain's growing industries.[21] Taking a page from colonial history, developing countries today forge ahead using the illicit until they can stand their ground as serious players in the global economy.

Not all firms are litigious toward piracy. In fact, companies get free market research by investigating pirated and illegal sharing sites to detect global trends. In September 2016, Samir Bangara, then managing director of the Walt Disney Company in India, declared at a conference in Singapore, "I'm going to put it out there. I love piracy."[22] This was a courageous statement, given that the attendees at the conference represented companies like Netflix, Spotify, Merlin, FOX, UFC, and Disney. What was his rationale?

Bangara told his peers that the industry is facing a new kind of challenge due to the proliferation of digital content. The competitiveness of this industry will rest on how aligned a company is toward "discoverability"—making content visible. The only way to find out what gets the attention of media consumers in this saturated content era is to watch piracy sites, because these are the favored sites of the majority of the world's consumers and reflect the great diversity in consumers' tastes. If certain television shows, for example, are found across different sites, downloaded by users from Mali to Mumbai, then producers can more confidently invest in the global scaling of those media shows.

Media conglomerates also benefit from piracy when it is practiced within spaces they control. Sony is a case in point. Sony supports and even encourages copying that takes place within their gaming sites, such as EverQuest and LittleBigPlanet, because the copying is central to the value creation of their games.[23] Given that playing with culture is intrinsically part of innovation, gamers constantly appropriate popular media sources, such as Monty Python, Dr. Who, and Star Trek. This enhances the game play and increases the value of Sony's game platform.

There is a double standard at work. As long as piracy increases a corporation's profit, it is a virtue; piracy that doesn't provide commercial returns is criminalized. Thus, the state and the media conglomerates are giving contradictory signals: they celebrate the innovative entrepreneurialism of the poor but simultaneously attack it as being immoral and criminal.

Media Consumption from Below

Nowadays in low-income communities, as we have seen, distribution channels are moving away from emporiums and mobile shops to social media as the youth go online. Informal production meets formal distribution. For instance, take the informal distribution of US television shows through Brazil's Orkut communities.[24] Online fans subtitle these shows and circulate them on their social media sites. Numerous sites have sprung up just to download these shows. They all have a formal presence and accounts on Twitter and Facebook. These piracy practices have made the international viewing of television shows become mainstream.

Global consumption comes at the cost of noncompliance with copyright laws. For instance, in 2017, Brazilians made 12.7 billion visits to piracy sites.[25] Because of the collective complicity of the digital audiences on sites like Orkut, YouTube, and Facebook, the risk is diffused and deflected. Even though this viewing is unauthorized, audiences do not see it as immoral. Instead, they see this as a hobby and part of the "gift culture" of sharing media with each other. One user put it: "There is no practice more beautiful than this one: it is an honest donation, with no hypocrisy."[26] This is a legacy of the bootleg cultures of the past.

Some viewers even see this practice as a favor for the media producer, promoting shows that otherwise would not be watched. Many people for whom income can be scarce believe that the current television industry has systematically excluded them through its high prices and delayed releases of content, and many complain that this is disrespectful toward them as media consumers. In the wealthy nations of the West, piracy is a common rite of passage for the young, most of whom, when they reach adulthood, become paying consumers of affordable plans via Apple TV and Netflix. However, most low-income countries in the Global South do not have alternative models of media consumption, so the young people remain limited to pirated media well into their adulthood.

In China, where government has tight control over content on the state-endorsed channels, most youth see media piracy as giving them the option to view entertainment created in many other parts of the world. The media programs available through Chinese public broadcasting are mostly oriented toward education and not entertainment, in accordance with communist ideology. There are tight import quotas on foreign films, most of which the government portrays as "cultural polluters," despite China's membership in the World Trade Organization. The Western films that have not been portrayed as polluters include the movie *Titanic,* which party leaders respected and allowed to circulate freely because it promoted Chinese values of aspiration, sacrifice, and valor.[27]

These factors have led to a phenomenal demand in China for Hollywood productions as well as European, Japanese, and Korean television serials—supplied through media piracy. Independent Chinese filmmakers who are censored by the state also find their distribution outlets through these black markets.[28] This is much to the consternation of the Chinese Communist Party, because the very technology that was made widely available across China in order to further national development has been turned against the state, in their view, by enabling unauthorized material to flow easily throughout the nation.

China has matured to become a powerful media market, and the government now allows the media industry to go beyond imitation to build an authentic creative entertainment economy. Most low-income countries in the Global South, however, have few resources to foster their local cultural and creative economies. Few nations can afford to build their cultural capital through locally produced films and music in their regional languages.

All the same, there do exist thriving indigenous media scenes that receive little aid from mainstream media investors or state actors. In Recife, Brazil, local musicians distribute their media products free of cost to mobile street hawkers, who sell them alongside pirated foreign films and music.[29] These street vendors have a strong motivation to sell this local music because their sales are pure profit and help strengthen local networks of community artists.

Years back, I was involved in a karaoke project by PlanetRead, a nonprofit organization that aimed to nourish literacy among low-income people in India. They came up with the innovative idea of using same-language subtitling on televised music content to engage as well as improve viewers' reading skills. We also created a digital jukebox of popular folk songs using subtitles for karaoke. The intent was to create high-quality local content and sell it cheaply to keep the project sustainable. We did wonder how local folk songs could compete with Tollywood, the Telegu-language film industry that dominated the scene. Folk music looked like a dying art form. Said one folk artist, "Young people no longer care ... they want to make money, listen to film songs and have no time for us."[30] What we soon discovered, though, was that few resources were being invested into producing quality local content. So this could have been part of the problem.

Eventually we also came to understand that in these Indian villages, folk music was a political medium and had been an expression of class consciousness for centuries. For instance, Gaddhar, a Marxist and folk activist of the Peoples War Group in Andhra Pradesh, would sing songs of oppression as he moved from village to village around the time we were there. His high popularity among the villagers drove the local police to put a bounty on his head.[31]

The project's song jukebox became enormously popular and went viral as young people made CD copies at the village cybercafé and shared them with neighboring villagers. It was impossible to get them on board with the idea of paying even a very small sum for this content. The artists involved were paid for their time, but their remuneration clearly was not enough to sustain them. Many of the locals involved in the project didn't take any pay; they simply wanted to get some of their own songs and other media out there for others to enjoy.

Nollywood, Nigeria's grassroots media industry, is now one of the largest film producers in the world, in terms of output, having taken over the African continent with little support from the state.[32] It is a good example of how an informal economy can create an African media empire and, through mass consumption, gain legitimacy. Much like the circulation of local Chinese and Brazilian media products through the established bootleg systems, Nigerian media products flow through networks that were designed for distributing illicit foreign media goods. Far from being a fringe or marginal film culture, these local, grassroots media products are extremely popular and widely distributed.

Given all these sorts of evidence, it seems clear that the diverse media industries of the Global South—the sorts of local cultural innovations that were suppressed for centuries under colonial rule—thrive today due to piracy.

Activists, Entrepreneurs, or Criminals?

Manifestos have unique appeal. They convert politics to passion. They go hand in hand with the rise of social movements. It takes inspiration to convert citizens into activists, and it takes perspiration to convert activists into reformers. There needs to be a strong common cause. Who would have guessed that in the last decade, piracy would transform from being a covert, criminalized activity into being a force in mainstream politics? The first Pirate Party emerged in Sweden in 2006. Their core founding principle in their manifesto was the radical overhaul of copyright laws.

> The Pirate Party believes that people with access to free communication, culture and knowledge grow, feel better and create a more enjoyable and humane society for everyone to live in. We see modern information technology opening up possibilities for people to take action for their own lives and participate in affecting the development of society. We see how a freer flow of information enables thoughts, cultural creation and the economy to grow.[33]

Today there are Pirate Parties in more than forty countries, including Brazil, Morocco, Slovenia, and the United Kingdom. Their shared values and political momentum led in 2010 to the formation of the Pirate Parties International, a nongovernmental organization supporting these diverse national parties.[34] Simply putting the word

"Pirates" in the name of a political party is a deliberate effort to appropriate a derogatory label, bestowed by Western media conglomerates, and transform it into a banner for a legitimate form of alternative governance.

Why have Pirate Parties risen so quickly and forcefully worldwide? What is their appeal to average citizens? How did something so technical—intellectual property—become a critical platform for average voters? And how does this concern the people of this world who live in poverty? The key to understanding this appeal is to look at what anti-piracy has come to stand for. The fight against media piracy is a fight against gift exchanges. Western economies are very successful in monetizing almost every aspect of life, including the very basic act of sharing with one another. Users of online technologies are constantly signing away their rights to the ownership of their own data as they simultaneously contribute to the building of social media empires every time they visit those sites online.

The mainstream digital version of the sharing economy, far from democratizing and redistributing capital, has concentrated wealth in the hands of the few. Those in power continue to claim that this is the new egalitarian way to social mobility and progress. The gap between political and corporate rhetoric and the reality of extreme social imbalances appears to widen by the day. These circumstances are well described in the United Kingdom's first crowdsourced political manifesto, "Manifesto of the Pirate Party UK," which gave voice to thousands of citizens and a variety of interest groups.[35] Along with its many ideas for transforming modern life into something more egalitarian and authentic, it speaks of people's pervasive alienation and the ordinary person's growing sense of helplessness that current political leaders have become deaf and blind to.

The Pirate Party stands as a reminder of an alternative perspective: that when the majority of people break a rule, the response should be to rethink the rule and not to criminalize an entire public; that when the dominant Western neoliberal system alienates the majority of the world's people, the sanctity of its ideology should be questioned. That is, rather than forcing the public to fit with a law, laws should fit the needs and wants of the people. Today governments tend to yield to the pressure of powerful Western media conglomerates, but progressive legal scholarship for the most part stands with the pirates.[36]

Contemporary scholars have provided ample evidence that copyright primarily protects the monopoly.[37] Copyright enforcement impedes the progress of emerging economies, and a simple look back at history shows that emerging economies have traditionally ignored copyright claims. Even in the United States, when budding entrepreneurs were building the US media empires, more than a century passed before Americans got around to complying with Great Britain's copyright laws.[38] Yet now that US media corporations have vast wealth and power, their policy is to amass more profit by trying to enforce copyright law against rising economies in the Global South.

When a social order is aligned with the interests of the bourgeois, it provokes the rise of self-appointed defenders of other people's rights. Somali sea pirates make for a fitting metaphor. The international news media have vilified Somali sea pirates, but a United Nations report in 2012 revealed that maritime piracy in this area was partly a reaction to illegal fishing by foreign ships and the corporate dumping of toxic material into Somali waters.[39] Because of this illegal fishing and dumping, several Somali fishing communities lost their primary source of livelihood. Many of the fishermen came together to protect their waters and soon came to be known as the Somali pirates. About 70 percent of the surrounding fishing villages supported their efforts. It was up to the pirates to deliver justice. One Somali pirate put it, "We consider sea bandits those who illegally fish in our seas and dump waste in our seas and carry weapons in our seas. We are simply patrolling our seas. Think of us like a coast guard."[40]

It is hard to hate the Robin Hoods of society. Media pirates transform media goods from a luxury into a basic commodity. They defy the rich to benefit the poor. Corporations that go after pirates look like bullies in this public media battle. It is bad for their brand. In the arena of digital media, the hunger to be entertained is stronger than the fear of criminalization, particularly in low-income economies where the gray market is the sole market in town for media goods. Survival economies are not conventional economies. Simply to survive from one day to the next is a struggle that requires making use of every tool available, and popular entertainment media provide much-needed escape and respite from the strains of such a daily life.

Yet, as happens with all ideologies and beliefs, pirates are bound to morph into diverse versions, from the enlightened to the destructive. Some Somali pirates have moved away from their common cause, pursuing acts of maritime violence and self-interest. And some political Pirate Parties have been accused of creating a layer of technology elitism, moving away from the original ethos of the public commons for expression, social justice, and equality. Media piracy, which still consists mostly of simple acts of sharing, has also created global monopolies of pirated goods—new underground empires.

One problem with vilifying or romanticizing low-income entrepreneurs as pirates is that this applies labels of morality to their ventures. When the activities of people living at the margins are viewed through a lens of virtue, what the viewer cannot see is the spectrum of possibility and probability that plays out when people with few resources transform their desires and demands into innovation, often on the margins of legality.

It can be argued that today's dominant digital media corporations all began as start-up pirate organizations.[41] For instance, Spotify, Skype, and The Pirate Bay in their initial years acted subversively to violate traditional business models. They challenged the status quo of the music, telecom, and television industries. They gained legitimacy through their scale, dedicated user base, and commercial value in Silicon Valley. Low-income residents of the Global South do not have a similar trajectory available to them, and much of their informal media economy will remain a survival economy. And as long as the Western media conglomerates remain unable to commodify piracy practices, these acts probably will continue to be labeled as criminal.

In Chapter 4 we will see that in the last decade, policy regarding those who live in poverty in the Global South has paradoxically shifted toward validating and even celebrating some aspects of their gray economy. The state, development agencies, and some corporate entities are increasingly reframing some of the poor's illicit acts as innovative. New business models and clever corporate philosophies are emerging on the foundation of doing "good" by being inclusive of the poor and simultaneously making a profit by expanding their consumer base. Much effort is currently being devoted to absorbing informal economies into the formal system and bestowing on them a long-withheld legitimacy.

The poor of the Global South are now often portrayed as being at the center of the innovation game. They are the "experts" in transforming scarcity into opportunity. They are perceived as having a strategic advantage over the privileged minority due to their life experiences with poverty. They know the needs of their market best and have creative ways to fulfill them with limited means. In this narrative, the community of the poor, far from having nothing to offer, is now at the forefront of societal progress. The poor embed the virtue that Silicon Valley values the most—entrepreneurship. From being criminals of the past, they are now the chosen virtuous ones. The question remains how and whether their gray economies can intersect with the resilient structures of capitalism to generate a new social order.

4

The Virtuous Poor

GOVERNMENTS AND BUSINESSES are starting to recognize that many residents of low-income communities are innovators who use the new digital technologies to transform scarcity into opportunities, and that such communities—natural entrepreneurial collectives—might be strategically harnessed to become key players in the digital economy. The work ethic of these innovators embodies the virtues of the twenty-first century—being creative and enterprising, they are no longer portrayed as passive beneficiaries but have made themselves into co-creators of the future.

However, as we have seen in their improvising, these innovators often break the law, disrupt institutional arrangements, and defy social norms. The gray economy is their way of life. Innovation is their survival skill. Living mostly on the margins of society, they have been compelled to pioneer entire parallel market systems to cater to their most basic needs. Hacking the system can be creative, but it is not generally a sustainable way of life and can be dangerous. And even though new communications media provide new opportunities that appear more empowering, more playful, and more gratifying, they can also be deeply exploitative—as illustrated by the example of gold farming in Chapter 1.

This does not deter Silicon Valley's new mission of pursuing "inclusive capitalism"—designing applications for and with the poor to make new customers out of the billions of people who have long been excluded and exploited by the mainstream market economy. These tech companies are determined to revive the trust in capitalism that took a hit during the 2008 financial crisis. This raises many questions: How do Silicon Valley and local governments plan to absorb these vast informal economies of the poor into the formal market system? Would such an absorption necessarily improve the lives of the poor in the Global South? Is it even possible to reconcile these two worlds of the legally innovative and the illicit? Is all improvisation innovation? If scarcity produces innovation, will this reduce the incentive to mitigate inequality?

To begin to answer such questions, we need to broaden contemporary notions of innovation and entrepreneurship by viewing them through the lens of the playful improvisation of those who live in scarcity. Mainstream capitalists currently are circulating various buzzwords and themes in discussing their newfound mission to transform the vast majority of the world's poor into consumers and producers in the mainstream capitalist system. To cater to the poor, they appear to suggest, one must think like them, speak to them, and work with them. Co-creation with the poor appears to be an enlightened approach. There is a thin line, though, between collaboration and exploitative commodification. In the process of making legitimate consumers out of the poor, technology companies harness their data. Playfulness at the margins is streamlined and diverted to strengthen and enrich the technology conglomerates. The question is whether this is equally beneficial for the vast underclass who, supposedly for purposes of social good, have been lured into these "inclusive" systems.

Discussions of innovation among the poor tend to lead into a morally problematic habit of glorifying poverty as an avenue for innovation. In the momentum to legitimize frugality and optimize the collective industrious play of the poor, states tend to transfer the responsibility for impoverishment back onto those who are impoverished. In framing the poor as "virtuous" for their entrepreneurial ways, mainstream capitalists and local governments conjure strategies to sideline the more subversive alleys of the gray economy, exploit the absorbable activities, and commodify the poor in the name of "inclusivity."

Hacking Poverty

In 2016 Travis Kalanick, then CEO of Uber, tweeted, "Fear is the disease and hustle is the antidote" on the trending hashtag #AlwaysBeJugaading.[1] "Jugaad" is a colloquial Indian term that means to improvise, particularly as a response to scarce resources and rigid social systems. An equivalent notion more familiar to Westerners is "hacking"— skillfully manipulating the system to one's advantage by working through loopholes. Hacking, or playing with, existing systems has been a survival tactic for the poor as they go about "jugaading" their way to get access to water, electricity, better transport options, and such.

For instance, tampering with the wires to get free electricity or modifying a two-wheeler to make more seat space for the family are some very useful quick fixes to satisfy immediate needs. The term "jugaad" has gone global among business leaders and governments, popularized by business books such as *Jugaad Innovation* and *Frugal Innovation*. It has come to mean innovation that is low-cost, simple, flexible, and inclusive—ingredients that are necessary in order to scale products and services beyond the predictable middle-class markets.[2]

A case in point was Uber's response when the Bangalore Transport Department, in March 2016, declared all shared bike services illegal. Ola, Uber's competitor, complied by taking the bikes off their app, but Uber rebranded its service as bike pooling, making this specific service nonprofit so that could not be banned by the government.[3] Sharing bikes is a natural way of life for people with few resources. Uber's jugaading of the bike system entrenched Uber's market share in India and provides a model for how other international businesses might increase their consumer base in India.

Jugaad innovation has led to many amusing and astonishing stories in the news media. A classic is the story about *dhabas*, roadside restaurants in North India frequented by truck drivers. The news media made these places notorious by reporting that they had modified washing machines to use them to make *lassi*, a yogurt drink. The multinational finance giant HSBC rode this media wave, making a popular advertisement in which a washing machine salesperson visits India to understand why sales have increased and discovers that his clients are using their washing machines in their kitchens instead of in their laundry rooms.

When I was on a development project in Kuppam, a rural town in India, I heard stories of some local farmers getting their five minutes of fame on television. I watched their interviews one night. Several farmers in South India had figured out that it was cheaper and more effective to spray Pepsi and Coca-Cola on their cotton and chili fields to kill pests rather than to pay the exorbitant prices demanded by the chemical companies for their pesticides.[4] This probably was not the kind of free publicity soft drink companies were looking for, but such stories nourished the emerging narrative of the poor as natural tinkerers and playful grassroots innovators.

The concept of jugaad, or "frugal innovation," has become pervasive. How to get more from less is the name of the game. A number of organizations are striving to enable grassroots innovation in their own ways. For instance, the Frugal Innovation Lab at Santa Clara University, in California, works on projects that use mobile phones for social benefit. Wakabi is an app that Ugandan farmers can use to plan the transport of their goods to market.[5] Another of the Lab's projects, AquaSift, is a response to one of the most persistent problems that plague the poor—the struggle to find and access safe drinking water. AquaSift is a monitoring device that uses the mobile interface to detect arsenic and nitrates in water.

The mobile phone seems to be a natural ally for jugaad innovation, helping to hack away at poverty in novel ways. Thane Kreiner, the executive director of the Miller Center for Social Entrepreneurship, also at Santa Clara University, is a strong advocate of applying hacking, which is a common improvisational practice in the technology world, to chronic poverty. He notes the current merging of two poverty hacks, mobile technology and social entrepreneurship—a combination that "supports solutions created within communities of poor and marginalized people, making those solutions more likely to be adopted and sustained over time."[6]

Perhaps the most lauded poverty hack is the M-Pesa project in Kenya.[7] Its story reads like a fairy tale in the world of poverty. This innovation took on the major challenge of the poor not having access to basic banking services, which can prevent them from taking out loans to start businesses or investing in their health and education. In 2007 the Department for International Development (DFID), a foreign aid agency of the British government, realized that many low-income Kenyans had worked out a way to transfer money in spite of not being part of the formal banking system: they were transferring mobile airtime as a proxy for money.

This inspired the DFID to partner with Vodafone and its Kenyan affiliate, Safaricom, to enable small electronic payments to be made with mobile phones, giving birth to M-Pesa. To date, it is one of the most successful mobile projects tackling poverty. Within a year, 40 percent of the Kenyan population had registered for an account. Almost a decade later, 20 million Kenyans use this service, and more than 70 percent of Kenya's poor use this app regularly. Vodafone's success impelled others in the private sector to direct their energies toward creating services that could be used by people with low incomes.

This was a promising change from the longtime practice of viewing the poor as a high-risk clientele.

Few thought leaders have been as influential in setting the foundation for jugaad innovation as the late neoliberal business guru C. K. Prahalad. He pushed companies to rethink their approach toward the world's four billion poor people, or what he called the "bottom of the pyramid." Instead of holding on to postcolonial notions of the poor as victims who constantly need foreign aid, he and his colleague Stuart Hart argued that this emerging collective "presents a prodigious opportunity for the world's wealthiest companies—to seek their fortunes and bring prosperity to the aspiring poor."[8]

The approach Prahalad advocated is not just about companies selling products and services to the poor. That by itself would be exploitative and imperialistic. It is about working with the poor communities, grassroots activists, and nongovernmental organizations (NGOs) to co-create projects that are a win-win solution for all. Prahalad's ideas caught the imagination of the CEOs of several major corporations, including Hewlett Packard, Microsoft, Siemens, Unilever, Procter & Gamble, and DuPont. Even after his death in 2010, Prahalad stands as one of the key prophets on innovation for the poor of the Global South.

Numerous other innovations have made jugaad stories the darlings of the mainstream news media, which have portrayed India as one of the world's main laboratories for frugal innovation. The race is to the lowest bottom line—the most affordable, the most accessible, the most flexible. In March 2016, India launched the world's cheapest smartphone, selling for less than US$5. Ringing Bells Freedom 251 is a 3G smartphone with 8 GB storage and cameras in the front and back.[9] Similarly, Tata Motors, the Indian automobile manufacturer, designed the world's cheapest car, the Nano, to cater to the swelling numbers of aspirational customers who yearn to upgrade from their two-wheelers to cars that can provide a safer journey for their families.[10]

Although the notion of jugaad has been in the news since the 1990s, the practice has been long-standing. As early as 1968, Ram Chander Sharma designed and developed the world's cheapest prosthetic leg, the "Jaipur Foot." It was named one of the fifty best inventions in the world by *Time* magazine in 2009. Compared to the US$12,000 price for a prosthetic leg produced in the United States, the Jaipur Foot costs only US$45. Today, the Bhagwan Mahaveer Viklang Sahayata Samiti, which provides free fittings of the Jaipur Foot, is the world's largest prosthetic leg organization. The mission of frugality is applied to both the product and the whole process, from start to finish. Devendra Raj Mehta, who heads the Jaipur Foot team, explains his zealous approach:

> From the beginning, I instituted a culture that did not allow the use of funds for any other purpose than our core objective. I did not even serve tea during our meetings, and tea costs two cents in India. . . . I believe that if I divert even one penny to an activity other than serving the poorest of the poor, I am committing a moral sin and a legal wrong.[11]

The dominant media discourse associates Indian culture with jugaad, which raises national pride. The Indian government has taken to celebrating the abundant creative energy of its citizens. From citizens to cities, the jugaad culture hype is spreading fast. The newspaper *The Hindu* declared Mumbai the "ultimate jugaad city," a "living lab," and an experimental playground with a potent mix of artists, technologists, and community activists.[12]

The Dharavi Biennale, a groundbreaking event in 2014, gained national and international praise for its unique approach to community building in Dharavi, India, one of the world's largest slums. The event tapped into the informal settlement's entrepreneurial spirit to tackle issues of health and livelihood. The biennale spanned two years, inspiring solutions to local problems through numerous workshops that combined art and science. Street murals, puppetry, tapestry, public cooking, storytelling, and music festivals across Dharavi drew the participation of a diversity of residents—potters, garbage collectors, welders, tailors, and so on—to bring awareness to their community problems.

The poor here occupy prime real estate in one of the most vibrant Indian economies. Urban developers are constantly subjecting them to new schemes in an attempt to pry this coveted piece of land from their hands. Given this constant tension—and the stalemate between the government, developers, activists, and residents—the Urban Design Research Institute in Mumbai, an independent city-planning organization, launched an international competition to hack away at poverty through urban design.[13] Several proposals came in, with the premise that these communities were collective entrepreneurs with strong social ties that needed renewal and not demolition. Cooperative connectivity was at the heart of the reimagination of this public space, where the residents become co-creators of their surroundings.

Involving the community to co-hack their future has become trendy among governments worldwide. Witness the rise of social laboratories, civic hackathons, innovation incubators, maker spaces, idea camps, and entrepreneur garages from Boston to Shanghai. In mimicking the private sector, many governments hope to achieve disruption and renewal through innovation for a more democratic governance. For instance, in 2013 the United Nations Development Programme, in partnership with diverse governments and local industries, launched a series of social innovation camps across Southeast Asia—in Bangkok, Cebu, Hong Kong, Jakarta, Kuala Lumpur, Manila, Seoul, and Singapore.[14] These camps served as a critical platform for citizens, programmers, and designers to generate novel ideas addressing local problems and to spread the implementation of prototypes using new media technologies.

This euphoria has caught on in the West. Michael Bloomberg, formerly mayor of New York City, has sponsored Innovation Teams, or "i-teams," to take on the grand challenges of city governance.[15] The teams use smart data to collate information across diverse sectors to devise holistic approaches to seemingly intractable problems. One such challenge was the high murder rate in low-income neighborhoods in New Orleans. Co-working with local gangs, citizens in poor neighborhoods, and data experts, a team was able to map local violence hot spots and provide targeted intervention. The targeted area experienced a 19 percent drop in crime in 2013 compared to the year before.

In fact, big data has become central to urban hacking projects. Citizens' mobile phones generate much of this data. Mobiles are ubiquitous and thus can be powerful instruments to encourage participation. This has given rise to a new kind of social entrepreneurship, capitalizing on collective action and social media technologies. The poster child for the new kind of humanitarian hacking system is Ushahidi, a nonprofit software organization founded in 2008 in Kenya.[16] It began as a response to the Kenyan elections in 2007, which almost caused a civil war. The mission was simple. Locals who witnessed or were targets of violence could report their experience through a text message. Ushahidi collected these reports and mapped them on Google Maps for the Kenyan public to keep track of the political crisis and build accountability.

From then on, Ushahidi has applied its open software to numerous projects driven by various social causes, including tracking the violence in Congo and Gaza in 2008–2009, mapping humanitarian aid after the Haiti earthquake in 2010, and creating alerts for the Ebola epidemic in 2014. It continues to support the Syria Tracker Crisis Map launched in 2011 to document human rights violations based on text messages sent by victims. This has become one of the richest repositories of data on the Syrian war, and is used by aid agencies and media outlets such as USAID, the *Washington Post,* and the *Huffington Post.* Since its inception, Ushahidi has contributed to numerous humanitarian efforts and has gained financial backing from the Rockefeller Foundation, Google, Cisco, the MacArthur Foundation, and many other organizations. This institutional support has enabled it to evolve into a far more sophisticated platform. From its beginning with text messages, today the software collates messages from various media feeds, including Twitter, RSS, SMS, and Facebook, and displays them on interactive maps.

Hackathons have arisen to support this kind of social entrepreneurship. In February 2016 more than 250 programmers, social change activists, and NGOs came together in the fourth annual IDHack—International Development Hackathon—to design mobile applications that could help reduce poverty through global development.[17] IDHack events are sponsored by the MIT Global Poverty Initiative, Harvard Hackers for Development, and the Tufts Institute for Global Leadership, and the participants receive input from corporations like Google, Microsoft, and JPMorgan Chase. In these events, university students in the Boston area become civic hackers for the day, working on developing digital applications that could help solve some of the problems faced by low-income communities in the Global South. Such events extend what's been called the "Californian ideology"—the belief in technology as a tool of egalitarianism, which was once the founding inspiration of Silicon Valley.

Apps for hacking intractable social problems have become a mainstay today. For every citizen complaint, there seems to be an app. If you want to complain about potholes, there is Street Bump and Pothole Alert on Apple, and Fill the Hole on Android phones. There are more than a hundred apps for reporting child molestation and child molesters. To help prevent rape, there are now numerous apps that will instantly signal for help—by creating loud alert sounds, automatic texts, calls to emergency lines, and instant notifications to family or friends—with a single touch or shake of the mobile phone. After the 2013 gang rape of a young woman in New Delhi, the app Circle of Six—which won a US White House "Apps Against Abuse" award—customized its platform specifically for the New Delhi region.[18]

Hacking poverty is not easy. Co-creating with the poor involves not just the community but also a host of organizations driven by highly diverse motivations. Corporations want to penetrate these undercapitalized markets and expand their consumer base by also doing good. Governments want to be more efficient in their delivery of services and to signal to the world that they are approaching chronic problems in a fresh way. Nonprofits want to serve as critical liaisons between the governments, the citizens, and the private sector to protect the interests of the poor while innovating cost-effective strategies to alleviate their chronic poverty. When the rules of the game may be the cause of poverty, hacking can be a powerful strategy to play with the rules and possibly reform some of them. Hacking's laboratory approach helps contain and control risk for hackers. Hackers in the most marginalized communities tend to scale their hacking innovations to lower costs and increase flexibility. Mobile technologies are powerful instruments that enable this scaling and are perhaps the most cost-effective hacking tools because they are embedded in the routine lives of the poor.

That said, while hacking via apps helps to circumvent barriers to a better social life, is it also instigating structural change? While jugaad innovation challenges the logic of the formal market system, will it continue to remain at the margins? While the heady mix of art, activism, and technology orchestrates such hacking, do these efforts inadvertently gentrify the very spaces they intend to protect? The hacking culture intrinsically is a counterculture to mainstream, institutionalized ways of doing things. What happens when the rebels become part of the system? Do they change the system or lose sight of their cause?

Formalizing Hacking for Development

In August 2015 the Institute of Technology and Society in Rio de Janeiro, Brazil, invited me to be a global policy fellow at their organization. The institute has built a reputation as one of the architects of the landmark "Marco Civil" legislation, an internet bill passed in April 2014 to protect fundamental rights, including privacy, net neutrality, and freedom of expression. They designed this fellowship program to attract researchers and professionals across the world to work with them and build an international network in this field.

It was an exciting time to be in Brazil, a country with some of the most avid consumers of digital technologies. Brazil continues to rank in the top five nations with the most users of platforms such as Facebook, WhatsApp, and Twitter. In 2015 almost half of all Brazilians aged ten and older used their mobile phones to access the internet. The *Wall Street Journal* declared Brazil "the social media capital of the universe."[19] Leveraging the high levels of citizen participation in the digital realm, Brazilian government agencies embarked on a number of open governance initiatives. These efforts at using technology for transparency were a response to the antigovernment protests in 2013.

When I arrived, the institute was in the midst of numerous projects to foster collective participation online for changing legislation and building grassroots awareness among Brazil's most marginalized populations, many of whom live in favelas, the slums of Brazil. Given the institute's deep involvement in the politics of internet governance, we fellows had unique access to key players in this game. As part of the program, they had organized a series of interviews with influential actors in the cities of Brasilia and São Paulo. It was a good mix of government ministries and committees, the IT industry, and civic internet activists and hackers. We met with officials and executives of several organizations, including the Brazilian Steering Committee, Google, Uber, Airbnb, Bitcoin, the Ministry of Culture, the Ministry of Information Technology, Facebook, and Vila Cívica, a civic hacker group.

What was particularly striking was the relationship between the government and the hackers. Exemplary of this strange new breed of partnerships was the Laboratório Ráquer, or "Hacker Lab," situated inside the Brazilian Chamber of Deputies (Congress). Prior to this, we visited Garoa in São Paulo, a typical hacker space where one could just stroll in. Their walls were covered in political graffiti, and the place was scattered with toys for the geeks. The hacker lab in the Brazilian Congress, however, was a different beast altogether. Entry involved going through a high-security entrance with police and metal detectors and personnel to accompany us to the right room through cubicles and corridors. This space was akin to a hacker in a suit.

However, upon entering the room, the hacker culture enveloped us as the group passionately explained their new role with the government. This space was born out of a hackathon event in November 2014. The Brazilian Chamber of Deputies hosted this event to make legislation accessible to the average citizen. The competition to design mobile apps led to three winning apps and, more importantly, an idea to create a sustained relationship between the public and the government, mediated by hackers. Within a month, the Chamber passed a resolution mandating a permanent presence within it that is "open for access and use by any citizen, especially programmers and software developers, members of parliament and other public workers, where they can utilize public data in a collaborative fashion for actions that enhance citizenship."[20]

Cristiano Ferri Faria, the director of this hacker space, showed us some of the work they were doing to enable citizen engagement, including visualization of government speeches that allowed citizens as well as officials to gain insight on the dominant talking points on diverse social issues. This overview could help politicians negotiate and make collective decisions, he explained. They were also building and extending their partnerships with hackers across Brazil to strengthen this initiative. Of course, an obvious question is how they managed to navigate the politics of possibly shaming the government by highlighting corruption, for instance, while continuing to be under the government's roof. What was the price for formalizing hacking under the umbrella of the government? Their solution was that when they came across contentious information that created a conflict of interest, they passed it on to other hackers independent of the government.

This initiative was not the only one in Latin America. In Mexico, the government spent 15 million pesos (about US$9.3 million) of the taxpayers' money on a mobile app for tracking legislation on mobile phones. This app quickly came to be called the "millionaire app" for having been created at a scandalous cost. In response, a group of young hackers held a mini-hackathon and produced a similar product for less than 12,000 pesos (about US$600), a minuscule amount in comparison. Surprisingly, the government decided to embrace the new cyberactivists. Within a few months Mexico became one of the first countries to launch a civic innovation office run by hackers.

These efforts are commendable, but apps do not necessarily solve structural and systemic issues. In the extremely competitive app economy, people might not even download the apps, let alone use them for civic causes. David Sasaki, an expert on open governance for the Latin American Omidyar Network, a philanthropic group, explains that apps can be mostly symbolic as they show what is possible. He believes that formalizing hacking is "about changing the mentality within government."[21] In the last few years, hacking of governance has become part of a larger movement across the globe, including Bloomberg's innovation teams in New Orleans and the social innovation camps sponsored by the United Nations Development Programme in South Asia. In the United States, June 4 has been designated the National Day of Civic Hacking. Hacking has become official.

Hacking has also become a powerful tool for rebranding nations. For instance, for decades Western governments labeled China an imitative, copycat, bandit nation. China's manufacturing industry did start up through reproduction—which, as we have seen, is standard procedure for emerging economies—but it has since diversified into numerous innovative businesses and products of its own creation. For many years the Western news media portrayed the Chinese wave of industrialization as the world's all-purpose factory. Creativity and Chinese culture were described as if they were positioned at the opposite ends of a spectrum. In recent years, however, headlines have shifted, somewhat belatedly, in their portrayals of China's innovation economy. BBC recently wondered out loud, "Can China Innovate?"[22] But in 2016 alone, news from China covered by *Forbes, The Economist, Wired, The Diplomat,* and others suggested that China has indeed broken out of the mold of its own making.

The Chinese government has committed to promoting a new agenda, one where "Innovate with China" replaces the "Made in China" message to the world. It has declared this the age of innovation for China, or "Chinovation." One of the top-down strategies for enabling this mission is institutionalizing hacking and maker spaces to foster creativity. Chinese hacker spaces are becoming legitimate cultural zones for production.[23] China's do-it-yourself (DIY) makers have become allies with the government to create social change.

China's first hacker space, Xinchejian, opened in Shanghai in the fall of 2010. Entrepreneurs, designers, bloggers, and artists congregated to tinker with new toys provided by the government—3D printers, sensor toolkits, soldering irons, and so on. This experiment became an instant success, and within six months similar hacker spaces arose in other cities, including Shanghai, Beijing, Shenzhen, Ningbo, Hangzhou, and Guangzhou. The Chinese government created a competition for proposals to build a hundred innovation houses across the country. Formalizing hacking, however, requires a break from the more negative connotation of hackers as rebels against government and the established order. This required a linguistic shift from the word *heike*—"black hacker," a person engaged in illegal activity—to the alternative term *chuangke,* "creative professional."

Contemporary China is working to become a creative China. In January 2015 the government initiated a new policy that aims to foster mass entrepreneurship among the Chinese people.[24] Unlike in the West, where hacker spaces have long been associated with privileged white males, Chinese hacker spaces are presented as democratic zones for innovation from below. The policy document starts with the premise that it is necessary to inculcate creativity and an entrepreneurial mind-set among those at the margins to enable them to mobilize themselves into prosperity. Leo Lee, the founder of a makerspace in Chengdu, argues that actually, China has always had creative entrepreneurship. At a 2015 innovation forum in Shanghai, he said, "In China, we are not in shortage of makers. We actually have makers all around us, the makers who build our infrastructures, repair our phones, and build our homes. China has so many makers, we just don't have a mechanism to identify them. We don't see them."[25]

He has a point. Take the cell phone industry, for instance. Hacking the cell phone by mixing parts and tailoring them for diverse markets is a typical creative enterprise from below. In the last decade this process has been gaining legitimacy—once an illicit activity despised by Western mobile companies, it is growing into an industry that global mobile conglomerates are grudgingly coming to respect.[26] Ming-Kai Tsai, the CEO of Mediatek, a key supplier of mobile phones, declared that what was *shan-zhai* (improvisation) yesterday has become mainstream design today.

How did this shift happen? It has been partly due to governments' unfair licensing policies, which deterred competition in this industry and made heroes of these entrepreneurs, who targeted their innovations toward the bottom segment of the country so that the neglected consumers of marginalized communities could enjoy the benefits of the mobile phone with cheap, accessible, and user-friendly devices. Through customization, tinkering, and remixing, this process became the great leveler, reducing the digital divide. While the formal system catered to the middle class, this informal system attended to the vast underserved poorer population, gaining the higher moral ground.

In October 2007 the Chinese government gave up its control over mobile licenses, opening up the market and allowing the new initiatives to get a legal foothold. The government hired 4,000 bloggers to publicize this shift in policy. This enabled *shan-zhai* entrepreneurs to build networks openly, and the media limelight gave them respectability—which in turn became part of the larger imaginary of China as a nation of authentic innovation. This highlights the relationship between fair regulation and good business practice. Illicit innovation often is more inclusive and democratic than existing legal arrangements. Morality and pragmatism compellingly combine to legitimize many of these bottom-up initiatives.

As governments continue to usurp hacker spaces, what began as countercultural spaces tend to become instruments of the state; what originally were creative outlets with subversive, revolutionizing potential become diligently controlled in the service of mainstream interests. This alliance with government might enable hardworking hackers to feel they are filling a newly imagined and expanded role of citizen, and many bandit entrepreneurs fervently wish to go legitimate so that they no longer have to operate at high risk under massive state surveillance. One problem here is that, in poor communities in the Global South, the original impetus to hack systems is to fulfill basic daily needs of marginalized populations—and if these hackers go legitimate, there is a strong chance that they might no longer persist in trying to solve problems for those populations. Quick fixes, remixes, and shortcuts are the rule of the day, to make products frugal and thus available and accessible to all, and the question is whether these products, once they and their makers are absorbed into the formal economy, will continue to be frugal. In other words, is there intrinsic virtue in frugality for the shaping and scaling of innovation for low-income communities in the Global South?

Frugal Innovation: At What Cost?

There is a cartoon by R. K. Laxman, India's legendary cartoonist, that shows a minister and his secretary standing before a slum, discussing its fate. The secretary says to his boss, "It will be a problem demolishing it, sir. Why not just put a sign saying 'low cost housing complex' and leave it?"[27] This sums up the most common criticism of frugal and jugaad innovation—that it perpetuates low-quality, short-term, and unsustainable solutions. The term "jugaad" has a long, indigenous history of being linked to dubious practices such as rural jury-rigging, corruption, and illegally tampering with vehicles. In recent years these associations have receded to the background while its more creative, improvisational, and spontaneous approaches to problems have caught the media's attention and the imagination of business thought leaders worldwide. Both, though, remain the two sides of the jugaad coin.

Sociologist Thomas Birtchnell gives us little cause to celebrate jugaad, the entrepreneurial improvisations of India's poor.[28] He argues that the development of aid policies for poor communities can be harmed by the myths perpetuated around the notion of jugaad—namely, that austerity is inherently positive for innovation, that it can be a solution to global recession, and that jugaad is an intrinsically Indian cultural practice that the world should learn from and embrace. Far from this being positively disruptive, he argues, it serves to legitimize government inaction.

Take one example of acclaimed frugal innovation common in India: the customization of vehicles by the poor to accommodate more passengers. India has one of the highest road accident rates in the world, especially with two-wheelers, the poor person's transport.[29] In this case, frugality comes at the price of safety.

One can argue that, all the same, such improvisation led to affordable models of transport, such as the small Nano car. But increasing the number of affordable cars for the poor increases negative environmental factors, such as air pollution and noise, so they come at the cost of the environment. Through this lens, it is not clear that these innovations—from jerry-rigged two-wheelers to a flurry of Nanos—made for positive change in the lives of the poor. Better public transport, especially if fares can be lowered, can have a better long-term impact on low-income populations if they cause less damage to their environment.

And even though mobile apps are exemplars of frugal innovation, many have only limited social impact. The AquaSift app, for instance, can detect toxicity in water but it cannot change the governmental and corporate policies and practices that allow dumping chemicals into the environment. Many low-income communities often have no way to get clean water even with apps like AquaSift. Ushahidi, the open software group that develops apps for users to track violence and other violations of human rights, doesn't provide a route by which to actually reform political structures. Like many such organizations, Ushahidi's business model rests on the failings of the state. The longevity of such social entrepreneurship depends on the state continuing to disappoint its citizens.

Numerous mundane acts of improvisation are not just illegal but unethical and harmful to others. Diluting milk with water to increase sales, relabeling old products as new, bottling tap water and selling it as spring water, putting weights on scales to defraud customers, and other such examples are also common jugaad devices of people at the margins. In 2015 a friend my mother has known since their childhood became ill on a road trip in Tamil Nadu with his family. He made the mistake of buying his heart medicine at a roadside pharmacy. Only when hospitalized did he discover that the pills were fake. This too is jugaad.

Of course, cell phones can empower as well as exploit through jugaad. There are numerous government-launched apps giving direct access to digital forms. This disrupts a carefully manicured bribery system built by low-end bureaucrats to exploit poor citizens in need of public services. On the other hand, there are several apps to detect police radar that help drivers speed without being caught. The mobile phone has become an indispensable tool for drug cartels, in a cat-and-mouse game of circumvention and detection through constant innovation on both sides. Banking on the poor to be entrepreneurial in the face of unsafe transportation, corruption, dilapidated infrastructure, and scarcity of essential resources can often foster perverse incentives to sustain the status quo. It is less about innovation and more about management of unfortunate circumstances. Their Dickensian deprivation becomes an asset for innovation.

The framing of India as the world's frugal innovation laboratory inadvertently sends a message that India is more a survival culture than a progressive one. The example of Indian innovation—"Indovation"—as a new business model was brought up at the United Nations 2010 summit on climate change. Rajendra Pachauri, then chairperson of a UN panel, declared that Indovation is "the key to taking us forward."[30] Essentially he was arguing that the country's low level of per capita energy consumption was a shining example of austerity innovation—but the low energy consumption is due to India's low per capita income.

Anyone who has studied the Indian economy prior the 1990s would find this trend ironic. After achieving independence from the British in 1947, India for decades had an image of being a "sleeping nation" with a "Hindu style of growth." Rather than attributing India's slow economic growth to the socialist policies of the Nehru government, thought leaders of that time blamed it on India's Hindu culture. Robert McNamara, the US secretary of defense in the 1960s, disparagingly spoke of a Hindu mind-set of "fatalism" and the lack of an Indian drive for progress, popularizing this image until the days of liberalization in the 1990s.

In the last two decades, Indian culture has experienced a makeover, this time as a desirable global model. Business guru Navi Radjou describes the differences between Indian and Western styles of innovation, comparing Indian-style innovation to jazz—free-flowing improvisations that build on themselves—and Western-style innovation to an orchestra where, "if you take the script away, people don't know what to do!"[31] While he advocates a merging of the two styles, he is unclear about how the so-called predictability of the West intersects with the supposed improvisation of Indian inventiveness.

Is this merger even possible? Do the West and "the rest" have irreconcilable differences when it comes to innovation? After all, the norm in American-style business is the culture of planned obsolescence— deliberately building deterioration into a product to shorten its life span and force customers to buy new products sooner. Many multi-national corporations across the West quickly adopted this strategy of making products disposable. In contrast, developing countries, where the majority of the world's poor reside, are pervaded by the repair culture—extending the life span of products through frugal and creative improvisation.

Repair is highly undesirable in most wealthy nations. It is an obstacle to corporate profit in their high-consumption and expensive labor markets. Take the telecommunications industry in the West. Every year they come up with new phones, extolling their new innovations, whether the consumers demand them or not. Over the years, Apple has made the iPhone increasingly less open to repair by the user. In older models the batteries were easy to remove and replace. In today's models Apple has made it very difficult to remove the battery (although energetic entrepreneurs, in harmony with our general narrative, have responded by making kits available online that can be used to replace the battery). Those iPhone users who would like Apple to repair their malfunctioning phones will find that Apple has made the process very expensive in both dollars and downtime. Other strategies used by mainstream phone manufacturers to increase their sales and profits include partnering with software developers like WhatsApp to prevent the latest versions of apps from working on older models of phones, creating new versions of chargers and other accessories for each new model of phone so that users who purchase new phones must also purchase new accessories, and even changing the size of SIM cards so they can't be transferred between different models of phones, much less different makes of phones. The game of constant upgrading is a serious deterrent to users being able to develop DIY repair skills.

In the developing countries of the Global South, on the other hand, cell phone repair shops are thriving. They can hack any phone for a small price. These young entrepreneurs cut SIM cards to fit new phones. They install pirated software so old phones can continue using WhatsApp. They mix and match Apple and non-Apple parts to create phones that provide robust connectivity and last longer. However, this hacking from below is becoming an uphill battle. Multinational telecommunications conglomerates not only are becoming more omnipresent in the Global South; they are making their technology more difficult to be hacked. So there is never a level playing field between innovation from above and innovators from below.

And, of course, it is not only an Indian virtue to find work-arounds for problems. DIY skills flourish wherever communities are having to make do with limited resources. They are "jugaad" in India, "shan-zai" in China, and "gambiarra," "bacalhau," or "jeitinho" in Brazil. Political scientist Alberto Almeida discovered through his surveys that two-thirds of Brazilians sought out ways, even illegal ones, to cut corners in order to solve problems. There is a reason so many Brazilians express little respect for the law. In just a decade, Brazil passed more than 75,000 laws, making it impossible for any citizen to know what all the laws are, much less to comply with them all.[32]

Given that improvisation is a way of life all over the world for people who live in poverty, how did India end up labeled as the leader of frugal innovation? Partly it is due to the rise of the call center industry and Western outsourcing. This brought India into the limelight as a center of behind-the-scene hackers who labored to reduce prices and solve problems for customers thousands of miles away. Partly it is due to the massive Indian diaspora in the United States and particularly in Silicon Valley, which ensures that these narratives circulate across strategic networks. But grassroots innovation itself has less to do with any national culture than with the universality of responding creatively to solve the problems of daily life in the face of limited resources and persisting obstacles. Over time, and everywhere, such work-arounds alongside slow institutional reform consolidate a culture that repairs the goods of daily life and does not fix the overall system.

Much like rebranding India—the land of "Hindu fatalism" is now "the jugaad nation"—the poor are experiencing a rebranding too.

They are now portrayed as industrious and virtuous, driven by necessity and aspiration, and coming to the table with infinite ingenuity. There is even acknowledgment of "reverse innovation," in which ideas flow from bottom to the top—from the poor, who are now portrayed as "experts" at scarcity and risk instead of as amateurs with little motivation or appetite for disruptive change.

Through this lens, the West stands alone in its hedonistic plenty. Quality is a desirable attribute for innovation in products for Western consumers, but quality is not necessarily the scalable attribute for new economies beyond the West. For instance, in April 2013 the German newspaper *Die Welt* asked if German products were too good for the global market.[33] Comparing the global scaling of award-winning German goods to "good enough" Chinese products, they discovered that Chinese goods were scaling far faster. The Chinese followed a more do-it-yourself and price-sensitive approach than the Germans. This raised the question of the role of quality as an essential attribute in contemporary innovation. Neither American-style quickly obsolescing and disposable products nor German-style high-quality, high-priced products are geared toward frugal innovation and the repair culture entrenched among those at the margins.

The growing evidence on collaborating with the poor has been disappointing for Western technology companies. Co-creation with poor communities is an oversold concept that is crumbling after a decade of failure.[34] Corporations were promised that they could make massive fortunes at the "bottom of the pyramid," through economies of scale, catering to the four billion poor who were untapped consumers. However, few companies have found this pot of gold, and probably few would now agree with Bill Gates's enthusiastic declaration, not many years ago, that this could be "an intriguing blueprint for how to fight poverty with profitability."[35] Companies that took up this cause, like Unilever and Procter & Gamble, have decided it was a pipe dream. Given the infrastructural and social complexities in creating markets for the poor, they were barely able to break even with their low-cost products. What started as for-profit products for the poor are now given away free or sold at a loss, and marketed as philanthropy.[36]

For more than a decade, management expert Erik Simanis advocated for the expansion of markets through the bottom-of-the-pyramid approach. Today his enthusiasm has dimmed. He admits that several business leaders and thinkers were seduced by this elegant and enlightened self-interest theory. They forgot that their main job was to earn profits and be accountable to their shareholders. In other words, they were not in the business of poverty alleviation but simply in business, where "development impacts have to become a byproduct of profitable business—not vice versa."[37]

The win-win solution of the 1990s almost two decades later looks more like the win-some, lose-some approach. Instead of deep social outcomes, these co-creative partnerships with the poor have often resulted in superficial effects like spreading the corporate brand in these communities. Companies buy the goodwill of local governments through such initiatives, which open doors to the middle-class market. The economy-of-scale factor runs into the challenge of educating the poor about these new services and convincing them to part with their limited funds to buy a product they are not familiar with. This is difficult to do in communities that are accustomed to improvising to solve their problems at little or no cost rather than buying new products.

The Informal Economy as a Way of Life

In 1996 I moved from Bangalore, India, to the Tenderloin, a poor neighborhood in downtown San Francisco. I took an apartment with Stephanie, a girl from New Jersey. It was the first week in the city for both of us, so we headed to a pay phone down the street to call our parents and tell them we were okay. It was two in the afternoon. As Stephanie stood dialing, a car pulled up and two men jumped out, rushed toward her, pulled her into the car, and drove away. I just stood there, stunned. I went to the pay phone, picked up the dangling receiver, and stared at it. A few minutes passed, which seemed like forever. Then the same car raced up again and came screeching to a halt. They threw Stephanie out, and as they drove off, I could hear one of the men yell, "It's not her, you idiot!" They had mistaken her for a sex worker who owed them money. Stephanie soon packed her bags and flew back home to New Jersey. That was my first week in the United States.

In the 1990s the Tenderloin neighborhood lived up to its name as the underbelly of San Francisco. Union Square, a popular tourist destination full of art galleries and cable cars, was just a few blocks away, and yet these two worlds could not be more different. The Tenderloin was a high-crime area known for theft, prostitution, and illicit drug deals. I had been oblivious to this when I moved there. All I knew was that it was all I could afford. I got a job working at a café down the street where I could help myself to the leftover muffins at the end of the day. The Tenderloin's poverty was visible and omnipresent. The apartments were run down, paint peeling off the walls. There were corner stores but no grocery stores. People without homes, many addicted to drugs, lined the sidewalks. By midnight the energy of the place changed. Transsexuals strolled up and down the street, playfully taunting the drivers who went by slowly to check them out.

It amazed me how contained the activity was in the neighborhood. Over the course of my two years there, I learned that there was an informal arrangement between the police and the sex workers. As long as they stayed below the radar and away from the tourist hot spots, they could conduct their business. There was also a vibrant sharing economy—not the kumbaya sort but a more practical kind. We all had something to trade. There are only so many muffins you can eat at the end of the day. Sometimes it was a trade for soup. Sometimes it was tutoring the son of the couple who owned the Indian restaurant in exchange for curry and roti. Sometimes it was being friendly with a bouncer of the club in exchange for his help with carrying furniture up the stairs. Sometimes it was buying a bottle of red wine for a sex worker so she would do her business under someone else's window and you could get some shut-eye. There was a thriving gray economy mediated through observation, neighborhood gossip, and chance.

Jugaad is a euphemism for coping with everyday life. The less institutional support there is, the more need there is to invent alternatives to make one's life easier. Some general needs in a community are opportunities for innovation. These innovations can create thriving micro-economies, which gain legitimation through consistency, reputation, and trust. Legality and informality have a complex and nuanced relationship. Take, for instance, the case of the Himalayan village Almora, which we visited in Chapter 2. The cybercafés I investigated often doubled as mobile phone shops with legal contracts with companies like Vodafone and Airtel that gave them a foothold in the formal economy. While these centers were legal entities with a positive contribution to the community, they also engaged in illegal practices.

Pirating software and hacking phones is the norm. Many local entrepreneurs break the law simply because setting up their enterprises legally would require filling out a mountain of bureaucratic paperwork. Sometimes there is complicity between local officials and small-scale entrepreneurs in poor neighborhoods to ignore unreasonable laws as long as this does little obvious harm. There are "white" and "black" ways of doing business. Official bills for services rendered go alongside under-the-table cash.

Wherever there is poverty and deep inequality, there will be thriving informal economies. Twelve million illegal immigrants support the formal markets in the United States. These economies make up about 5 to 15 percent of the entire market in most wealthy countries, whereas they constitute more than half of the market in low-income countries.[38] Clearly, this is not a marginal issue but an ongoing global concern.

Peruvian economist Hernando De Soto argues that the informal economy is actually the norm across the world. Ninety percent of the world's population live in developing countries and former Soviet states, and these people participate in the informal sector.[39]

De Soto's research reveals the bias of the market system, whose bureaucracy systematically excludes the majority of the world's population.[40] For instance, he observed that in Peru there were 700,000 laws in place. This gargantuan maze of rules produces loopholes for the privileged. Simultaneously, it creates traps for the poor, not only because they are unlikely to be familiar with most of the laws but also because they are the most likely to violate them, given that complying with many of the laws requires paying exorbitant fees. These impositions force people with limited resources to operate instead in a parallel, informal market system.

In the eighty-fifth anniversary edition of *Forbes* magazine, in 2002, De Soto was listed as one of the fifteen innovators "who will reinvent your future."[41] While his work has been deeply influential for decades, he is not without critics. The recurrent point of criticism is De Soto's advocacy of formalizing the gray economy by incorporating it into the already existing neoliberal market system. Grassroots movements such as Movimento dos Trabalhadores Sem Teto (The Homeless Workers Movement) in Brazil and Abahlali baseMjondolo (the "Red Shirts") in South Africa attack De Soto's proposal on individual land ownership rights.[42] Instead, they passionately promote a "commons" approach to the severe problems of homelessness in their countries. Collective ownership, they argue, will protect the most marginalized and will prevent gentrification of these neighborhoods, which is usually the fate of progressive efforts in urban reform.

The informal economy, however, can reinforce rather than reduce inequality produced by the formal economy.[43] There are few viable options available for tackling the informal economy. Governments cannot afford to ignore illegal practices, but neither should the poor be criminalized for their survival tactics. Less regulation can have the adverse effect of less governmental oversight over the actions of powerful multinationals in a developing country. Even though inclusive governmental policies seem like a best option here, the poor have deep-seated distrust of authorities.

Also, the nature of informal economies cannot be truly grasped without acknowledging their deeply gendered aspects. Women run most survivalist enterprises. This places them in perpetual vulnerability. Sectors such as trade and commerce are the women's forte. For instance, the proportion of women who are self-employed in the informal sector is 64.2 percent in the Middle East, 88.6 percent in sub-Saharan Africa, and almost 90 percent in Asia.[44] Consider South Africa after apartheid.[45] New legislative programs such as the Reconstruction and Development Program were aimed at building a "democratic, non-racial and non-sexist future." They had a long way to go. Women there, often with the assistance of their children, run informal enterprises with little access to capital, few skills, and few opportunities for transitioning to the formal economy. Very often, entrepreneurship is equated with masculinity. Popular media portray the average entrepreneur as male, whether in the West or in the Global South. Alongside the acknowledged feminization of poverty, it is time to start acknowledging the feminization of entrepreneurship.

Where do the rising digital economies of the Global South fall on the spectrum from formal to informal? Cell phones and the internet, with all their offerings for connectivity and engagement, have become needs and not just wants. For the poor, just like for the wealthy, the new technology tools are necessities rather than luxuries. The media and the mobile industries lag far behind in satisfying the rising aspirations of low-income youth as they seek friendship, romance, and entertainment. As we have seen, this urgency to consume new media technologies has spawned numerous enterprises primarily operating within the informal economy. How do governments and the formal market reconcile with these new creative initiatives from below while simultaneously maintaining their institutional order?

Inclusive Capitalism

The current popular model is "inclusive capitalism." Jamie Dimon of JPMorgan Chase, Bill McNabb of Vanguard, Siv Jensen, the Norwegian minister of finance, Indra Nooyi of PepsiCo, and Paul Polman of Unilever have found a common purpose. They came to the front lines for this new market ideal at the October 2016 Conference on Inclusive Capitalism in New York.[46] Many credit C. K. Prahalad with bringing this concept to the limelight as early as 2005 when he asked, "Why can't we create inclusive capitalism?"[47] However, only in the past few years has any structure been proposed for making this ideal into a reality.

At its most simplistic level, the idea of inclusive capitalism is to do good and make a profit at the same time. Value is to be defined in terms beyond the monetary, and the self-interest that has long dictated conventional capitalism is to be replaced with societal interest—instilling morality into economics. As social inequality widens and poverty persists, inclusive capitalism has become the chosen pathway for some key governmental and corporate leaders. Today, few would assert that profit should be the sole motive dictating market practice. But it is difficult to achieve consensus on how to level the playing field between the haves and the have-nots.

Katherine Garrett-Cox, the CEO of Alliance Trust, has said that "profit and purpose are a powerful combination: to earn the right to a more prosperous future, we must show that we are socially useful today."[48] This suggests that people are not entitled to a good life, but instead must earn it. They have to be the agents of change for their own good. Apparently this is said to apply not only to the wealthy, regarding their achieving even more prosperity in the future, but also to the poor—for poverty to be alleviated, the poor should become change-makers themselves. This is consistent with the West's celebrating the poor as entrepreneurs and marveling at their collective ingenuity. There is much incentive to recognize grassroots innovation and to support and scale it. New social media technologies are timely tools that stimulate creativeness on their platforms that can be harnessed for social change.

The corporate and the government sectors have invited the poor to collaborate with them. Public-private partnerships are the goal. The poor are encouraged to bring to the table their expertise gained in their long-standing exposure to chronic scarcity and their ability to pioneer alternatives under such constraints. Hacking poverty is the poor person's creative play. The corporations, aid agencies, and the state, for their part, promise to bring to the table their institutional, legal, and technical support to identify, consolidate, and scale such innovations from below to create sustainable social development.

Many thinkers and leaders from the inclusive capitalism coalition agree that market economics has an ethics problem. For the market to truly repair itself and create radical reform, the system needs to be instilled with a new set of moral principles. Sir Evelyn de Rothschild, chairperson of E. L. Rothschild, remarked at the 2016 Conference on Inclusive Capitalism that the old ways of doing business need overhauling: "Old dogs must unlearn their tricks."[49] To ensure that the benefits of this new version of capitalism are distributed fairly, Joe Kaeser, president and CEO of Siemens, advocates an "ownership culture," one that is genuinely participatory, so that businesses, governments, civic organizations, and citizens can all have a stake in the pie. Inclusive capitalism as harmonious capitalism.[50]

The problem, as we have seen, is that as attempts at inclusive capitalism play out, they are inundated with numerous contradictions and parallel conflicting systems. The root issue for this conundrum is what counts as legitimate virtue among the poor—where legitimacy is defined by the dominant market structures. The creativeness of the poor is viewed as entrepreneurial and innovative as long as it extends the vision and end goals of the corporate realm and aligns with the classic economies of scale. The improvisations of the global poor feed into the laboratories of ideas for the global market leaders.

This helps them expand their consumer base to include the marginalized majority who have long evaded commodification. In the digital economy this is even more prescient, as the poor have been the fastest-growing user group in the last five years. From the government side, as long as the poor confine their creative play to their own backyard, the authorities can keep an eye on them and contain the effects of their activities. This also diffuses and distributes state responsibility onto their citizens.

The irony is that the poor's creative initiative and improvisation are largely the result of how the market and state continue to exclude the poor. It is difficult to include the interests of the poor, in spite of the rhetoric of joint governance and innovation for the common good. The narrative of the poor as virtuous beings working hand in hand with the corporate and the government sectors often seems to be merely public relations rhetoric. This cosmetic approach casts a lifeline to neoliberal capitalism instead of promoting global solutions to inequality.[51]

Mainstream media today generally avoid the derogatory labels— "mobs," "the masses," and so on—that for centuries were commonly used to refer to the poor. Today the poor are "the collective intelligence," "crowds with wisdom," and "self-organized learners" who are able to help themselves overcome adversity in spite of the many challenges in their daily lives. Their creativity is said to have the power to change their lives and society. Nowhere has this rhetoric been more pervasive than in the field of education, as we will see in Chapter 5.

The decades of data on education in developing countries show teachers absent from the classrooms and state policies that minimize low-income youths' chances for a public education. Many actors in development work—government agencies, aid foundations, corporations—express faith in the enterprising nature of the poor: with the aid of new digital technologies, the poor, as natural problem-solvers, will collectively teach themselves and provide for themselves the education they need to raise themselves out of poverty. However, this unwavering faith in the poor and their self-organizing ability threatens the very fabric of public education. As the next chapters reveal, technology companies are pushing this faith-based approach so they can justify replacing traditional learning institutions with the apps they develop for personalized learning.

5

Slumdog Inspiration

"WHAT THE HELL can a slumdog possibly know?" asks the police officer. To which Jamal, the boy from the slum replies, "The answers." This is a powerful scene from Danny Boyle's widely acclaimed 2008 movie *Slumdog Millionaire,* which at its heart celebrates the ingenuity of the poor. The movie is set in Dharavi, India, one of the world's largest slums and home to almost a million residents in the heart of Mumbai. It follows the life of Jamal Malik, who manages to survive the cruelty that slums bestow on children like himself. Through his ability to learn from his experiences, he lifts himself out of poverty, becomes a call center employee, and although uneducated, succeeds in winning in the Indian version of the TV show *Who Wants to Be a Millionaire?* Life furnished him with all the knowledge he needed to answer all the questions asked on this television show. Life was his school. Street knowledge trumped book knowledge.

The inspiration for this movie, which was adapted from the novel *Q & A* by Indian author Vikas Swarup, came from a 1999 social experiment conducted by Sugata Mitra, the chief scientist at NIIT, an IT Learning Solutions Corporation. Curious to see what children in a slum in New Delhi would do with a computer, Mitra set up a computer in a hole in a wall in a public space so children could play with it. Within a short time, children with little prior knowledge of computers began to use the computer with no formal instruction. Mitra then replicated this "Hole-in-the-Wall" experiment in a rural area.

In his TED talk, Mitra shares the amazement he felt when, after returning to the rural area a few months later, he found children playing games on the computer.[1] When the children spotted him, he reports, they immediately demanded "a faster processor and a better mouse" and complained that he had left them with a machine that only worked in English so they had to teach themselves English to use it. The unsupervised child becomes the teacher. These children taught themselves a new language so that they could play games. Mitra's "School in the Cloud" work has won him numerous accolades—including the 2013 TED Prize, which provided US$1 million funding to expand his project of enabling children to learn through playing on the internet.

This kind of play—self-organized discovery—is widely celebrated by the media as a new "revolution of the masses." The poor are called upon to leapfrog over their poverty with the click of the mouse. The shortage of teachers will not stop the children from getting an education. There will be no lost generation here, because the children can take charge and become like Jamal Malik. They too can carve out their future with digital education games on their mobile phones and tablets. Play is synonymous with informal learning. When the poor play with their gaming apps and teach themselves, they shed the failures of schooling that suppressed their ancestors for centuries. Play is freedom to learn, freedom to think, and freedom to become. Such is the rhetoric, propagated by technophiles like Sugata Mitra, that is seeping into educational and technology policies.

In my own projects in rural villages in South India and the Himalayas over more than a decade, I have faced numerous difficulties in the scaling of computers, both within schools and at stand-alone kiosks. I have witnessed major organizations like the World Bank, Siemens, and Hewlett Packard brought to their knees by the significant disconnect between their ambitions and their understandings of these communities. I have encountered Mitra's Hole-in-the-Wall experiment, not as a hub of thriving autonomous learning but instead as abandoned gaping holes, forgotten by the passerby.

Why do we burden these children with expectations that their play should be instructive, transformative, and revolutionary to their lives? Is this a way of abdicating our responsibility toward youth in low-income communities in the name of child empowerment? I argue in this chapter that child-centered play with technology is no substitute for education. In spite of what technology has to offer, children still need good teachers, good content, and sustained reform of the educational system. The poor are not miracle workers. When they play, let them not be expected to choose math games over adrenaline-inducing car-chase games. The self in self-organized learning needs support structures, even more so in these deprived communities. Good learning and teaching cannot be automated. This is a mundane plea, hardly TED-worthy. It is not surprising that a technophile prophet such as Sugata Mitra can sustain an ideological cult of play-driven, self-organized learning as a way out of poverty. To dismantle this cult, we need to bring down the prophet.

Evangelizing Play-Driven Learning

The British news magazine *The Spectator* calls Sugata Mitra the "guru of self-organized learning." The Smithsonian Institution in Washington, DC, has recognized him as the "evangelist" who has sparked this movement. The technology news website ZDNet has called him the "prophet" for a radical new way of thinking about education.[2] Mitra often gets a standing ovation in his public talks as he immerses his audience in the lives of children in a slum in a developing country who, once given access to the internet, open the world of education for themselves. This vision propelled him to place a computer in a hole in a wall in a slum to show how children's play with new technology has an infinite capacity for them to self-educate about anything, even molecular biology.

Since the 1999 launch of the Hole-in-the-Wall experiment, Mitra's claims about the power of play-driven, self-organized learning have expanded significantly. It is one thing to demonstrate that a child can use a computer without instruction and learn various ways to manipulate this new toy, such as bringing up the paint program or playing games. Tell that to any parent, rich or poor, and they will shrug their shoulders—they have already seen their children master their mobile phones without any guidance. To claim that children can teach themselves genetics, mathematics, biology, and physics in the same way, however, is a different ball game.

Mitra first procured major funding to test his ideas from the International Finance Corporation, a subset of the World Bank group, in 2001.[3] He set up thirty learning stations in poverty-stricken areas in and outside India. With a team of his own researchers from NIIT, he conducted studies to support his theories. The first round of evidence his team amassed allowed him to argue that children in resource-constrained areas in developing countries learn how to use the computer and the internet on their own through sustained play with the new technologies.[4] Findings from his later experiments, he argued, revealed that play can lead to productive outcomes as children teach themselves educational content they encounter online. With a friendly encouraging adult, a poor child can, in this manner, do just as well in educational achievements as a child in a good school.[5]

One of his more astonishing and popular claims delivered in his 2013 TED talk is that children in a remote village in India learned molecular biology on their own:

Can Tamil speaking children in a south Indian village learn the biotechnology of DNA replication in English from a street side computer? And I said, I'll measure them. They'll get a zero. I'll spend a couple of months, I'll leave it for a couple of months, I'll go back, they'll get another zero. I'll go back to the lab and say, we need teachers. I found a village. It was called Kallikuppam in southern India. I put in Hole-in-the-Wall computers there, downloaded all kinds of stuff from the internet about DNA replication, most of which I didn't understand. The children came rushing, said, "What's all this?" So I said, "It's very topical, very important. But it's all in English." So they said, "How can we understand such big English words and diagrams and chemistry?" So by now, I had developed a new pedagogical method, so I applied that. I said, "I haven't the foggiest idea . . . And anyway, I am going away." So I left them for a couple of months. They'd got a zero. I gave them a test. I came back after two months and the children trooped in and said, "We've understood nothing." I said, "What? You don't understand these screens and you keep staring at it for two months? What for? So a little girl . . . raised her hand, and she says to me in broken Tamil and English . . ."Well, apart from the fact that improper replication of the DNA molecule causes disease, we haven't understood anything else."[6]

This punch line gets an appreciative laugh from his audience.

Mitra is no stranger to controversy. Over the years he has provoked educators by calling his early experiments "minimally invasive education" and by peppering his talks with claims that these initiatives demand "the end of schooling as we know it" and that "every teacher that can be replaced by a computer should be."[7] His faith in googling for information led him to declare that "knowledge is becoming obsolete."[8] Why know when you can just google? Since receiving his 2013 TED award, he is propagating his educational doctrine through the online Self-Organized Learning Environment (SOLE) Toolkits.[9] These allow anyone in any part of the world to take on the mission of playful learning and spread it in her or his own community. Play-driven learning promises to go viral.

Taking Down the Prophet

The *British Journal of Educational Technology* invited me to do a face-off with Sugata Mitra in the "Afterthoughts" section in their journal.[10] It turned out that Mitra and I had submitted papers at the same time on the Hole-in-the-Wall experiment, based on our fieldwork. Mitra and his team had completed the experiment in Kalikuppam, a remote Indian village, where, they reported, they had found evidence that Tamil-speaking children, once they were given access to computers and the internet at one of Mitra's learning kiosks, were able to teach themselves basic molecular biology. The researchers reported that these children could achieve test scores comparable to those of students at a local school who had received instruction in this subject. They also reported that, with the help of a "friendly adult mediator," these children were able to achieve results similar to those of children in a high-performing private school in New Delhi who were fluent in English and were taught this subject by qualified teachers.[11] This was one of their boldest claims yet.

These children from the village, Mitra reported, had proven that with a little help from new technology, they could be "equal to their [rich] peers."[12] More importantly, he reported, a qualified teacher with abundant resources at a wealthy school was no more effective than a doting adult mediator with no knowledge of the subject coupled with a child's productive playfulness with the computer.[13] If we are to take this report as sacrosanct, we should start replacing all teachers, even the most qualified ones, with technology. Surely, if they both have the same effect, why shouldn't we? Mitra even prods us to look at the bright side: scarcity leads to positive outcomes. This path leads to celebrating poverty because the poor find creative ways to cope with it.

My evidence was not that fanciful. I spent eight months in a remote area in the Himalayas where I investigated two of Mitra's abandoned learning stations.[14] In my investigation, I found community indifference and resentment toward this project. Through conversations with teachers, children, and parents in this area, I discovered that these kiosks were primarily portals for entertainment used by a few boys. Within a few months the kiosks fell into disuse for lack of maintenance. One teacher put it, "I'll tell you, they spend so much money on computers and so little on taking care of it. They gave the keys to the chaukidar [watchman] and told him to clean it and take care of it. Now you tell me why should he take care of it? He doesn't get paid for it at all. He sleeps here below and works at the school so why should he go up and stay up just for this?"[15]

These computers did not threaten the teachers. They already had computer labs set up in their school. They were more annoyed by the poor learning habits these kiosks were creating in their children. Prior to this, I had worked for six months on a Hewlett-Packard project that installed internet kiosks in Kuppam, a rural area in Andhra Pradesh, about five hours from Mitra's Kalikuppam site. The intent was to create learning portals and 24/7 information hubs for the community. By the end of my stay there, several parents had complained to me that their boys were skipping school to spend their time playing games at these kiosks. They also expressed anger that pornographic material was so easy to access on the web.[16]

Clearly my evidence diverged substantively from Mitra's. What do we make of such contradictory findings? What disturbed me at the outset was the fact that as I dug deeper, I found that almost all the published papers that celebrated Mitra's experiment came from his NIIT team. NIIT is a for-profit Indian company that offers educational technology software solutions, serving governments and private schools in India. It makes perfect business sense for such a company to sell the idea of replacing teachers with software and to celebrate a child's play as educational.

However sincere the team may be, they have a conflict of interest when they seek their own empirical evidence that serves their business model. When news media asked the NIIT team about the impact of unsupervised play on learning, they replied, "Instinctively we know [that their theory is true], but we need to show it . . . the clue is in their [children's] eyes. They are smiling, laughing. You don't get that in a classroom."[17] Even if we assume that they are being objective here, we are still confronted with a number of flaws in the design of their study that cast doubt on the validity of the results. Mitra defends his use of the methods of physics in studying this social science subject. "It is the subject that I know, and I didn't study social science." Down the line, he backtracked by saying, "I cannot confirm each of these findings."[18]

Confirmed or not, his reports are out there and they fuel the gospel of unsupervised, playful learning. That gospel was not simply an anecdote in a TED talk—it inspired funders to throw millions of dollars into similar projects. His approach has become a fundamental criterion in the awarding of education technology prizes, influencing future education innovation for the poor, as we will see in Chapter 6. So let us look closely at the experiment that equates a qualified teacher with a computer and a mediator, where being rich or poor has little impact on learning as long as the child has access to the internet. Mitra does not dispute that on the internet children spend most of their time entertaining themselves with games and spend 20 percent of their time just "looking at things."[19] In that time of discovery, he claims, such children have learned molecular biology on their own from a downloaded English-language text written for adults.

When asked why he would impose English-language adult material on Tamil-speaking children, he argued that because English "is the most common language in which children would find information on the Internet" and because digital content is primarily written for adults, it was important to expose the children to this reality.[20] This discounts the numerous scholars and advocates in the past decades who have argued that the world would be richer culturally if local and regional languages were supported. UNESCO, local governments, and several activists and nonprofits are on board with creating new content for the internet that is linguistically diverse and child-friendly, to achieve the best learning outcomes.[21]

These efforts have already borne fruit. A year before Mitra's experiment, UNESCO reported on the decline of the English language on the web, down from 75 percent of content in 1998 to 45 percent in 2005.[22] As of 2017, there are about as many Chinese-language users of the web as there are English-language users. Nobody disputes the uphill challenge involved in linguistically diversifying the web, but few see monolingualism as inevitable or desirable. Even Silicon Valley is doing its bit, developing polyglot software to capture a new market of diverse language users.

Companies like Google have launched ambitious projects, such as the Indian Language Internet Alliance, with the aim of quickly getting half a billion more Indians online by providing content in their local languages.[23] Facebook today already defaults to the local language, acknowledging that their future markets are in the Global South. Mozilla and GSMA, a trade body of mobile network operators, are currently working on unlocking relevant web content in multiple languages for billions of the world's poor.[24]

Disregarding these prominent movements, Mitra has put his weight behind English and adult content as the future of the web and of children's learning. But aside from these values embedded in the design of his project, let us look at the comparative testing that led him and his team to assert that quality teachers are equivalent to a computer accessorized with a nonteacher adult guiding the children who are using the computer.

In essence, Mitra and his team entered the village, pretested a select group of children on their knowledge of molecular biology, downloaded a text on this subject to the computers, instructed the kiosk mediator not to instruct but to affectionately encourage, and then left the village. Seventy-five days later, they were back with their testing gear, allegedly finding results comparable to those of students at a local school and at an affluent private high school in the city.

Critical information is missing. For instance, Mitra and his team have not stated that the selected children were school dropouts, so we can assume that the children attended a local school that followed the same typical state curriculum as the neighboring rural school to which they were compared. This would mean that at their traditional school the children he selected were getting the same instruction as the other children, including instruction in basic molecular biology. They were not blank slates. By 2009, when Mitra's experiment took place, the Indian government had already equipped the country's schools with computers. Mitra and his team have told us nothing about what these children learned with their textbooks and the computers in their school. They have told us nothing about the role of their teachers in their learning of molecular biology. How can we, then, assess the actual effects of the out-of-school, Hole-in-the-Wall experiment? What we can assume is that the children's local, traditional schooling and their use of Mitra's computers influenced each other. We also have been told nothing about how the children's parents and other elders were involved in the children's learning during the period of the experiment. The ultimate upshot is that no causal relationship has been established between the children's learning basic molecular biology and their exposure to Mitra's Learning Station and the helpful mediator.

Another kind of issue that the report neglects to discuss is the fact that seventy-five days is a long time to work on one document. Few schools would devote so much time to one text, because that would come at the cost of neglecting other subjects. Mitra's selected children were assigned an adult to prod them along. We have been given no reason to believe that the adult moderating the kiosk did not become teacher-like, did not help these children with this text, and somehow remained simply an enthusiastic but neutral observer. We also are not told what incentive, monetary or otherwise, the supervisory adult was given to dedicate seventy-five days of her life to the project.

In this span of time, when these children learned some basic facts about molecular biology while being exposed to one text for two and a half months, did they learn anything else? To make a fair comparison between the education provided by Mitra's kiosk computers and a quality teacher in a local or an affluent school, we need to measure these children's learning on other topics besides molecular biology—and compare their learning on those topics to the learning that took place under the guidance of quality teaching in a traditional school. The reports by Mitra's team do not even touch on issues like this. Pedagogy is not a black box. And the very design of the experiment—leaving these children unobserved for seventy-five days, with no interventions by the experimenters and no knowledge of what actually transpired for these children during this significant period—certainly does not satisfy fundamental criteria for good science.

Over the years, the few independent researchers and practitioners who did investigate the Hole-in-the-Wall project came to similar conclusions. The education technology entrepreneur Donald Clark discovered that the computers provided for the children rarely worked, the DSL connection was often down, and when it was up, the kiosks tended to be dominated by a few older boys who used the computers for gaming.[25] Education professor Mark Warschauer attributed the failure of this project to the poor content available on these kiosks, which was not in the local language. His study revealed that the children's parents were concerned because during the experiment their children quickly lost interest in studying and instead reverted to gaming.[26]

Such documented failures did not put a halt to Mitra's continued education "experiments." After he was awarded the US$1 million TED Prize in 2013 for his "School in the Cloud" dream, he leveraged his Hole-in-the-Wall media coverage and the positive reports coming from his own NIIT team to convince Silicon Valley of the virtues of his mission—to spread universal education by fostering "self-organized learning environments," or SOLEs as he calls them, in poor and rich communities alike. There is a SOLE toolkit available online that anyone can download and put to use.[27]

The formula for this supposed radical pedagogy includes two major elements. First, the mediators need to ask big questions and let the children browse for the answers with their peers without further instruction. In poor communities, connecting to "grannies" via Skype can help the children develop language fluency and search for skills that will allow them to confront the big questions. Second, mediators need to allow for chaos in the classroom by not imposing any premeditated curriculum or agenda on the children. In other words, let the children play unsupervised. As we follow the instructions from the toolkit, we are told to pose the question that triggers the maximum curiosity among the children. Examples of big questions are "Can anything be less than zero? Will robots be conscious one day? How do my eyes know to cry when I'm sad?" We are told to take notes of this learning process and monitor the changes. We are told to "encourage debate" and facilitate discussion.[28]

The most startling and welcome aspect of Mitra's new project is the discarding of the principle of zero intervention. Clearly, there is more structure here. The toolkit itself is a format for learning. The entire SOLE manifesto seems to address a "somebody" who will download, organize the students to organize themselves around the internet, ask the big questions, and moderate the sharing of the discoveries. It is quite evident that the toolkit is a proxy for a curriculum and the "somebody" is a teacher.

Yet the word "teacher" is nowhere to be found. This time around, the mediator is not supposed to merely express awe at the children's learning, as in the initial Hole-in-the-Wall experiments. This time the mediators are expected to do much more. They are to inspire, question, facilitate, and connect. The sites where the current SOLE experiments have been established are traditional schools, with teachers, in poor communities worldwide. The self in "self-organized learning" has shrunk to its rightful size.

Let us step back a moment from the big promises, seductive TED talks, and clever anecdotes for this experiment. We are left with a call for teamwork among children and a teacher who is well trained in managing a classroom by leveraging children's play into learning. How is this different from the last few decades of best practices documented in education research?

Since the 1960s, educators have been writing about such a method, employing multiple labels.[29] Blended learning, hybrid learning, technology-mediated instruction, personalized learning, web-enhanced instruction, mixed-mode instruction, STEM learning—given these established methods, there is nothing innovative in the SOLE approach. If anything, even though it can provide some relief for students who are averse to formal instruction, the toolkit method provides little guidance on how to transform play-based learning from superficial engagement to deeper thinking over a sustained period.

Googling for Wisdom

Google is godsend to Mitra and his team. Play, they say, is curiosity-driven search. Mitra promotes a vision of critical self-organized learning through search engines. He has much faith in the discipline of young people and the power of googling as a pathway to productive discovery. In a 2013 interview with the *Huffington Post,* he makes his case:

> Disbelief has followed me for 25 years. They [his critics] say children will just use computers to play games all the time. And actually, they get tired of games in two or three months. They might play occasionally, but it's around this time they discover Google.[30]

He argues that the very act of googling is learning. Through Google, children will teach themselves mathematics, particle physics, genetics, and so on. Mitra admits that the children in poor communities may need a little help with their searches. Three hundred "grannies" have been recruited as volunteers for the School in the Cloud project. They will use Skype to guide the children on their search adventures in Google.

In a BBC interview Mitra confessed that "there are hundreds of reasons why it [the project] doesn't work."[31] Teachers are not interested in taking on this project, Skype does not have reliable connectivity in remote areas, and there are cultural misunderstandings when British grannies talk remotely with children in Indian villages. "The schools were predominately Muslim and, with hindsight, that may not have been the best choice," says Mitra.[32] The grannies plodded on nevertheless. They read aloud *Not Now, Bernard,* a British story of a child who is ignored by his parents. One day a monster eats him up and replaces him, but the parents do not notice that the monster is not their boy. The children enjoy these stories—when Skype works, of course.

Without Skype grannies coming to the rescue for the poor, will Google step up? Carole Cadwalladr of the British newspaper *The Guardian* investigated how children use Google without supervision. In one of the SOLE experiments, the children are encouraged to explore the world of the painter Cézanne and share their discoveries with the group. One group embarked on this quest by spending the first ten minutes googling "Susan" and "Suzanne." Another group instructed others to go to Wikipedia for the answers. A group of girls decided to write the name Cézanne on a sheet of paper and color in the letters, and only one of them pursued the search online. Cézanne was not a compelling subject for these girls.[33] They made a choice for themselves not to learn.

Mitra attributes this to "conditioning" of girls who "have been told to be quiet so they don't talk. That obviously pulls their results down."[34] Never mind the fact that it is widely known that girls today do better in school than boys.[35] A 2015 study revealed that even in countries where gender inequality is severe, girls still outperform boys.[36] Data from the Programme for International Student Assessment (PISA) for the period from 2000 to 2010 revealed that among 1.5 million fifteen-year-olds, the girls scored higher than the boys, even in countries—such as Qatar, Jordan, and the United Arab Emirates—that are infamous for their gender divides.

In one 2016 SOLE experiment, teachers reported that by the third session, "learning seemed to have plateaued."[37] Students hit a ceiling as it becomes more challenging for them to sift out relevant information from their searches. When they keep reaching a dead end, without helpful intervention, they grow frustrated and disengage. The sheer amount of available information can overwhelm a child who does not receive guidance. For instance, the "big question" on world population growth resulted in a list of promising leads to the question on Google. However, the children navigated away from this page, going straight to Wikipedia.

Other studies have been done on the googling of information without guidance. For most British children, the answer to the question "What is the British Raj?" is "An Indian takeaway restaurant in South Shields."[38] Journalist Rebecca Mead observed that some students, when searching for "seals" on Google Images, came up with numerous results including a corpse of a porpoise split in half by a seal attack. The search also yielded portraits of the singer Seal—an image of his head had been photoshopped onto a sea lion's body.[39]

In my own project in the rural Himalayas, I encountered the miseducation that takes place through googling without supervision. By volunteering at a popular cybercafé in the village where many children accessed the internet, I was able to observe the informal learning that took place among the children away from schools. A group of high school girls came in, ready to tackle a school assignment on "Western versus Indian painting." They chose Google Images as a starting point, as they wanted "nice images" to go along with their argument. They typed "painting," which overloaded them with a huge number of irrelevant images. They honed their search by retyping "Western painting." Forty-nine million images came up. The first pages primarily displayed cowboy images and horse paintings. This excited them.

They chose a Native American Indian painting by the artist Carl Sweezy. They chose another cowboy and horse painting and added it to their portfolio without clicking on its link. That painting turned out to be the work of the artist Hsu Pei-hung, a native of Kiangsu Province in China. (After going abroad to Paris and Berlin, he returned to China inspired by the symbolism of cowboys, which to him best represented modern China.) Self-organized learning guided by Google's algorithm led the children to categorize a traditional Chinese ink painting style with Western thematic influence as Western art. With no teachers or parents to argue otherwise, the girls took their misinformation to be a meaningful fact. After forty-five minutes, somewhere far down the pages, they encountered an image of the *Mona Lisa* right next to an image of Spanish bathroom tiles. Fortunately, Leonardo da Vinci won and was added to their portfolio.

On the Indian front, their search yielded a number of Madhubani paintings, village folk art from the state of Bihar. This is not a coincidence. The National Databank on Indian Art and Culture is an ambitious government project that is digitizing India's vast cultural heritage.[40] Through the digitizing and unleashing of millions of Indian painting images into the digital sphere, certain images have gained visibility. The government has invested in marketing Madhubani paintings as one of the authentic precolonial cultural art forms of India through e-greeting cards, free downloads, and easily available reproduction rights.

The students' search yielded complex results. Madhubani art was given more visibility than other Indian art partly because of the newfound confidence India has gained over the last decade. India is moving to rebrand itself culturally as well as economically. During two centuries of colonial rule, the British had introduced a Western aesthetic to India and validated it as fine art. Famous Indian artists such as Raja Ravi Varma, a figure taught in the national art curriculum post independence, have started to become controversial. After all, Varma got his endorsements from the likes of Lord Curzon, the Viceroy of India who described Varma's work as "a happy blend of Western technique, and Indian subject and free from oriental stiffness."[41] History is hard to shed. When the girls found Varma's art online, they quickly recognized it and selected for their portfolio.

Mitra is right about one thing: Google does instruct. But Google's algorithms favor the older and the well connected. Network theory suggests that the longer a node has been in existence, the greater the likelihood that it will obtain connections in the network, and connections lead to other connections. The rich get richer. Google's instructional guidance follows the logic of regional context, user popularity, relationship effects, and the marketing and promotional strategies of the state, corporations, nonprofits, and other actors that leverage these network systems to become visible.

For example, the girls' first page of search results on "Western painting" profiled the artist Carl Sweezy because he and his commercial gallery were good at marketing his work online—so good that they won an award for being the best online marketer of products. *Mona Lisa* and Raja Ravi Varma win in terms of the longevity of their work online. Madhubani paintings achieved equal prestige with Varma due to recent political and economic commitment. With massive funding to promote this art form as "Indian painting," commodification wins in the googling game. In other words, the educational curriculum Mitra believes in is the "curriculum" of Google, driven by commercialism, politics, popularity, and historical precedent. So what if Google is a little chaotic, he says. He likes chaos theory. Sure, the internet can be dangerous, but so are roads, he argues.[42]

Mitra is not a man who easily steps back. Facts, scholarship, evidence, and history do not disturb his faith in self-organized, play-based learning. Regarding the possibility that children will learn "incorrect things" from the internet, he states that in all these years he has "seen no evidence of this."[43] To Mitra, Skype failures, poor connectivity, googling frustrations, misunderstandings, and mistakes are all just excuses for not embracing the new gospel. He believes in the "self-correcting internet," where googling will eventually yield the wisdom that the child seeks. An optimist indeed.

Granny Clouds and Village Wells: The Dangerous Metaphors

Mitra loves metaphors. To help us picture the role of the Skype mediator for the children in remote communities, he gives us an image of a British granny. She sits at the other end of Skype, guiding these children in their learning. Suneeta Kulkarni, then research director of the SOLE project, clarifies that not all mediators are "grannies."[44] They are volunteers from various walks of life. But the granny image stuck, Kulkarni concedes: "It is the granny cloud now." In another primary metaphor, Mitra speaks of the internet as the "village well"—a valued and shared resource enjoyed by the whole village.

Metaphors make his talks engaging, his concepts graspable, and his ideas come to life. It makes sense for him to use such language to inspire the public. Metaphors have a long legacy of influencing how we think and act. Some are images that help us to feel we have some comprehension of the incomprehensible, some imagining of the unimaginable. Since the birth of human language, metaphors have been employed faithfully to make abstract notions tangible.[45] By their very usage, they seem to transform fiction into reality.

Think about how many metaphors come to the rescue as users try to wrap their minds around new technology. Since the nascent years of the internet, "digital space" has been conceptualized through metaphors such as chat rooms, electronic frontiers, home pages, information highways, web pages, and the cloud. Each metaphor comes with an expectation, a hope, a new way of envisioning the future. In fact, we have amassed tremendous evidence from psychologists, cognitive scientists, linguists, and other experts that it is impossible to understand novelty without metaphors.[46]

Metaphor is not just a cognitive tool but a policy tool. Senator Al Gore stood before a crowd in 1992 and promised them that they would soon all enjoy getting on the "information highway." He reassuringly compared it to "a network of highways, much like the interstates of the 1950s . . . highways carrying information rather than people or goods."[47] He was leveraging the history of hope that the building of highways had provided for many of the world's populations. People craved speed, connectivity between the rural and the urban, and good roads seemed to promise that inequality would be reduced if everyone could easily access the resources of the city. All of this was packed into a single metaphor—"highway."

Information scientist Mark Stefik argues that the highway metaphor considerably set back the development of the internet.[48] For decades the metaphor shaped public perception of the internet as a mere instrument of access rather than focusing on the quality of content.

Legal scholar Kristen Osenga similarly criticizes the usage of the "cloud" metaphor to understand the storage of data. It gives us the false impression that information is "out there," saved in a vague, nebulous form with no tangible ownership. This prevents people from critically questioning the data mining that is taking place through this very deliberate and systematic warehousing of users' personal data. The cloud metaphor provides a romantic and poetic vision of our information floating freely, circumventing questions about who owns our data today and what they are doing with it.[49]

For his vision of learning, Mitra offers us the sexist and ageist metaphor of the "granny cloud." There is a reason this metaphor is hard to shake off. For most people, the image of a grandmother is comforting, familiar, and nonthreatening, a common imagery in children's storybooks. Feminists have long argued, though, that grannies are portrayed as feeble, two-dimensional, and forgettable characters in many of the familiar narratives.[50] Picture the old granny spinning wool in the tower, or the granny eaten by the wolf in the Red Riding Hood story. We are not meant to shed a tear for them, because they are objects to quickly dispose of in the business of storytelling. In the granny lexicon, we encounter numerous pejorative terms, such as "granny dress" and "granny glasses," signifiers of pathos and unfashionableness. A powerful "nexus of ageism and sexism," the term "granny" becomes the norm and goes "virtually unnoticed and unchecked," argues Sylvia Henneberg, a humanities scholar.[51]

Mitra explains that adults often intimidate children, especially the teacher who looms over them. This deters them in their pursuit of productive play. Grannies are different. Mitra claims that, for children, "it would be better, in a way, if any adults present were completely un-educated. There is nothing children like more than passing on infor-mation they have just discovered to people who may not already have it—an elderly grandmother, for instance."[52] Here Mitra skillfully adds ignorance to the list of an elderly woman's characteristics. If this were not enough, the stereotype of grannies being filled with emotional em-pathy seals the deal. Mitra's reductionism of older women for the sake of creating a clever and viral buzzword for a learning project has coupled education with sexism and ageism.

Mitra's "granny cloud" is not just a poor choice of words, but a dan-gerous metaphor with a dangerous message. It perpetuates the image of elderly women as ignorant, helpless, two-dimensional, innately em-pathetic, and traditional. The fact that the granny position in Mitra's project is voluntary confirms the long feminist discourse on women's work as unpaid labor. He replaces the role of the paid local rural teacher in Colombia, for instance, with that of a British granny volunteer. This signals that teaching, rather than being a crucial job in education, can now be simply a hobby for retirees—and that we can dispense with tra-ditional education, one of the primary domains that have brought real attention to linguistic practices that belittle and demean.

Mitra's metaphor of the internet and computers as "village wells" comes with its own set of problems. An internet-connected computer for the children, he claims, is like "a village well, where children assemble to draw knowledge and, in the process, engage in meaningful conver-sation and immersive learning activities that broaden their horizons."[53] Not all village wells are such egalitarian places, though. For instance, in India, access to village wells is contingent on caste.[54] Higher castes, although a minority, often exert careful control over who is allowed to draw water from wells. Well ownership also often goes hand in hand with land ownership.[55] Water is a scarce resource that is subject to di-visive politics around the world, with the poor at the losing end. The "village wells" metaphor can suggest that computers are in the hands of those with power and can be instruments to further divide the community rather than bind it in a shared endeavor.

From their outset, Mitra's projects have been all about the "self" in learning; they have given no attention to the role of the community in this play-driven process. In his reports on his experiments over the years, Mitra has commented that many teachers are obstacles to children's learning because they are poorly trained and incompetent, but other than that the community is conspicuously absent. When Mitra and his team do mention the community, it is usually just to characterize it as a nothingness, a void so remote and so devastating that any intervention is a godsend. This portrayal is a defensive response to the critics who question the project's outcomes.

For instance, when Mitra's team was criticized because their experiments did not produce deep learning, they responded by saying that they deal with a "part of our planet where children, with nothing other than a street-side computer, are able to answer tests on their own. They have no teachers or educational support from their parents or anyone else in the community."[56] This portrays criticisms of the experiments as criticisms of the efforts of the children, and Mitra's teams present no evidence to support these negative characterizations of poor communities as places where children receive no support from their parents or schools. Mitra's teams also disparage their critics as people with limited and "shallow" worldviews who are blind to the fact that what the children do achieve is "nothing short of miraculous."[57] Who can argue with miracles? In response to criticism of the SOLE project, Suneeta Kulkarni, the research director of the project, attacked back, reminding the critics, against all real evidence, that we are dealing with places where "there's nothing."[58]

Any practitioner who has spent time in villages and slums in developing countries would have a hard time defending such a position. In my own experiences in rural villages over the last two decades, I have come across many community activists, parents, teachers, and elders who are doing good work for their villages with few resources. I spent six months living in a rural town close to the village where Mitra's experiments were going on. While undoubtedly poor, the villages in the area were not black holes of oppression with absolutely nothing to give, as Mitra and his team would have us believe.

Where there are people, there will always be something to give. To say otherwise is condescending. By purveying a notion of nothingness, Mitra and his team assert a need for technological intervention while downplaying the rich human resources that are present. They conduct "experiments" intended to prove that computers and the internet alone should get credit for the children's learning, so it is convenient for them to ignore the presence of an involved community.

Arun Chavan, the SOLE project's poster child, participated in one of the early experiments. He is currently doing his doctorate in evolutionary biology at Yale. From Hole-in-the-Wall to Yale—a Cinderella journey made possible by Mitra and his team! Yet when Chavan was questioned about the most important influences in his life that led him to Yale, he said it was all the people in his life who opened his mind to numerous things. When asked if he had to give a TED talk, what it would be about, he said it would be about his father. "My father writes and directs plays. As a kid, I acted in many of them. These plays have significantly influenced my thinking and have greatly contributed to who I am."[59]

One may ask: Why direct so much energy to criticizing one project and one person? The answer, quite simply, is that we are in an age of TED celebrities where a popular idea can attract funding more easily than a sound idea. Academic pop stars, such as Sugata Mitra, have armies of social media fans who attack anyone who criticizes their guru. Mitra's evangelizing of the granny cloud will continue to deepen the association between education and sexism and ageism, and we need to put a stop to this. To take down a dangerous idea, we need to take down its prophet.

Myths, Messiahs, and Miracles

For almost two decades Mitra's projects have continued to receive abundant funding, despite all the evidence disproving his claims about their success. This is cause for concern. It is worrisome that Mitra and his particular notion of play-based, self-organized learning have become an inspiration to numerous influential persons and funding organizations. Myths, miracles, and messiahs have long engulfed us. The birth of each new technology comes with a promise of miracles that will overcome adversity. Human action, it seems, has reached its limits, and prophets of technology convince development agencies and grant organizations that the global poor need the miracles of technology to survive and eventually thrive. This potent fiction has been sustained by elaborate obfuscations. Myth has been allowed to trump fact in the name of doing good. There is often global complicity among governments, aid agencies, and technology conglomerates in supporting systems and regulations that continue to disempower the poor in the name of their empowerment.

The geeks are the new messiahs deployed to seduce development organizations with simple and clean technological solutions to the complex and messy realities of poverty. International technology development projects are launched with missionary zeal to convert the digital-have-nots into digital-haves. The poor, of course, must live up to their end of the bargain—when they play with the new technologies provided to them, they are expected to produce the results desired by the technology conglomerates in their sacred mission. Play is under orders to open doors to the impossible.

The first myth is that *extreme poverty needs extreme measures.* Poverty porn is pervasive. Dominant media are saturated with narratives of starving children and the helpless poor, pushing the notion that only a miracle can save the global poor. Many people desperately want to believe that there is a quick remedy to this suffering and a short-cut to social change—and turn to the modern version of faith: faith in technology. New technologies tend to be imagined as new opportunities to achieve the impossible. The technology innovation projects that promise quick and simple solutions have come to be the most appealing to organizations that fund development projects.

Bold change apparently needs bold ideas, such as leaving slum children alone with computers for a few months and coming back to find the children transformed into digital aficionados and renaissance youth. Projects that capture the imagination by envisioning the miraculous are tempting to funders. This is dangerous for the future of tech innovation for development, because it channels funding disproportionately toward "sexy" projects that are sold with entrancing rhetoric over pragmatic projects that are rooted in evidence. More importantly, it creates even more unrealistic expectations for future technology and child play, dooming them to failure from the outset.

The second myth is that *the poor have nothing to lose.* On the contrary, they have everything to lose. The impact of failure can be devastating for the poor in developing countries. Entire nations suffer when they place their faith in misguided projects. An entire generation loses the opportunity to learn when development funding is spent on acquiring fancy laptops instead of on training teachers. The reductionism involved in portraying people living in poor communities as blank slates, as completely helpless and apathetic, is a powerful script used to justify even the most unrealistic interventions.

The third myth is that *the poor are different from everyone else.* The war on poverty has gone on for decades. Development agencies say that the poor are different, and have their own values, mind-sets, and cultures that hold them back. What works for those who are better off does not work for them. Such views help to rationalize treating the poor in ways that members of development organizations would never dream of treating their own families and friends. Such views are used to justify hypocrisies in policy and practice. When the Hole-in-the-Wall project launched and revealed that poor children worldwide were curious, creative, and playful with new technologies, the funders went crazy. Money started to pour into this specific "experiment" and it scaled up around the world.

This enthusiasm was fueled by a belief that poor children in the Global South were different from children in the West. Their poverty made them far more resilient, and infinitely creative, in the face of what can look like insurmountable challenges. While schools and parents in the West struggled to get their children to study, these slum children were said to move to a different tune. They were autonomous beings, who would rise above their station with the click of a mouse. Note, also, the additional divide implicit here in the ascriptions of "difference"—the children are ascribed a luminous difference that propels them forward into success, in contrast to the difference ascribed to their communities, which are described as hopelessly tied to failure.

Ascribing autonomy to them, however, is another way of transferring responsibility to the poor through the ruse of glorification. Poor children are framed as radical users of technology, entrepreneurs and true innovators, carving out the future of technology innovation. They are described as being able to do anything they put their minds to, given that they are survivors against all odds. This romanticism has fictionalized the communities of the poor. How can development projects devise genuinely useful applications for technology in poor communities when they are thinking in terms of fictions, not real communities?

The bottom line is that there are no miracles. Groundless faith, not evidence, has shaped these templates on child play and learning with new media devices. Mere enthusiasms have distracted attention away from the evidence-based fact that in reality, children living in poverty do not tend to use new technologies to educate themselves. They use them predominantly for play. And yes, they will teach themselves skills they need in order to use the technologies for play. But their online behavior is not the fictionalized, purely instrumental activity of self-organization and self-enlightenment. Clearly, we need to move away from such groundless faith and its fictions. In the serious work of providing developmental aid, there is no room for miracles or false messiahs. We need to uncover and dismantle the myths being circulated that low-income children use new technologies for self-organized learning. Let evidence and not sensationalism be the guide.

Chapter 6 explores how Mitra's ideas have become the foundation for the prize industry.[60] Philanthropists are investing their resources in novel gaming applications to educate disadvantaged children in developing countries. We can largely credit Mitra with perpetuating the mutated version of self-organized learning as a black-box miracle for future educational technology innovation. The hype about Mitra's projects has led local governments and development agencies to give the green light to technology conglomerates to use poor communities as human laboratories in the name of self-organized, play-based learning.

6

The Poverty Laboratory

NICHOLAS NEGROPONTE, the founder of MIT's Media Lab and the One Laptop per Child (OLPC) Association, told his audience at the 2011 San Francisco Open Mobile Summit that he planned to airdrop tablets into the Kalahari Desert in Botswana for the children to teach themselves to learn. "It [the tablet] is like a coke bottle falling out of the sky," he exclaimed, referring to the 1982 movie, *The Gods Must Be Crazy.*[1] He had apparently forgotten that in the movie, the bottle, initially welcomed into the tribe as a gift of the gods, becomes an object of evil. His other inspiration came from Sugata Mitra's Hole-in-the-Wall project.

Since then, 2.4 million OLPC laptops were distributed to children in several deprived regions of the world.[2] In Uruguay alone, 570,000 laptops were handed out through a deal between OLPC and the Uruguayan government. Rwanda chose to spend its annual primary education per pupil budget of $109 on this $100 laptop.[3] In remote Ethiopian villages with little access to running water or electricity, OLPC spread laptops with educational games and English-based apps for the children to play with.

After three years, in 2014, OLPC was declared a failure, in spite of the massive financial investments and sponsorships. Reporter Tom Murphy reviewed the outcomes from numerous external OLPC evaluation reports, including one from the Inter-American Development Bank that found no increased learning achievements through this initiative.[4] Uruguay officially declared no improvement on math and reading scores with the adoption of OLPC. Wayan Vota, then spokesperson on OLPC News, confessed, "Let us be honest with ourselves. The great excitement, energy, and enthusiasm that brought us together is gone. OLPC is dead."[5]

Even though the project died, this worldview lives on in the name of experimentation. Negroponte has found a new avenue to propagate his vision of autonomous learning as the chairperson of the Global Learning XPRIZE Foundation, shaping future education for the poor. Autonomous learning is the fuel for further investment in technology innovation for social change. Silicon Valley is at the heart of evangelizing this message, spawning numerous experiments in areas ranging from the villages of Paraguay to the slums of Nigeria.

The idea of autonomous learning is hardly new. It is built on learning theories from a century ago, such as Lev Vygotsky's constructivism and John Dewey's notion of progressive education. These theories were put into practice in the 1960s in the free-school movement in the United States and England—and ended in failure.[6] As for replacing teachers with technology, government agencies and development groups have experimented with the poor for decades—including using radio broadcasts to "civilize the masses" in the 1920s, television-led schooling in the 1970s, and computer-assisted learning in the 1990s.[7] This history has proven that technology cannot replace teachers. So why do these ideas persist and even gain strength with the rise of each new technology? How long must a discredited idea be pushed before it will stop being called an experiment?

The poor have long been used as test subjects for social experiments. They are approached in the same way as patients for an experimental clinical trial who have run out of all conventional options—as people who have nothing to lose. But it is more likely that they had few genuine choices to start with. The failure to provide real options to the poor can occur in spite of major commitments by a nation to reduce its educational inequality. Fixing education and poverty is not an easy or quick task. Scarce resources, political turmoil, and discriminatory cultural practices are just some of the obstacles. Sometimes poor nations, driven by national pride, choose shortcuts out of an urgency to "catch up"—hoping that technological innovations will magically erase long-standing inequalities in education.

Despite Thomas Edison's prediction that motion pictures would replace books as the dominant medium for learning, they did not; but they set the precedent for the radio as an alternative hope. Analogously, the cumulative failures of mass communication technologies to end educational inequality are continually followed with nominations of newer technologies as the answer. Failed schooling is unforgivable, but failure of the technologies implemented as substitutes for schooling is seen as an acceptable trajectory for innovation. This vision is still promoted as sacred by technology companies, in a continuing cycle of implementing still more new technologies for the poor—technologies that, even when they fail, are still a success for the companies because they increase sales to captive clients.

Governments make the best clients, as they are vulnerable to the media rhetoric of novelty. This is a meal ticket for many, including funders, technology companies, celebrity researchers, and politicians who want their own flagships of innovation. False messiahs such as Negroponte and Mitra have made governments and funders believe in the miracle of autonomous learning with new technology—holding people responsible for their own governance and, quite naturally then, for any failure that emerges from these experiments.

Myth of Novelty

Anyone claiming that autonomous learning is a novel idea need only brush up on education history. Two powerful figures in the world of education are development psychologists Lev Vygotsky and Jean Piaget. In the early twentieth century, they advocated the theory of constructivism that remains a buzzword in learning circles today. This theory emphasized children's ability to learn actively through play with their peers, independent of the teacher. Controversial at that time in the Soviet Union, Vygotsky argued that the teacher should be more of a facilitator than a content provider and that it is in unstructured social interactions, such as play, that children can accomplish their "greatest achievements" and go beyond their age in learning.[8]

Another towering figure in the previous century was the American philosopher John Dewey, who radically changed the education system with his experiential learning theory. The child, Dewey said, gains "command of himself" by acquiring knowledge through meaningful and lived experiences.[9] As in Vygotksy's constructivism, play takes center stage as an essential and innately positive human experience that transforms into learning. French philosopher Jacques Rancière also adhered to this doctrine of child autonomy in learning.[10] He tells the story of a French teacher who found himself in charge of a class of Flemish students who spoke no French. Given this challenge, he provided a bilingual French–Flemish text and asked the students through a translator to provide their critique in French. With no formal French instruction, the students amazed him by producing their work in French. They figured out how to construct French sentences, grammar, and vocabulary. Through this illustration, Rancière makes his case that we need to reexamine dichotomies between the schoolmaster and the student, the "knowing minds and ignorant ones."[11]

Autonomous learning is not just a theory, but also an ideal, an alternative vision, and a promise for social change. Determined to confront the deep and persistent social inequality and the dearth of qualified teachers in impoverished communities, several intellectuals have come to the fore to promote this doctrine. Many thinkers are attracted to the theory of education as an arena where they can have their say. Education has long been viewed as critical for leveling the playing field between the rich and the poor. People who are not educators are especially fond of proselytizing for innovations in this field.

Few disciplines give so much credence to outsiders. Sugata Mitra is a physicist and technologist by training who stumbled upon education. Ivan Illich, an early proponent of child-directed education, was an Austrian philosopher and a Roman Catholic priest. Bertrand Russell was a philosopher and mathematician. Prominent outsiders like these have promoted seductive new solutions to age-old problems, but their learning theories have failed to prove themselves.

Take Beacon Hill, one of Britain's most famous educational experiments, which was set up by Russell and his wife, Dora Russell. As part of the sweeping "free school" progressive movement of the 1920s, the Russells decided to put their ideas into practice. It was a time when almost everything was up for question, including marriage and monogamy, sexuality, feminism, and parenting.[12] Education was especially a candidate for change—because many social values emerge from schooling, transforming society through the socialization of children. The Russells believed that the key was to put children in charge of their own learning.

In an essay for the school's periodical in 1933, Dora Russell advocated that the children must govern themselves, arguing that educators must not ask "What do I wish this child to learn or to become?" but should instead ask "What does this child wish to know or to make of himself?"[13] The children formed part of the governing board of the school, with a say in its running. Parents were given a school prospectus that stated:

No knowledge of any sort or kind should be withheld from children and young people; Respect for the individual preferences and peculiarities of the child, both in work and in behavior; Morality and reasoning to arise from the children's actual experience in a democratic group and never of necessity from the authority or convenience of adults.[14]

This was the ultimate democracy, the founding principle by which educators recognized the individuality of the child over all else, including the will of the teacher. The authority of the teacher was dangerous to the child's well-being.

As the years passed, this grand theory began to crumble. Children did not view self-governance as freedom but instead saw it as a chore. Apathy set in. Much like other radicals and progressives of their generation, the Russells wanted to believe that children were innately benevolent and egoless. In practice, they found that the children were often driven by self-interest and needed to be taught to rein in their needs for the good of the group. They found that given a choice, a child would rather climb a tree than do math. Human nature got in the way of a beautiful theory. Bertrand Russell admitted in his autobiography that he had been mistaken in a number of his beliefs, particularly regarding the role of unstructured play and self-governance in education. He had come to recognize that children did need a certain amount of guidance, order, and routine, and that "left to amuse themselves, they are bored and turn to bullying or destruction."[15] In 1943, Beacon Hill was forced to close after years of financial difficulties and low enrollment.

This did not stop later intellectuals from reviving this idea and in fact expanding the claims for self-directed learning, especially when it came to the poor. In 1971, Ivan Illich called for the dismantling of schools. He framed schooling as a powerful institution that reproduces social hierarchies. The traditional school, Illich argued, is geared toward teaching the poor to subsume themselves to the social system that works to the advantage of the elites. The poor should break these chains and free themselves from such indoctrination. Poverty is a "loss of personal potency," and the only way to rise from this state of help-lessness is to reclaim control over one's learning.[16]

To make his point, Illich quoted Fidel Castro's declaration that universities could be abolished, that life itself is an educational experience. Decades before social media, Illich advocated for new technology to serve as a pathway for personalized "learning webs." He envisioned peer networks to support all activity that individuals deemed valuable. He believed in the power of technology to create new institutions that would allow the poor to be autonomous, creative, and at last independent of the trappings of social oppression.[17]

Not surprisingly, Illich was a friend of the Brazilian educator Paulo Freire, who became world-renowned for his critical pedagogy movement. The bible of this movement, Freire's book *Pedagogy of the Oppressed* (1969), created a major stir in Brazil and beyond. It became so controversial that Freire was forced into exile. Freire compared the Brazilian educational system to a banking model that deposited information into the minds of the poor. The only way for the poor to rise against this was to become cognizant of their oppressors and conscious of the oppression that surrounded them. He argued that a peasant could teach his neighbor more effectively than could a teacher brought in from the city. Autonomous learning was free from power and hierarchies.

The World Bank funded rural development programs and campaigns in the 1970s based on the Freirean literacy method. Freire served as an advisor on education reform in former Portuguese colonies in Africa, particularly Guinea-Bissau and Mozambique. His ideas resonated with marginalized groups across the world, including South Africa's Black consciousness movement in the 1970s under the activist Steve Biko. Over the years, however, several failures emerged in instituting this radical pedagogy among the poor.[18]

If teachers were oppressors and the curriculum an instrument of control, how were the poor to gain the skills necessary for social mobility? How can one sustain any educational initiative without institutionalizing it? And once it is institutionalized, how is it different from the traditional school? How were the poor to partake in the politics and economy that demanded a common language? How can a unified society be created when its members are described as opponents—oppressed and oppressor, the good and the bad? To this day there is little empirical evidence to support Freire's grand claims. Freire's ideas are rooted in a utopian perspective on human nature. Clearly, manifestos move people. Idealism's virtue will always be in its ability to inspire.

Alternative Education in India: A Personal Journey

My own journey as a teenager is a testament to the draw of autonomous learning. I am a product of Victorian Catholic schooling in Bangalore, an IT hub in the south of India. Remembering was prized over understanding. Rote learning was the template for education. When I was a teenager, I voraciously consumed Bertrand Russell, Henry David Thoreau, and Jiddu Krishnamurti, an influential Indian philosopher who advocated autonomous learning in the 1930s when India was still under British rule. At the age of eighteen I decided to quit college and take control of my own learning. I left home and along with a group of radical educators moved to a remote village in the state of Kerala. Our dream was to set up a unique learning space for ourselves, a cross between Walden Pond (Thoreau's experiment in simple living and self-sufficiency), Russell's Beacon Hill, and Black Mountain College, a school founded in the 1930s in North Carolina under the influence of Dewey's philosophy of learning.

In our radical learning space there would be no grades, no curriculum, and no central authority. Play, as discovery and self-governance, would dictate learning. We would learn as a community and as individuals, pursuing our education through an expression of our own choosing. I chose painting and writing. I wrote poems about fireflies and penned reflections in my journal on the adventures of living in a village. I ranted on in my weekly letters to my family about how society and its institutions had trapped them in a formulaic life. Having been brought up in the city, everything rural was exotic to me. I admired the life skills of the villagers as I saw the challenge of growing one's own food or fetching water or starting a fire.

Within a month, the adventure turned tedious. At the start, the silence of the village was a magical contrast to the constant din of city traffic. A month later, it was absolutely deafening. Perhaps I was too arrogant, I told myself. I needed to learn from other experiments before embarking on my own. During that time, an artist friend in Kottayam, a small town in Kerala, alerted me to an opportunity to teach at an alternative school called Corpus Christi. I jumped at the chance.

The founder of this school, Mary Roy, was a formidable woman. An Indian educator and women's rights activist, she fought an archaic 1916 law that discriminated between the sexes on matters of inheritance, and she won. Today she is known as the mother of the 1997 winner of the UK's Booker Prize, author Arundhati Roy, but she will always remain an unforgettable character who made a mark on many, including me. Self-organized learning and play were the central mottos of Roy's approach to education. "The more fun they have, the more they learn," she would say.[19] I related to her anger about the Indian education system, which emphasized book learning over joy.

Roy believed that learning spaces should reflect the values of the school. Laurie Baker, a British-born Indian architect known as the "Gandhi of architecture," was able to realize Roy's dream. He built simple, organic, open spaces respectful of the surrounding natural areas. Even though this school was, indeed, a high point of inspiration in my life, it was hard to ignore that it was a deeply privileged school. It drew the attention of affluent forward-thinking parents and fine teachers with freedom to experiment in their pedagogy. There was clearly a structure within the play to make it succeed.

This quest took me to a far more experimental setting, this time not just a school but an entire community in the making. I was nineteen.

Auroville, also called the "city of dawn," was a township built on arid land on the outskirts of Tamil Nadu in the south of India.[20] It was based on the teachings of Sri Aurobindo, an Indian philosopher and political activist during the British rule, who promoted self-realization as the fundamental human pursuit. After his death, his French companion, "the Mother," embarked on establishing a model universal township to "realize human unity." The government of India backed this communal experiment, and in 1966 UNESCO lent its full support, endorsing it as a commendable project for humanity. When it was founded in 1968, it had 400 residents from twenty countries. By 2014 it had grown to 2,500 residents from forty-nine countries, with two-thirds of its residents coming from India, France, and Germany.[21]

The charter declares that money is not the prime medium of connection between humans. The communal fund supports all. Aurovilians make their unique contributions to the growth of the community in monetary and nonmonetary ways. Everyone has something to give. Individual ownership was discarded for communal ownership. This was a leaderless utopia. Harmony between the rich and the poor, between diverse nationalities, between the young and the old, all starts with self-realization. In this spirit, education was about self-governance. The central principle guiding all schools in this community was that true teaching is "nothing that can be taught."[22] Play is the purest and most authentic form of self-realization.

When I think back to my days in Auroville, I remember cycling between communities with names like New Creation, Aspiration, Arati, and La Ferme, reflecting people's diverse preferences and nationalities. I spent one evening sitting at a dinner table with Danish and Swedish scientists who talked for hours about the hundreds of varieties of tomato seeds they were striving to preserve. I lived in the same commune with an elderly American psychologist who viewed it as his retirement home and a British architect who wanted to create houses in the manner of large kilns, by baking them from inside out. My shower had no door or roof. It was a thinly curved cemented structure like a shaving of a pencil. Someone was bartering their homemade peanut butter in exchange for help with their plumbing system.

I decided to volunteer at the school. I would facilitate and not infringe on the youth's will. I tried hard to inspire. They showed little regard for authority and preferred to gossip with their friends. It felt like a personal failure when I could not get them interested in anything intellectually challenging. For me, the utopia started to fray at the edges. I have since followed the progress of Auroville through a number of visits over the years. One good friend, an Indian trained as a web designer, decided to become an Aurovilian after falling in love with a German woman. They had their child in Auroville. Over the years, I noticed his idealism transform into cynicism. The politics of Auroville were vicious. Given their antipathy to leaders and aversion to ownership, it was hard to have an open dialogue and transparency about building a house or about the savings that members put into this community to secure their future. And although in principle the community was open for all, in reality there were deep divides between the Aurovilians and the people in the surrounding villages.

News of Aurovilians engaging in money laundering and land appropriation make the headlines time and again, and there is an ongoing campaign to shut down this experiment.[23] Tensions escalated when BBC began reporting on pedophilia in Auroville. Children in nearby villages are said to be particularly vulnerable. Reports about this commune continue to emerge citing rape, abuse, suicides, and even murder, reading more like a dark thriller than the realized utopia it originally was intended to become. The community has defended itself, arguing that Auroville is a "living human laboratory" and that, as with all ongoing experiments, failures are bound to occur.[24]

A number of children who grew up in Auroville have written about their experiences. Loïc Rich describes the time when he was nine years of age.[25] He was left to run wild, as parenting was given a low priority.

Play was about absolute freedom. The adults' corresponding freedom—freedom from their children—transformed into emotional disengagement and an abdication of parental responsibility. Rich compares his childhood to *Lord of the Flies*, as he and the other children made up the rules as they went. Their rules included being discriminatory—they collectively decided to hate the local Tamil children.

When we look back in time, the education theory of autonomous learning has enjoyed a long life. The theories of Dewey, Vygotsky, Piaget, Rancière, and other educators have been normalized as doctrine in the contemporary educational systems in much of the world. These philosophies have traveled far from the West to the indigenous peasants in Brazil and the utopian cult of Auroville in India. Decades of experiments with this learning ideal reveal its most dangerous mutation—the misplaced glorification of children and their supposed innate ability to leverage their unsupervised learning for social and individual betterment.

Many proselytizers of self-driven learning are privileged, as I was. I romanticized free learning in my early years to escape the stranglehold of Catholic schooling. Bertrand Russell craved for an alternative paradigm as a reaction to his stifling aristocratic homeschooling. Sugata Mitra comes from a well-off family and went through schooling similar to my own in India. Autonomous learning can serve as an intellectual sabbatical and a good story, for the wealthy. But for the poor, it is Russian roulette with their future.

Eye on the Prize: Innovations in Mobile Learning

In March 2016, I found myself sharing the stage with Matt Keller, the former vice president of the One Laptop per Child program and current senior director of the $15 million Global Learning XPRIZE. We were at UNESCO's annual Mobile Learning Week event in Paris.[26] I was presenting a report commissioned by UNESCO on the impact of prizes on innovation in education in developing countries.[27] The room was packed with representatives of foundations, think tanks, agencies, entrepreneurs, and educators involved in projects experimenting with mobile- and game-based learning in developing countries.

Keller captivated the audience as he talked about the launch of the 2014 Global Learning XPRIZE, a $15 million competition held every year. Elon Musk, the South African–born business magnate and founder of Tesla, is behind the funding. Musk's dreams are audacious. Musk talked of changing the world and preventing human extinction. His solution? Settling at least a million people on Mars to ensure humanity's future.[28] The Mars colony is just one idea among many. Negroponte appears tame, even conservative, in comparison. We can rest assured that Musk expects great things from the Global Learning XPRIZE.

At the UNESCO event, Keller made his case for technology innovation to come to the rescue. It rested on the "stunning market failure" of investing $129 billion "on schools that have no impact on learning." Instead, the prize is designed to encourage the best minds to come up with learning apps with which children can "teach themselves and each other reading, writing and numeracy." OLPC is born again. This time it is different, though. It is about inspiring every Negroponte-like entrepreneur out there—Negroponte multiplied—to come forth, compete, and replicate this experiment around the globe.

This experiment has clear guidelines. Because it is a competition, there are common criteria that must be satisfied so that entrants can compete fairly.[29] All XPRIZE competing teams are to design self-learning apps using open-source software for Android tablets.[30] Their inventions will be field-tested in Tanzania for eighteen months in 200 villages, involving a total of 4,000 children. The app that shows the highest measurable increase in learning and is the most child-friendly, so that children can operate it alone or in self-organized groups, will win this prestigious prize.

The atmosphere at the UNESCO event was infectious. Several XPRIZE teams attended this event. It was to be followed with XPRIZE's first "Hub" Summit for this new crop of competitors and the XPRIZE management team. The competitors were a motley group, from garage tinkerers in Brussels to a company in Kenya tweaking their already existing software to get recognition for their invention. Teams ranged from university students who had come up with an app during a school project to NGOs carving out their paths for further funding. While the competitors were diverse, many shared a common approach to the educational challenges.

I talked with Team Lara, a group of young European developers and designers enthusiastic about children controlling their destiny by dispensing with the school and the teacher. Their vision was to create a "full school inside the app."[31] Jo Grimstad, from Norway, the team leader of Educativo, was similarly ignited by the idea of inventing an app that could serve as a playground for learning. Their app aimed to empower children to "take control of their own learning and their own future." To Grimstad, it is clear that the traditional model of education is "no longer scalable nor sustainable."[32]

All of the 135 teams came up with similar celebrations of technology both to promote autonomous learning and to put an end to schools and teachers. It is hard to blame them. After all, the XPRIZE criteria defined the acceptable parameters for innovation, with self-learning at its heart. The more autonomous an app, the greater its chances to win the prize.

In the last decade, prizes in the world of global education have exponentially grown as a tool to spur radical change. The language of "market failure" is applied readily to public institution such as schools. Innovation in education has become synonymous with technology intervention. Most of the research on innovation and disruption in the last few years has emerged from the business sector, whose values, objectives, and systems of accountability clearly are different from those of the public sector. As early as 2009, McKinsey & Company reported on the state of the prize industry and its biases, noting that "corporations and new philanthropists have provided more than two-thirds of total prize capital since 2000 and are pursuing arenas closely linked to their commercial interests or individual philanthropic passions."[33] The private sector provides the funds while the public sector carries out its bidding.

This has not gone without notice. In recent years there has been growing criticism of such partnerships. They reduce the risks for the private companies and allow them to experiment on public institutions with little accountability.[34] Because the prizes are designed to encourage the development of mobile apps for innovation, the resulting apps tend to cater to basic literacy instead of deep learning. Apps for learning mathematics, for instance, are far easier to prove successful than are apps for learning to read, which need to factor in children's cultural and linguistic backgrounds.

The more complex a human task, the less likely it is that apps will be worthy of the task. Focusing on apps to teach low-income children in developing countries would create a two-tier system in which children who are poor learn the basics while the better-off, who will have not only apps but also the benefit of traditional schools and teachers, can be immersed in more creative and critical thinking. In my UNESCO assessment of the prizes for educational innovation, I found a troublesome trend. The Global Learning XPRIZE was not alone in promoting children's self-learning and autonomy. A majority of the projects that have been funded recently through the education prize industry have focused on independent learning through mobiles. They treated teachers as obstacles and schools as failures. These were the starting points.

We need to be cautious when it comes to the claims made for mobile learning.[35] Mobile learning cannot replace the school. There is growing evidence proving that mobile phones work best in out-of-school contexts and for limited learning tasks.[36] As learning tools, phones cannot replace computers, which provide for a wider and deeper spectrum of learning. And computers cannot replace teachers, who can take children's learning even wider and deeper and who understand their students in terms of their culture and language. And educational apps for mobile phones can themselves be more effective if teachers are taught how to use these tools to train themselves and manage their teaching tasks. This approach would be contrary to the gospel of self-organized learning, and few of the prize projects pursued it. For app developers, child autonomy continues to be more attractive than teacher autonomy and effectiveness. And even though it has been shown that mobile phones do increase children's engagement with apps, there is no conclusive evidence that they improve learning outcomes.

At the Mobile Learning event, international development practitioner Juan-Pablo Giraldo expressed his skepticism about incentive prizes: "They are not a bottom-up process . . . you need to start with the children, not the technology and then when you understand their needs—you start designing for them."[37] Over the course of the week, I met several thoughtful practitioners who had little choice but to toe the prize-incentive line, given the dominant climate of prize-based funding.

In the last few years there has been a significant rise in the marketization of public funding. In most countries that are members of the Organisation for Economic Co-operation and Development (OECD), an alarming shift has taken place in the financing of public research and development (R&D). From 1981 to 2013, the share of public-financed R&D declined from 0.82 percent to 0.67 percent of GDP. By contrast, industry-financed R&D increased from 0.96 percent of GDP in 1981 to 1.44 percent in 2013.[38]

Corporations and philanthropists today run the show on innovation. Economic sociologist Linsey McGoey argues that today's age of billionaire philanthropists induces dangerous alliances and a possible negative impact on the world's poor. For instance, the Bill & Melinda Gates Foundation and Big Pharma joined forces to pressure governments to maintain strict patents on lifesaving drugs, which increases inequality in access to those drugs. Instead of collaborating with local farmers and grassroots NGOs in developing countries, the Gates Foundation invests in partnerships with Goldman Sachs, Coca-Cola, Monsanto, and Rupert Murdoch.

McGoey reports on perfectly functioning educational projects that are getting the axe because they do not feed into the feeling of being God that many philanthropists crave. Funders seek projects that promise earth-shattering change rather than incremental shifts in society. Negroponte's tablets dropped from the sky and Musk's Mars colony are cases in point. Given the maze of egos, power imbalances, and dubious experimenting, McGoey wonders "whose interests are most served."[39]

If in doubt, we are reminded that market efficiency is the reason private-sector involvement is tolerated. Nowadays, "responsible innovation" is a buzzword among funding agencies.[40] This type of innovation necessitates that public–private partnerships find common ground for sustainability. Public funding's end goal is to produce the largest social impact for the most marginalized populations, even if doing so is not profitable. Governmental agencies and aid foundations encourage anything that facilitates this mission, including the public disclosure of valuable knowledge. However, industry-funded prizes may not share the same societal priorities. From the perspective of the private sector, information asymmetry—the withholding of valuable information—provides a competitive advantage.

So what approach or approaches would be best, regarding innovation for learning among the poor? If the benchmark for success is to generate as many apps as possible, then clearly a model like XPRIZE works. If the goal is to devise diverse solutions for diverse populations, the prize approach will come up short. The prize industry in general appears to adhere to uniform strict boundaries, from the device parameters to the learning ethos of self-directed learning. This constrains the innovator's imagination and ability to think outside the box. One must also consider that there are limits to how much innovation a social system can take on at a given point in time. Innovation is inherently unpredictable and disruptive. It will produce more failures than successes. That is the nature of the beast.

It is also worth keeping in mind the "Collingridge dilemma": We cannot predict the social consequences of a technology until it plays out in its entirety. By the time the negative aspects surface, these technologies have been absorbed into the system.[41] This is not an argument against innovation in general. If it is possible to create change for the better for the world's poor, then it must be pursued. However, technology should be peripheral to the social system it aims to transform. Innovation does not automatically reduce inequality. That assumption is clearly a myth. Experiments by their very nature privilege one group over another, one village in Tanzania over another village in Kenya or Nigeria.

Furthermore, projects that fund educational innovation in developing countries have been fixated on one type of innovation—technology innovation—negating other kinds of innovation that involve a change in social systems and attitudes. Those latter types of innovation require long-term investment, which does not appeal to most policymakers and politicians. They are also difficult to monetize, making them less appealing to the new corporate funders and philanthropists of public systems.

Michael Hollaender, current director of Die Deutsche Gesellschaft für Internationale Zusammenarbeit (GIZ), expresses his concern over the hype around prizes as the new strategy to alleviate poverty:

> One major concern is that innovation, on one hand, which opens up the risk for failure, does not necessarily fit well with long-term solutions for sustainability. Just to add to this paradigm, and this is more specific to the tech sector, the development cooperation became more political and economical and many donors are not just concerned with development goals but also private sector development. These prizes can combine this so they can claim they have an overarching development goal, but also, without putting it on the agenda, they also do private-sector support.[42]

Technological innovations that can be adopted, adapted, and integrated to enhance learning and teaching outcomes are often incremental improvements to proven educational interventions—not radical transformations. Neatly contained solutions, such as autonomous learning, are unrealistic and damaging. That kind of storytelling should not be the foundation for educational innovation.

Silicon Valley's Learning Labs

Project Hello World, a nonprofit based in the United States and the United Kingdom, is founded on a belief in autonomous learning.[43] The project sets up solar-powered outdoor internet kiosks, called "Hello Hubs," in deprived communities in Nigeria and Uganda. The goal is to offer underprivileged children the "power to educate themselves, communicate with others, and share their voices with the global community." In a given week, about 500 children use these kiosks of educational games.[44]

Hugh Jackman has endorsed this so-called new paradigm in education, and blogged his support for this project in 2015.[45] He describes an abysmal picture of the social and economic isolation experienced by the poor in Asia and Africa, and how the Hello Hubs give the children the rare opportunity to educate and empower themselves through their play online.

Project DEFY (Design Education for You) is another such endeavor, in India's IT hub Bangalore, that builds "schools without teachers" in its rural region. The founder, Abhijit Sinha, used to be an IT employee but decided to quit his job and launch this project. He bought a few computers, loaded them with educational games, and set them up in a room. It was up to the children to figure them out. Before long, Sinha reports, they were "playing games like they were pros."[46]

The doctrine of autonomous learning has reached such a crescendo that even the rich are taking note. Max Ventilla, a former Google engineer, has raised $175 million to build the AltSchool, starting in the San Francisco Bay Area, as a way to redefine the American classroom.[47] The plan was to scale this new type of school in Manhattan, Chicago, and other parts of the country. The core of this "rebooting" of the school system involves teachers making way for educational technology. Ventilla explains that his goal is to shift the role of an educator to being "someone who is more of a data-enabled detective."[48] The classroom has cameras to record the children's every movement, guaranteeing an unlimited stream of data for the teachers. The model requires students to spend about 30 percent of their day on their laptops, completing "playlists" that are personalized learning sequences designed for the students. The assumption (or faith) is that this autonomous play will lead to unparalleled and complex learning.

Journalist Rebecca Mead described AltSchool classrooms as being like IKEA showrooms, with beanbags and clusters of chairs of varying sizes scattered across the room. She observed many of the children lounging in solitude with headphones on and playing with their tablets, much like passengers in a subway car. She reminds us that this is not just a school but also one of the most expensive educational technology investments in Silicon Valley, with significant debt.[49] The Silicon Valley gurus placed their bets that the future of education is in autonomous learning software.

Mark Zuckerberg and his wife, Priscilla Chan, through their philanthropic Silicon Valley Community Foundation have invested millions in AltSchool with the goal of scaling this software into all public schools. The Bill & Melinda Gates Foundation has committed billions of dollars for research into digitizing play-centric autonomous learning. Laurene Powell Jobs, the widow of Steve Jobs, has channeled $50 million into this cause and currently is an investor in AltSchool. In 2017 alone, according to the research firm CB Insights, venture investors spent about $2 billion on education-technology startups globally.[50] Major ambition has coupled with tremendous faith in educational technology. Silicon Valley has given its blessing to this worldview. Yet, in 2016, a number of AltSchools started to shut down. Several parents have accused this company of prioritizing technology over their children. Playlists were not updated regularly. Students' work on their devices were not monitored much. Assignments were not personalized as promised. Some parents felt their kids were being used as "guinea pigs" to test out new educational software. As one parent attested, "We kind of came to the conclusion that, really, AltSchool as a school was kind of a front for what Max really wants to do, which is develop software that he's selling."[51]

What the Poor Need Is *Less* Innovation

The twenty-first century is the age of innovation. At least this is what many of the world's thought leaders tell us. Sir John Chisholm, current chairperson of QinetiQ, an international defense and security company and an expert on change management, declares that technology will change "the very future of the human race."[52] Not to fear, though—technology pundits are working hard to make innovation serve the common good. Ryan Allis—the current chairperson of Connect and Hive in San Francisco and an angel investor in twenty-five companies, including SpaceX, Elon Musk's Mars project—provides a startup guide to ease us into this new era. All we need to do is reimagine "everything," says Allis. With just "a laptop, a smartphone, and the cloud," we can access any service anytime—including, of course, education.[53] Negroponte would concur.

In the last decade, much has been written on the long-awaited disruption of that archaic institution—the school. The educational system in low-income communities in developing countries is regarded as a "stunning market failure."[54] Fortunately, the market "success" of new technology will step in and take its place. Smart technology will replace not-so-smart teachers. Educational technology entrepreneurs are busy making all-inclusive, self-contained schooling apps for the poor. Self-help is the foundation of the innovation age. Centralized schooling should be discarded for personalized play-driven learning. Playlists take precedence over playgrounds. This gospel seeks to do away with the school, the teacher, the community.

The flaw in the master plan is to mistake the school for a market investment. The school is an egalitarian ideal. Children—regardless of whether they are rich or poor, or of a particular gender, age, caste, or race, or with special needs—come together for the common pursuit of learning. It is an important public domain where all share an equal right to an education. The school is an embodiment of society's belief in fair play. This institution is accountable not to the market but to the public, to its community, to its children. When it fails, which it does repeatedly, we do not discard it like obsolete technology but instead work at reforming it. It is here to stay.

That is more than we can say about the spectrum of technology projects that have entered the world of education. Silicon Valley's pet project, the AltSchool, in spite of its massive venture capital backing, found itself drowning in losses in 2017. Ventilla spun their failure, as they started to shut down their AltSchools, as a business shift to software sales, or what he called "challenges and opportunities."[55] He ended on an upbeat note, declaring that they had built "an operating system for a 21st century school system."[56]

The market is more forgiving of technological failure than of human failure. Technological failure is a necessary and even celebrated ingredient in the process of technology innovation. The solution is always around the corner. Silicon Valley excuses the millions of dollars spent on failed education technology projects as worthy experiments. Failure breeds success eventually, they promise. To invest in teachers is antithetical to this new creed. Technology is allowed to err, but humans are not.

Technology corporations have convinced themselves that they are the new activists. The invisible hand of the twenty-first century comes from Silicon Valley. This is hardly surprising, given that much of today's technology world sprang from the "Californian ideology" movement of the 1960s.[57] Campaigns against homophobia, mindless consumerism, pollution, racism, sexism, and militarism were the principles defining the time. The industry was designing an alternative to the status quo. Companies like Google put themselves up on a moral pedestal with their "Don't Be Evil" byline. Technology determinism and libertarianism became the mainstay for the information age.[58]

The new version of the Californian ideology manifests in the notion of liberating the self from the institutions of the past. Compassionate capitalism translates to Twitter for democracy and Google for learning. If there is a need, there will be an app to fulfill it. Technology becomes an all-purpose institution. Poverty is an opportunity. Scarcity breeds innovation, or as Sugata Mitra put it, "a reduction in resources can cause something nice to happen."[59] The neoliberal belief in the marketplace translates to elevating inequality as an asset for innovation.

A critical factor in this game is that the private sector gets to be innovative while the public sector takes the risk. Every educational technology experiment thus far has been based on public subsidy. Postcolonial nations, strapped for cash and desperate to accelerate their economies, channel their scarce resources and high hopes into these new technocratic solutions.

These partnerships come with conditions, rules, and boundaries created by the geeks. Nobody should interfere with the child's learning unless explicitly instructed to. This is an experiment, after all. The world's poor are the recipients of novelty. Poverty is Silicon Valley's laboratory. The poor get to be first in line to try out cutting-edge solutions to learning and teaching. Who would not want that? The most fundamental caveat here is that with self-directed learning comes self-responsibility—and, if anything goes wrong, self-blame.

There is a justifiable fear of going against the gospel of innovation, new technology, and self-governance. To lambaste new technologies is to be labeled a luddite. To denounce the extravagant claims for self-directed learning is to be a mere traditionalist. To condemn the prophets is to condemn the future for the poor. Those who criticize celebrity figures like Negroponte and Mitra are accused of building strawman arguments—indeed, over the years these celebrities have declared that they are not against schools or teachers, they just want to help the most marginalized and most deprived children, who would otherwise not have a fair chance in life.

Nobody should be placated by such claims. It is important instead to look at what these prophets proselytize and how their theories have become sacrosanct. How do they approach the design of projects—their assumptions, evaluation measures, attitudes toward the poor communities—and what are their personal stakes? How do they explain the fact that they dismiss the vast evidence for the failures of previous play-driven, mass technology experiments in self-learning? How do they handle criticisms of their own projects? What kind of role—if any—do they assign to the community and the teacher? The answers to these questions show that these prophets give precedence to anecdotes and mesmerizing metaphors instead of objective evidence.

The poor do not need more innovation. If innovation is a proxy for pilot projects, the poor are better off without them. They should not be guinea pigs for new technology. The simple fact that a given technology is new should not in itself justify using it to experiment on the poor. No new technology can be a stand-alone solution. Without motivated communities, no technology will succeed. Yes, play-driven, self-organized learning is here to stay—as an already established, legitimate, and widely practiced approach used in schools by good teachers worldwide. Unfortunately, its most appealing mutation, currently, is its most extreme mutation—technology apps used by children in isolation from schools, communities, and other traditional support systems. Developers of educational gaming applications sell their wares by claiming that they can replace teachers and schools.

In Chapter 7 we will see how poor communities have historically been used as social labs to test digital surveillance. The system that is stacked against them appears even more gargantuan in this big-data era. Because the poor experience digital life primarily through cell phones, they increasingly find themselves inside walled gardens—digital leisure enclosures controlled by the state and the media industry. It is worth asking if the global poor's collective enterprise and improvisational character will enable them to play hide-and-seek with these surveillance systems that have become a normative presence in their daily lives.

7

Privacy, Paucity, and Profit

AFTER AN HOUR of navigating traffic from the city center of Belo Horizonte, the sixth-largest city in Brazil, the taxi driver entered the residential area called Minas Caixa. The hilly streets were lined with bars, mom-and-pop shops, and houses, all fenced off by concrete walls that blended into one another, forming a long uneven barrier on either side of the street. My research team was there to interview young Brazilians about their digital privacy. We chose Escola Municipal Dora Tomich, the local public school, to conduct our interviews. A ten-foot concrete wall fenced off the school, and the only way to get in was through a large metal door.

The young people we interviewed were enrolled at a night school program for nontraditional students. Many of the students faced challenges typically associated with low-income urban neighborhoods such as this, including violence, limited access to public services, and high rates of health problems, teenage pregnancies, poverty, and school dropout. All of the students lived with their parents or siblings, except for one who lived alone and another who lived with three roommates. In spite of their young age, they all held jobs—

as security guards, construction workers, babysitters, cashiers, factory workers, and so on.

We encountered difficulties in talking about privacy. There is no obvious translation of this term in Portuguese. At the start of the interviews, the standard response was that they had "no idea" about what they considered private and public space online. After some discussion, they described privacy based on the digital medium through which they sent their messages. This translated to them using messenger apps for private communication and Facebook for public communication. Facebook is a public sphere to them. We found that they did not trust digital platforms. Raquel, a nineteen-year-old student who works as a waitress, captured a shared sentiment when she remarked that "there are many people that use it [the internet] for evil."[1]

This is not to say that young Brazilians are not obsessed with social media. On the contrary, many of them are addicted to living the digital life. "Even when I'm sleeping, I'm connected," said Pablo, a young man who is an assistant mechanic. When asked how frequently they check their Facebook or WhatsApp, some responded, "the entire day" or "every day, every hour," and reportedly take a break from these only when they are sleeping.[2]

Mobile phones are personal property for these young people, not meant for sharing. Carlos, a young man who worked many night shifts to save up to buy a smartphone, was protective of it. "I don't like that people touch my personal stuff," he said, "If they want to see something, I, myself, will show them. I do not let them use it."[3] However, when in relationships, they have no problem sharing their passwords with their partners. Romance unlocks the private worlds of these teens. Different rules of privacy apply to different people in their lives. Deep distrust of the internet coupled with a passion for broadcasting oneself online complicates neat demarcations between the private and the public. In this way the low-income students in this neighborhood resemble typical teens in the West when it comes to their digital privacy practices.

There is a growing need to protect young people as they share intimate details of their lives online with little thought of the consequences. Since the early 2000s, people in the West have been increasingly concerned about the lack of control over their networked lives online. Revelations that the US National Security Agency tracks and stores users' online social interactions has escalated these fears. There seems to be no place to hide. A surveillance society promises to be the new reality. Sandwiched between corporate and government watchtowers, the user has little hope for anonymity.

According to a 2015 PEW Report, 91 percent of Americans in the survey "agree" or "strongly agree" that consumers have "lost control over how personal information is collected and used by companies."[4] Moreover, 70 percent of them are concerned about information they share on social networking sites being accessed by the government without their knowledge. While adults are concerned about state and corporate surveillance, teens are more worried about family and friends invading their privacy without consent. The news media stress that cyberbullying, online sexual predators, and revenge porn are also dangers inherent in posting personal information online.

Most of the data currently available to researchers on digital privacy and surveillance is drawn from the West. Given that the poor in developing countries have become consumers of new media technologies in the last few years, companies have only recently started to target them online. Because they constitute 85 percent of the world's youth, they promise to be a lucrative market. How do low-income people take to this new corporate surveillance? In the previous chapters we have seen that the poor inhabit informal economies and that the new digital platforms extend these gray economies. Can the poor escape the sophisticated online tracking systems that are now in place? Do they even desire privacy, a value long privileged by the West?

Many of the poor live with extended families in one-room houses, often in illegal settlements. Daily surveillance by their families, their neighbors, their employers, government officials, police, local slumlords, and welfare workers pushes their lives further into the public domain. This is the world they know. A 2013 Meeker report on internet trends found that different cultures demonstrate remarkably different levels of public sharing.[5] For instance, about 60 percent of Saudis surveyed reported that they share "everything" or "most things" online, compared to 15 percent in the United States and 10 percent in France.

Even if those outside the West do value privacy, it seems they will face an uphill battle to keep their lives private online. Digital privacy is a new luxury, with the rise of a new divide between the haves and the have-nots—the divide between "the privacy rich and the privacy poor."[6] The marginalized majority cannot afford to pay for privacy or may lack the knowledge to disable "super cookies" that stalk their every move online. Do the world's poor have the basic skills to block a person, create a good password, or change their privacy settings? Does the walled garden of Facebook's Free Basics trap them and infringe on their right to privacy?[7]

This chapter investigates how low-income young people, particularly in Brazil and India, play with privacy. As they discover new digital worlds that promise them connectivity and community with a global public, do they also compromise their privacy? Play takes the form of circumvention and at times resistance. Play is the crafting of visibility and invisibility, depending on what the situation demands. We find that teens in these low-income communities differ in how they value privacy. They have, however, accelerated their learning curve when it comes to managing their private lives online. They have developed strategies to balance their desire to play openly with strangers online with a need to protect themselves from unwanted attention.

Digital Surveillance of the Poor

Surveillance has a colonial heritage. Most countries outside the West underwent long periods of colonial rule. The rulers designed new techniques to control colonized populations to prevent uprisings. The criminologist Simon Cole argues that colonizers were the pioneers of identification technologies.[8] For instance, in the mid-nineteenth century, the British Empire instituted fingerprinting to track its subjects. It was a brilliant means of linking the individual body to the state. The very essence of personhood, the fingerprint, was used against the self in the name of social order. The collecting and recording of fingerprints forced all colonized subjects into a classification system. This early biometric technology, used on criminals back home, became a standard method to record all natives from the colonies, framing an entire populace as latent criminals.

Previous to this, people were identified through sensory recognition. Recording of body descriptions was common. For instance, "a mole on the cheek," "small eyes," "large forehead," or "thin lips" were typical ways of identifying people based on their physical attributes. Notes on whether the person had marks from smallpox, or if they had a gunshot wound, as well as if they stammered or talked slowly, were all documented as added inputs to profile the individual.[9]

An issue arose when it came to recognizing and profiling Indian natives. British bureaucrats of the time noted in their logs that they found it tremendously difficult to "tell one Indian from another."[10] That was problematic. It was important to be able to differentiate the "troublemakers" who could provoke an uprising from the law-abiding masses. The fear of political upheaval was a constant motivator to identify and track the so-called unruly subjects. The fingerprinting technique was timely indeed.

In order to make bodily surveillance more palatable, the British rulers repackaged this elaborate system of acquiring such intimate knowledge as a paternal act.[11] The natives were told that fingerprinting was a way to protect them and give them access to certain public services that many had been deprived of, such as pensions for the native clerks working for the British bureaucrats. Connecting surveillance with the everyday lives of the native subjects normalized this system and gave it the appearance of benevolence. Unfortunately, the native elite learned well from their masters how to perpetuate this disciplinary surveillance apparatus. When the colonizers left, the system they had set up did not leave with them but instead became the foundation for many of the postcolonial institutions that today are ongoing obstacles to social equality.

Interestingly, in the British industrial era the British proletarians were treated in much the same way as colonial subjects. British administrators in the eighteenth century described policing as the "science of happiness."[12] The poor needed to be saved from themselves. Sir John Fielding, a notable English magistrate and social reformer, viewed the poor as a "contaminating force" who needed to be contained to protect the dignity of society. The poor needed to be constantly scrutinized, diagnosed, and monitored lest they get out of control, he argued, and those from outside the locality should do the policing.[13]

Poor people's "idleness" was particularly threatening. Police were instructed to strictly monitor the leisure activity of the poor in order to tame their debased immortality.

> The most intimate features of the activities of the poor and the wayfaring—their habits, customs and resorts—should be made accessible to the intelligence of a new improved police. The poor were to be tracked down, classified, counted, and ordered. Their behaviors were to be prised open and catalogued.[14]

Today we see similar patterns in the policing of the poor.[15] New technologies of surveillance are aimed at poor communities, supposedly to provide welfare services or to institute law enforcement. These communities, particularly in developing countries, have long been used by the state to test out new surveillance techniques. Hence, it should not be a surprise that the poor have come to expect and even live with these tools of control. Take the Snowden revelations in 2013. While the media went into a frenzy over these leaks, for the poor this was old news. Their privacy is violated daily. The stop-and-frisk policy in the United States allows police to frisk and question any person on the street on the grounds of "reasonable suspicion." This has translated into profiling, and African American and Hispanic people in low-income neighborhoods have become targets of interrogation.[16] The homeless are surveilled through closed-circuit television cameras at shopping malls, shelters, urban parks, and city benches. Welfare mothers are closely monitored under an "ethics of care" approach, as social workers demonstrate their concern through regular inspections.[17] The welfare state is a surveillance state. The state demands an unequivocal naked transparency as a trade-off for services provided.

New systems of government surveillance are more sophisticated than ever before. The global media praised the Indian government when they launched the ambitious Biometric Identity initiative in India, known as the Aadhaar project. BBC endorsed this effort, reporting that the poor, "with [previously] no proof to offer of their existence will leapfrog into a national online system, another global first, where their identities can be validated anytime anywhere in a few seconds."[18] The goal of the project is to provide a unique identification number (UID) to each of the 1.2 billion Indian citizens through the capturing of their fingerprints, iris scans, and photographs. This consolidated digital identity serves as a primary portal through which citizens gain access to government services such as welfare, banking, and food rations for those at the margins of society. It aims to bring all of the undocumented poor into the system. R. S. Sharma, then secretary of the Department of Electronics and Information Technology in India, declared, "Digital India is not for rich people . . . it is for poor people."[19]

India is not alone among nations in the digital tracking of citizens. China has revealed a comprehensive plan to reify its vision of a good society and a good citizen by creating a unified digital system—the Social Credit System—which it plans to fully implement by 2020.[20] By combining citizens' financial records, online shopping data, social media behavior, and employment history, the system will produce a "social credit" score for each citizen. This rating system will be used to measure the citizens' trustworthiness. Each citizen will earn credit through good behavior, online and offline. This will directly affect their access to all kinds of public services, including the nation's financial credit system. In essence, it is a value-embedded system meant to encourage good behavior and discourage bad behavior. According to the Chinese government's Planning Outline for the Construction of a Social Credit System, the system aims to measure and enhance "trust" between the citizen and the government and within the commercial sector by strengthening the "sincerity in government affairs, commercial sincerity, social sincerity and the construction of judicial credibility."[21]

China's Social Credit System is being built on an already existing system—Sesame Credit, owned by Alibaba, the eBay of China. This gamelike application helps document a person's actions on the site and provides a total score of the "goodness" of the individual. The person can then share this profile with his or her family and friends. Users are encouraged to make decisions about whether or not to interact with other users based on their credit scores. This is not an unprecedented idea. Since the Mao era, the Chinese government has maintained the Dang'an system, which closely monitors each citizen in every aspect of their daily lives.[22] A file is kept on each Chinese citizen, beginning at their birth. The file includes their grades in school, their housing situation, their families, and other details over the course of their lives. Employers receive these files to help them in their hiring decisions.

While the Social Credit System is an extension of the Dang'an system in many respects, it differs in one significant way. This digital system can now harness the nuanced choices, personal behaviors, and social networks of Chinese citizens that eluded surveillance in the past. Digital platforms give governments a portal into citizens' homes, lives, and bedrooms. In a digitally mediated life, nothing is private. Unsurprisingly, the administrators of this system are the technology companies. Armed with exclusive licenses to sell credit-rating services, eight Chinese companies, including the internet giants Tencent and Alibaba, mine as much data as possible about their consumers.

The calculations affecting ratings give insight into what the society prioritizes as worthy. For instance, Tencent, a major Chinese social network portal, found that people who bought curtains or scuba gear somehow evoked more trust from people reviewing their profiles, while those who purchased photography equipment were deemed as less trustworthy. Those who play video games got lower scores, as gaming is seen as a wasteful activity. Buying baby-related items brings one's score up. Things get more worrisome when seemingly unrelated web portals start collaborating. Alibaba's Sesame Credit joined hands with Baihe, China's biggest matchmaking service.[23] This partnership allows people to publicly view the credit scores of romantic prospects in order to decide whether to date them. This can lead to public shaming, as these scores are visible to friends, family, and colleagues.

This system can become highly discriminatory, as the scanning of social media accounts can sentence people to unemployment, slow internet connectivity, and travel visa bans based on their liking an anti-government post or being friends with those who don't share the state's communist values. Technology companies that do not comply with these "ethics" could be fined for supporting so-called immoral and indecent content. The poor usually suffer the most, as they have much to resist, much to protest about, and much to transform through collective action.

Take the Hukou system. Instituted in the mid-1980s, this residence registration system controlled the flow of migrants from rural to urban areas.[24] Few would dispute that the 300 million such migrants worked hard and served as the engine of the Chinese economy in the last decade. Yet they are denied public services like education and health care. Their movements are severely curtailed, leaving them in a persistent state of vulnerability. The new digital monitoring through the Social Credit System promises to exacerbate an already desperate situation in need of urgent reform.

On the surface, Brazil seems to have taken a different path in its internet regulation. In 2014, Brazilians celebrated the landmark internet regulation initiative called Marco Civil, a progressive bill designed to protect citizens online and keep the internet free and open to the public.[25] This included provisions for privacy rights, net neutrality, safe harbors for internet service providers, open government, and freedom of online speech as an exercise of civic rights. What was particularly novel in this effort was the collaborative process that shaped the making of the bill. In the draft phrase, more than 800 contributions came from nonprofit organizations, municipalities, and activists.

However, the actual law that was enacted was far from the draft version approved by the diverse stakeholders who participated in the drafting phase. For instance, freedom of speech was limited by adding provisions that gave the government further powers to monitor citizens online. Nonetheless, the Brazilian law can be a template for developing countries that are looking for models different from those of the Chinese and Indian datafication systems.

Whichever system of surveillance the state uses, the poor continue to be catalogued subjects. States continue to pioneer new techniques to enhance surveillance of the disenfranchised in the name of social and economic development. It is clear that the so-called information age did not arrive as a result of the digital age; it began long before. What is less clear is how the global poor understand and play with these new surveillance systems that can simultaneously liberate and entrap citizens with their very own data.

Favelas and Slums Go Digital

Legal scholar Helen Nissenbaum argues that privacy cannot be understood without examining its context, because "people don't choose in the abstract, but in a particular context."[26] While teens will be teens wherever they live, their contexts do matter to their privacy. Privacy for a teen in a suburb in California can be quite different from privacy for a teen in a favela in Brazil.

According to UN Habitat, nearly one billion of the world's poor live in slums and favelas, and this figure is expected to double by 2045.[27] Slums for the most part are illegal squatter settlements, and their residents are criminalized simply for living in them. By default, young people here are born criminals. In such zones of deprivation, which lack secure public infrastructure such as water and sanitation and come with few or no rights to the land inhabited, how do these youngsters carve out for themselves spaces of security and privacy on the internet?

Very little research has been done to understand privacy among these young people, so in 2015 I set up a comparative project on privacy in the Global South. My team and I embarked on investigating how low-income teens in the favelas of Brazil and the slums of India conceptualize and practice privacy under their challenging social conditions.

In Brazil we chose two favelas to visit, one in Rio de Janeiro and the other in Belo Horizonte. In Rio, roughly a quarter of the city's residents, popularly called "cariocas," live in favelas.[28] These favelas are dense concentrations of poorly constructed buildings, many of them makeshift shacks constructed of bricks and discarded materials, built on hillsides bordering the city. Typical of favelas, both sites were part of larger complexes in which one favela blends into another, and often only locals can detect the invisible boundaries that differentiate these neighborhoods.

Favelas have specific points of entry, making it possible to monitor who comes and goes. A favela's legal ambiguity gives the government the right to police its residents. Young people living in favelas are subjected to regular public humiliation and physical violence. Human dignity is a privilege few are granted. State surveillance gains further credence due to the high rates of violence triggered by turf wars among drug gangs, particularly Comando Vermelho, Amigos dos Amigos, and Terceiro Comando. They account for many of the armed homicides in Brazil's favelas.[29]

Drug gangs constantly recruit new soldiers. The average drug soldier is a ten-year-old boy, and 80 percent of the youths involved in trafficking do not live beyond twenty-two years of age.[30] Given the high levels of unemployment, racism, and general discrimination they face, many young people are drawn to the drug trade. Hence, they face layers of surveillance—surveillance from the state, from the drug lords, and from their own community associations wary of violence.

One of the favelas we focused on, Santa Marta, came into the limelight in 1995 when Michael Jackson shot a video there for his song "They Don't Care about Us." The lyrics struck a deep chord as they brought to the surface the chronic insecurities, the feeling of daily violations, and the state of neglect and helplessness experienced by many young people, especially those who live in poverty. This song became an instant hit, much to the dismay of the local authorities who came under global scrutiny because of it. While Santa Marta now has an active community association that provides a number of social programs, it still suffers from problems typical of favelas—the violence of drug gangs and the police, and restricted access to public services. Within this social vortex, what does privacy look like here as young people take on social media and share their everyday lives? As the public sphere suffocates them with surveillance, will they open up and express themselves online? Will they trust the digital world more than they trust the physical world they inhabit?

In contrast, in the slums in India that we visited—the first in Isnapur, close to the global metropolitan city of Hyderabad in southern India, and the second in Ludhiana, in northern India—we did not find the culture of violence we found in Brazil. In the last ten years Isnapur has emerged as a hub for the use, sale, and repair of mobile phones, especially for the young population. This transformation is attributed to the proximity to Hyderabad and its booming educational and industrial scene, which has spilled over to this low-income neighborhood. Though still rural in character, surrounded by farmlands, Isnapur is also a manifestation of the emerging aspirations of the young people in slums.

Through their digital consumption, they are starting to partake in new worlds of commerce and social exposure to ideas and people from all over the world. Nonetheless, this urbanizing slum still suffers from tremendous social and economic constraints and limited access to the opportunities that are available just a stone's throw away in Hyderabad.

The settlement in Ludhiana is also surrounded by agricultural land and farming communities, with a mix of urban and rural occupations. Unlike Isnapur's proximity to Hyderabad, Ludhiana is a distance away from the nearest metropolises, such as Mumbai and Delhi. Ludhiana has some modern infrastructure, but the young people continue to be entrenched in social traditions and conventions that influence their privacy practices on social media. Both of these slums we studied are on the border between socioeconomic changes reflecting the rise of India as an information technology hub and the cultural traditions and norms that hold power over these youth.

"The Internet Was the Land of Marlboro"

Facebook is a public square for Brazilian and Indian youths. In 2018, India and Brazil ranked first and third, respectively, as countries with the most Facebook users in the world.[31] In the next five years, Facebook expects to double the number of users in these emerging economies. In both countries, Facebook is so pervasive that for many young people, it is their internet. In our conversations with them, it became clear that they viewed Facebook as a place to be seen and heard. The pursuit of "likes" is their main preoccupation.

Facebook is a "happy" place. This matters a lot in favelas, where young people's day-to-day lives are entrenched in poverty and violence. For instance, Rodrigues, in Rio de Janeiro, fills his Facebook wall with positive messages. He does not want Facebook to be an extension of his reality; he wants it instead to be a safe space away from it:

We live in Rio de Janeiro that is extremely violent. We have many tragedies, many bad things happening. If you only post bad things, soon my page on Facebook will only have bad things. So, if I'm a guy who wants good things for me, I'll only post good things and soon there will only be good things on my Facebook page. If you open my Facebook page today, you'll only find positive things, happy things.[32]

Young Indians similarly portray Facebook as an open and positive space. Facebook for them is a place to post jokes, spiritual and motivational sayings, and nice photos of beauty and inspiration.

Sharing mainly positive posts requires an effort at self-presentation, making sure to not reveal one's vulnerable side or too much of one's actual life. Said Milana, a teen mother in Rio:

On Facebook, depending on the day, I share a thought. For example, a short while ago, three days ago, I noticed I am getting bald, so I posted a joke. Christmas is coming and I posted, "Dear Santa Claus, I would like to ask for hair!" But in a more spontaneous way, I try to be spontaneous. I do avoid using Facebook for outbursts. I don't like it, I think it's overexposing. Feelings I think is something particular, it's unnecessary, because not everybody who is on Facebook is someone you know. I wouldn't like them to know about certain things of my life. So, when you expose yourself, it's as if you're exposing yourself to judgment.[33]

Studies across cultures about self-presentation have found that young people are obsessed with controlling their image online. Teens do their best to manicure their self-brand to promote a particular identity to their Facebook world.[34] Much like young people in the West, Milana worries about how she presents herself to the eclectic audience she has gained over the years on her Facebook page. Her Facebook friends include many of her neighbors from the favela, as well as a few boys she met recently at a street party, and some of friends from the school she dropped out of when she became pregnant.

It is challenging to manage the different groups that inhabit one's network, like family, colleagues, friends, acquaintances, and strangers. Keeping everyone happy is not easy. Sanitizing one's Facebook presence by avoiding controversial topics is a typical way to go. For example, Raquel, a waitress in Belo Horizonte, talks about how she brings up her religion on Facebook:

> We know there are many beliefs, people believe in many gods. That's something we have liberty with. We live in a secular country and people have a right to that. I'm Evangelic Christian, Protestant. I'm very careful in trying not to monopolize goodness, to think that only evangelic people are good, or only my belief is right. For example, if I post something, "My God is the only God of Love," I end up offending a person who believes in another God and who thinks that her God is also a God of Love. I need to understand that people think differently than I do and I can't offend them with my post. So I try to hold back a bit. If I'm going to talk about God, I'll talk about my God, it's my right and I'm not offending anyone or anyone's belief. The same way with sexual options, same way with color, and race.[35]

While young people seek affirmation through geniality, they also greatly value authenticity.[36] Their notions of authenticity are influenced by their concepts of who their audiences are. The more their online audiences are tied to their real lives and the environment around them, the more they are likely to be truthful. For instance, while many of the youth feel a need to create a "happy" place on Facebook to counter the high levels of violence and racism in the favelas, they also strive to carve out an honest space. Says Rodrigues from Rio:

> Many people will say that I'm a criminal . . . so for those who know how to use the social network, for those who use the virtual world

in general to talk about those things [about being systematically discriminated against], it's good. Because in many places that we go to talk about those things, we go and knock on the door and they will slam the door on our faces. We won't be able to talk. But the social network is there and you say whatever you want.[37]

Several of the young Brazilian males felt that traditional media like television are stacked against them. The constant stereotyping of favela boys on television has become an exhausting and hard-to-battle image. On Facebook they can be more themselves, say what they think and feel. Pablo, in the Belo Horizonte favela, explained to one of our researchers who is white:

> I'm not a prejudiced person, but I'm going to explain to you how it works more or less. If I have your skin color, your biotype, straight hair, bright eyes, and I appear on television singing a song or saying anything, there will be people who applaud. There will be people who will say they found it cool. But, if I show up on television with my black hair, with dreads, with loose clothes talking about politics, social problems, hunger, misery, corruption, living inside a [poor] community, many people will say that I'm a criminal, that I'm saying many silly things.

On Facebook, however, Pablo felt he could really discuss issues that concerned him and he felt that people kept a more open mind in these conversations.

Some youths, however, complained that there was more integrity in the early days of Facebook when people argued, had genuine dialogue, and said things that were profound. Today "people use it to post appealing and provocative content, seeking some kind of fame," lamented Carlos from Belo Horizonte, who posts less because of this shift. "The internet was the land of Marlboro," he remarked, "everybody would say whatever they wanted and that would be it. Not now. Now, people know there's a limit."[38]

The internet of the past was envisioned as a digital Shangri-La, an inclusive and open public sphere. Metaphors from the 1990s give a sense of the utopian visions surrounding what was then a new technology. The internet was supposed to be uncharted territory available to anyone and everyone to explore and inhabit; it was to be the "new frontier" and the "Wild, Wild West." These metaphors signaled that whereas those with power monopolized the real world, technology had a chance to create social equality by opening this infinite digital space to everyone.

The premise for this new land of opportunity was that nobody would have sole authority to own or regulate this new digital terrain.[39] People regardless of their social or economic status would have the right to inhabit and express themselves in this affirmative domain, creating a culture of shared intimacy, community, and aspiration. Today, however, much of the internet is behind walls, closed, and fortified. Facebook users are selective in their acceptance of "friends" and in what they share of their daily lives. There is a reason this nostalgia appears to be growing among young people, in spite of their enthusiasm for this digital sphere.

Although they continue to remain positive about Facebook, teenagers have also quickly developed an impressive array of strategies to deal with the growing insecurities stemming from social networking sites. In a short time, many of them learned how to use the different media available to them for different purposes. For example, with the popular application WhatsApp, different rules of conduct and privacy expectations kick in for the Brazilian and the Indian youths. They developed the habit of erasing their histories quite often on WhatsApp but found this task pointless on Facebook. They viewed the publicness of their histories as an integral part of the Facebook culture, which fosters the accumulation of the past to facilitate the public permanence of the self.

Meghana, a nineteen-year-old in Ludhiana, compared these two apps and expressed a preference to be anonymous on WhatsApp but not on Facebook: "With Facebook, when you post a picture you post where you are, and who you are with. With WhatsApp, I don't. If I want, I can stay anonymous with it. Nobody will know what I'm doing and for me that's better."[40] This matters for Meghana, who lives with her three brothers, her parents, and two older cousins, all of whom are constantly watching her. She is of marriageable age and therefore is viewed as vulnerable and in need of protection through this familial surveillance.

Other young people are skeptical about the differences in applications, believing that they are now converging into the same open culture. Raquel from Belo Horizonte does not trust any of these apps to keep personal matters private. While she acknowledges that WhatsApp is "something more secret" than Facebook, she argues that "if something happens on WhatsApp, it passes from one contact to another. Then once you look at it again, it's all over the world, all over the internet."[41]

Generally the youths were accepting of the downsides that come with the internet. They believe that when you put something online, even if you intend it to be private, you should be ready for it go public. Milana, the teen mother in Rio, expressed a pragmatic view on this matter: "I think that even things you put on private, you have to think if it'd be worth for it to go on the internet, because once it does, you're not the owner of that anymore. It may be used against you. You have to be very careful on that."[42]

In Brazil there is an added reason for caution, particularly about indicating one's location. In the last decade, kidnappings have become common. When I was in Rio in 2015, many locals instructed me on the dos and don'ts of my movements. People told me not to carry my phone in my hand or much money in my purse, and to not cycle by the beachfront after four in the afternoon. Stories emerged from some of my Brazilian colleagues of kidnappings of people they knew. A "quick" abduction involved capturing an individual and releasing them once they withdrew funds from the ATM. Jason Lee, a jujitsu athlete from New Zealand who came to Rio to participate in the 2016 Olympics, tweeted to the world that two people dressed as police officers had kidnapped him. They forced him to withdraw money from his ATM to secure his release.[43]

It is not surprising that young Brazilians are careful about revealing their locations online. "If I go to a friend's wedding, I end up posting pictures," said Rodrigues from Rio, "but I'm always careful with this thing of tagging places, due to all the warnings about crimes, about groups that plan kidnappings, these kind of things."[44] In fact, a study done on location awareness via smartphones in Rio de Janeiro and São Paulo revealed that the youth feared these new technologies, as they believed that criminal gangs would use them against people.[45]

Organized crime continues its business even behind the prison walls, often with the help of mobile technologies. The incarcerated make and receive calls and track others on social networking sites like Facebook and even update their own profiles to show they are still in the game. Gangs are notorious for tracking profiles online and making people their targets for robbery and kidnapping. Hence, young Brazilians have developed an aversion to any location-disclosure behavior, including tagging, to protect their personal safety. This is part of a larger coping strategy they live by, which includes checking their wallet when someone bumps into them and looking around before unlocking their homes.

How does this compare to the West? According to the 2013 PEW Internet Statistics Report, 74 percent of Americans use their smartphones to get location-based information, but only 12 percent of them use location-based social networks, such as Foursquare, to check in and hunt for friends nearby.[46] Location tracking is an unwanted feature of digital life, regardless of whether one is rich or poor. The difference is in what drives this desire for locational privacy.

For some in the favelas, this is now less of a concern. A popular mobile used by many people in the favelas—the diretão—has a special

SIM card illegally obtained from service providers that allows users to be unidentified when they make calls. This kind of anonymity is prized by members of criminal gangs. Such anonymity is limited to calls shorter than ten minutes. After ten minutes, the provider can triangulate the cell position, disable the diretão, and possibly find the service thief.

Another way of escaping detection is through the cloning of analog mobiles. It is easy to retrieve the unique electronic serial number and telephone number by hacking into these old phones. This allows one to duplicate the information on another handset, making it indistinguishable for the cell tower, resulting in another person footing the bill for both phones. Given that mobile theft is a lucrative and common business that supports many favela residents, this technique transfers the financial burden to their wealthy neighbors.

Hacking is a way of digital life, with corresponding violations of privacy. Many of the young people in the favelas were victims of hacking. Their Facebook passwords had been hacked. They reported the incident to the cyber-police but they were told that without proof, nothing could be done. Most of them did not expect the police to be able to do anything about this anyway. It was their own problem to solve. As Pablo, the young man in the Belo Horizonte favela, put it, "When using the internet, we accept that risk."[47]

They notified their friends to ignore any messages coming from the hacked Facebook account. They changed their emails. They set up new accounts and reported the hacking to Facebook. Some were hacked on other sites, such as World of Warcraft and Tíbia. Rodrigues, from Rio, was not a man to take this lying down. He decided to turn the tables. He tracked the IP address of the person who hacked his account, looked up the fixed local address, and went to confront his hacker. He was grateful that it was someone his age: "If it were someone older than me, I wouldn't go," he said with a laugh. Having confronted his hacker, he was able to get back everything that was his. Others, like Milana, tried the affective approach:

I touched the emotional side of the person [hacker] while they were in my face. I went through the Facebook of a friend of mine and asked for them to give it [her account] back, because I had there the profiles of people who passed away and there was no way for me to add them again. I guess after a while they gave up.[48]

When we asked the young people if they would feel more protected with stronger privacy laws, most were skeptical. Some felt it was all theory, as it would not really stop them from experiencing harm. Rodrigues bluntly stated,

Honestly, I don't feel protected, but I feel a bit more comfortable for knowing that I have someone to run to. I would feel protected if I'd know that what I post would not be linked to other things. I would feel protected if I didn't need this law.[49]

While relatively new to the internet, these teenagers in favelas have become veterans at navigating public space online. While they use sites like Facebook to get some respite from their current struggles, they are no fools. When they sugarcoat reality, they are well aware that it's a candy pill. They don't have many illusions about the internet being a sphere of security and freedom. They see it as a leisure space where they can escape, connect, socialize, and engage on day-to-day matters. They recognize that this digital play needs to be carefully managed, manicured, and manipulated. They are savvy hiders when they need to be, and active seekers when they need to be, especially when seeking happiness online.

Friending Corporations

The attention of the poor is a valued commodity. Technology companies gift laptops to schools and tablets to hospitals in villages in developing countries, in exchange for goodwill from the state. The goodwill buys them a captured market. Free laptops for the few today should earn many new customers tomorrow. During the last two decades, this has become the modus operandi for multinationals to get on the fast train for capturing the digital market outside the West. Take the classic case of the Indian state of Andhra Pradesh and its former chief minister and self-proclaimed "CEO of the State," Chandrababu Naidu, a businessperson at heart. He wooed Hewlett Packard, Intel, and other companies to set up their corporate social responsibility efforts in his rural constituency in early 2000.[50] He was well ahead of his time.

In September 2015, Narendra Modi, the prime minister of India, hugged Facebook founder Mark Zuckerberg on his visit to India and tweeted a selfie with him to his 12.5 million Twitter followers. Highlighting the persistent digital divide in India, where more than a billion people still do not have access to the internet, Zuckerberg promised that "one day, we will connect everyone, and the power of the internet will serve every community across India and the world."[51] Of course, it does not hurt to have the first-mover advantage with the world's second-largest population, many of them young and digitally hungry.

In earlier chapters we have seen that this so-called corporate friendship with the poor had not always existed. The private sector needed serious convincing to engage with the world's poor, which were long considered a high-risk market for them. As we saw in Chapter 4, one of the most convincing was the late neoliberal business guru C. K. Prahalad. In early 2000 he began his mission to push the corporate world to view the poor as consumers instead of charity cases. His timing was fortuitous. This concept came at a time when social media were emerging and taking the world by storm.

The rise of social networking sites inspired a cultural shift toward perceiving users not as mindless masses but as co-creators with collective intelligence and wisdom. Business folk were called upon to exercise their imagination, to envision the poor as future digital consumers and agents of change. After all, the existing market had not taken into consideration that the informal economy accounted for up to 60 to 80 percent of all economic activity in developing countries. With few ties to legal and formal institutions, this massive segment of the world's population remained largely invisible to the corporate world. At a time when the consumers in the West are demanding invisibility and the right to be forgotten, the poor seem to have earned their right to visibility. Progress is often bittersweet.

Today there is much discussion about social media corporations exploiting users' data to the advantage of their multibillion-dollar industry. The appropriation of value from user-generated content happens through a variety of creative strategies via the platform of choice.[52] Affect is at the center of this digital economy. How people feel is reflected in what they comment on, whom they friend, whom they follow, when they decide to tag themselves to an event, and what they like. Often their personal activities, their user names, and their profile photos appear to endorse an event, a product, or a service to their circle of friends. This effectively commodifies that person's experience while it personalizes the endorsement online.

Those concerned about their privacy frown upon targeted personalized advertising. Consumers tend to describe this trend is "creepy."[53] Given that the technology industry has developed sophisticated techniques to target consumers' needs and desires, how much farther can they go with this before they lose their customers because they have violated their privacy? Corporations want to speak to their customers on a personal level, and they have built an impressive system to do so.

Facebook, for instance, can create a thousand different ads for a thousand targeted audiences, depending on their age, family background, and income. They collect data not just on one platform but across platforms—"cooperation in competition" at its best. The big-data monopolies—Google, Facebook, Twitter, Amazon, and Apple—are hoping that most of their customers choose this personalization over privacy.

Would that be the choice for our young men and women in the Indian slums and Brazilian favelas? We got them talking about corporate surveillance of their digital life. What did they think about targeted advertising? Were they aware of the business models of their new digital playgrounds like Facebook and Twitter? Did they also get "creeped out" by ads that addressed them by name or seemed to be there at the right time and the right place with the right product at hand? Did they feel special for becoming visible to these global brands or just more exploited by the outsiders?

What became quickly clear was that the young people in the Indian slums seemed more open and positive about online advertisements than were the Brazilian youth. Given that being online is still a costly endeavor for the poor, the Indian youth felt that these targeted ads saved them time and money. Meghana in Ludhiana was enthusiastic about them: "It [targeted online advertising] is good. Because it depends upon us what we will buy. If we find something good, we can buy it. It will save us time. It is beneficial for us and even to the seller. Because in today's world the social network is used a lot. Putting ads on there is very good. Because many people read this. Buying is also easy. They can purchase on the internet itself." Keep in mind that in comparison to ordering online, their options offline are extremely sparse. Many spend hours looking for a good deal. Few quality brands are available to them within their vicinity. Few shops sell what they want in their neighborhood. When there is a captured market, there is little incentive to satisfy the customers. The internet compels the shops in slums to improve their services and quality of goods. After all, now the poor are not optionless customers but come with digital alternatives to satisfy their wants. Observed Surain from Isnapur, "A person can find whatever is best for him. Whenever the person is searching for something, the ad gives other options."[54] It also gives these shoppers a sense of worldliness as they become aware of a myriad of products and services available to global consumers.

Not all ads are good. Meghana distinguishes the nice ads from the "vulgar advertisements which harm"—pornography. She and her family, she states, are different from city people when it comes to such media consumption. There must be a reason these ads come up, she explained.

Somebody must be clicking on them, watching them. But not her, and not her family. "I belong to a village. In cities, I don't know what is happening. But in villages, people are concerned about self-respect."[55]

In contrast, most of the Brazilian young people shared primarily negative emotions about targeted marketing, from being upset to downright angry at this intrusion into their digital life. Many viewed these ads as spam that unnecessarily filled their pages and needed constant ignoring, blocking, or reporting—efforts that often amounted to sheer tedium. Some complained how annoying it was, "because we think it's something, that it's someone wanting to talk to you. But no, it's just another advertisement."[56]

Bots are not friends, not in Brazil. Rodrigues, like several others, felt that the advertising is an imposition and a violation of personal space online: "I think it's forced, not everybody wants to see advertisements that they're not really interested in. When it's something forced, it ends up not having much acceptance." Regarding targeted ads, the creepiness factor goes up. "It feels as if someone knows that I researched that. It is a bit weird. I think it's unnecessary," lamented Milana.[57]

Some gave deeper thought to what bothered them about data mining and customer tracking online. Raquel, for instance, acknowledged that there is no free lunch and that Facebook needs to support itself through such tracking and advertising. It is a business after all. Yet, she finds it a cruel practice.

> I think the bad part of it is that, because sometimes you search for things to buy, but if you don't have the money, and when Facebook comes and keeps offering and offering, I think that's bad, and that hurts. It's something you want, something you need. You work and yet you don't have the money and the internet keeps massacring you, throwing this at you for you to buy. It's the model of capitalism. They want you to buy and you don't have the money to buy, and they don't make it easy for you to buy it. Now that's mean.[58]

Distrust levels were high among the young people in the favelas of both Rio and Belo Horizonte; they viewed the online marketplace as a mirror image of the frauds that surround their day-to-day lives. Milana was convinced that these ads with their promises came from the jails, where many of the people she knows are held:

> The majority of the ads go, "Oh, you won a television!" and it's from jail. Because sometimes the prison inmates, from their cells, call our number. "Oh, you've just won some money!" or a smart phone or something. You shouldn't believe it though because it can be from jail. I don't know how they do it, but they manage to get our number and send the messages.[59]

Many feared that what they felt was private would somehow circulate into the public domain through their search behavior. They felt the need to constantly monitor their privacy settings and block certain ads that popped up through their private searches, as they did not want their friends to know about them. A case in point is browsing for porn. Pablo, the young man in Belo Horizonte who is addicted to the internet, acknowledged that sometimes he searched for pornography but worried that the sites he visited would appear as ads on his Facebook page. Viewing pornography is something that he does in private, and he feels that he is entitled to this privacy.

Even brands that Pablo likes, such as Dafiti, irritated him because they bombarded him on Facebook with their products. Dafiti is a Brazil-based fashion and lifestyle site and is the fastest-growing e-commerce site in Brazil and the Latin American region in general. This is a highly trusted company, a brand synonymous with e-commerce in Brazil. Since its founding in 2010, its outreach has been impressive—it now has 50 million unique visitors per month. Even though Pablo is a loyal customer of this online shopping site, he felt hounded by it, and "exposed."[60] Not all shopping preferences and habits needed public attention, he felt.

So what happens to lesser-known sites when they target their customers online? Inspired by Dafiti's tremendous growth and success in such a short time, competing sites have sprung up in recent years, many of them fake and untrustworthy. Some of the young people shared stories of having been tricked—for example, Milana's sister-in-law paid for a phone on the internet but received a fake product—which made them rethink online shopping in general. These experiences can cause a serious backlash against e-commerce.

Compared to their Indian peers, the Brazilians revealed a sophisticated understanding of the issues at hand regarding privacy, security, and commerce. They talked about being careful about the kinds of information they share online, particularly information that can be used by hackers to draw from their bank accounts or to shop using their accounts without their knowledge. They had developed strategies to distinguish the levels of safety of online shopping sites. For instance, Carlos from Belo Horizonte checked sites "to see what the people who bought previously said." He closely examined reviews, comments, and forums before proceeding to buy on any site.[61]

Brazil does have a Consumer Defense Code that requires companies to inform their customers about their policies for including customer data in their databases, and in July 2018 the Brazilian congress passed a personal data protection bill.[62] In comparison to other Latin American nations, this is rather late in the game. Chile enacted its data protection laws in the 1990s. Argentina has been complying with European rules on privacy for decades, and in 2010 Mexico passed a federal law on personal data protection. These measures are important to institute if e-commerce is to have a large and sustaining impact on these marginalized groups, who, like all other online users, need protections from hackers and other dangers.

We know that e-commerce comes with promises to end the traditional consumer alienation of poor people. Online shopping can be liberating for the poor, as it allows them flexibility and choice—in contrast to the older markets, which did not treat the poor as legitimate consumers. This is even more reason for corporate transparency and personal data protection laws to be at the heart of the process. In return for their participation in e-commerce, these vast populations of low-income young people should be guaranteed data protection and online security.

The Digitized Disenfranchised

A common theory of rule is that it is essential to simplify those who are ruled into manageable units to be tracked, collated, and computed. This reductionism dehumanizes the poor, making it easier to impose inhumane rules of conduct onto these now-faceless beings. Colonialism would have been impossible without the data-driven bureaucracy that enabled the few to rule the many, particularly of the "exotic" kind. These surveillance machines were easy to justify, as they appeared neutral to the lay public.

Postcolonial nations continue to build on colonial bureaucracies through the digitization of human activity in the name of national interest. The current systems rest on an assumption of citizen trust, which is as yet unearned and undeserved. It will take a radical dismantling of archaic laws and the restructuring of the legal and administrative systems for these surveillance systems to truly serve the common good.

Digital life for the poor appears to be public life. Never before have our mundane acts gained such validation. Data is the new economy, and data-mining the poor promises to make national systems and multinational corporations data-rich. With this wealth of data, it can leave them privacy-poor. Anonymity is difficult to achieve in the digital public sphere. The reason the chronic surveillance of the poor has not raised as much as an eyebrow in governments and development agencies is the persistence of the myth that privacy is a value held more by the higher classes as they retreat into their own gated communities. The poor, in contrast, are romanticized as tightly woven communities with less of a need for privacy. What they lack in wealth, it seems, they make up for in togetherness. Three generations under one roof, closely packed in dense mazes of makeshift shacks, are their signature "joint-families." The state describes the apparatus of surveillance as an apparatus of care, in these contexts. Surveillance at its best looks like a concerned community, a protective village, a watchful neighborhood.

Contrary to this myth, however, is the fact that low-income youths are usually deeply vigilant under the social microscope. That they are accustomed to being watched does not mean that they are consenting subjects. In spite of their newness to the internet, this disenfranchised demographic has quickly learned the lay of the digital land and how to navigate this new frontier. Privacy is often a necessity and a critical tool for survival as they invent strategies to circumvent surveillance.

Data gathering is not just a state or corporate prerogative but is also an instrument used by the poor to survive. Mundane, humble, day-to-day information about the who, the why, and the when of those in the social network creates local knowledge. The poor harness such collective intelligence to avoid harassment. Webs of relationships nurtured in these deprived areas serve as channels through which data of the collective circulates and people share knowledge—how to hack a phone, how to not be scammed, and so on are part of the new literacies they develop in this digital era. These localized data collection strategies lend a culture of stability to environments that are chronically unstable. Together, the people of the neighborhood have each other's backs.

Now that these young people have gained the attention of the corporate world, companies seduce them with advertising just like they do with users in the West. Facebook has become an equalizer between the rich and the poor in online corporate marketing. Many brands do not discriminate algorithmically as they attempt to lure the poor with choices beyond their means, contributing to the already existing aspirational economy fed by conventional mass media, be it Bollywood films or Latin American soap operas.

Selective visibility is desirable. Throughout the Global South, visibility is intrinsically tied to intimacy and romance. Sites like Facebook enjoy special status as romance sites for low-income communities, encouraging more publicness among the young as they go about self-manicuring their image and their activities to attract true love. As Chapter 8 shows, romance appears to be the big trade-off for relinquishing privacy.

8

Forbidden Love

TODAY, TO BE young and in love is to share the most intimate of things—passwords. It is fashionable in the West for young people who are in love to reveal to each other their passwords—the keys that unlock their digital lives. In an age when trust is hard to come by and digital vulnerability is high, what better way to say "I love you" than to make oneself public in the most private of relationships. Boyfriends and girlfriends sometimes create identical passwords as a way to be an open book to each other.[1] Some change their passwords to display their love by putting their partner's name in their password, expecting the same in return.

Many teens say that they feel secure swapping passwords. After all, if one of them violates this trust, it would lead to mutually assured destruction. Some feel protected through such sharing. There is a sense of safety in knowing that someone is out there who you can fully trust and is looking out for you online. The digital public world can be a lonely place, after all. The unending flow of information, compounded with endless networking possibilities, can create a sense of isolation in the crowd.

Not everyone sees this sharing of passwords as romantic. Educator Rosalind Wiseman argues that the pressure to share passwords is similar to the pressure on girls to have sex.[2] A possessive boyfriend often demands his girlfriend's password to keep track of her social life online. Sharing digital passwords can further complicate any adolescent's life, as online actions are hard to erase.

In 2011 the PEW Internet & American Life Project conducted a survey of American teens and their sharing habits and found that one-third of online 12- to 17-year-olds shared their passwords with a friend or a significant other, and that almost half of 14- to 17-year-olds did. Girls were almost twice as likely as boys to share their passwords.[3] A 2015 PEW Report underlined that 31 percent of teens are heavily surveilled during their relationship by their partners, who regularly check where they are and who they talk to. Disturbingly, 22 percent of those who have ended a relationship have experienced internet abuse from their ex-partner, including name-calling, spreading rumors, and sharing embarrassing information on their online social networks.

Is this trend prevalent beyond the West? Does this aspect of American teenage life cross borders? What do trust and romance look like for young people in low-income communities outside the West? This chapter reveals that low-income youths in the Global South, who are desperate to partake in new digital worlds of romance, experiment with what to make public or private on their social networks. This is essentially an everyday negotiation of self-preservation versus desire. Romance is a critical window into the world of privacy. Going public becomes worth the risk with the promise of a soulmate. Digital media carve out new opportunities for companionship while also posing new threats to teens' safety, especially in low-income and patriarchal societies.

Complicated Courtship

Many societies in developing countries are patriarchal and have strong norms concerning romance. Most young men in low-income communities in the Middle East and South Asia have barely spoken to a girl outside their family circle.[4] Arranged marriages are often the only pathway available for a young person to connect with someone of the opposite sex. Many of the young men we spoke to in Ludhiana and Isnapur explained how few opportunities they had to converse with a girl in their communities. Even talking to a girl could affect her reputation. Strong sexual segregation rules applied in their communities. Few public spaces allowed the crossing of these strict gender borders. It is no wonder that Facebook and WhatsApp are tremendously popular among these young people. Online chatting is one of the few ways they can explore this vast and unexplored territory of romance.

The digital world opens up new possibilities of communication and, more importantly, a new mating ritual and space for romance. However, given the social risks involved, girls learn quickly to balance this opportunity for autonomy with the social expectations for their behavior. A 2014 study of young Indian Muslim women revealed the challenges of disclosing visual aspects of themselves, given that their physical modesty is closely associated with the upholding of their family honor.[5] In the West, most young single women choose their most attractive photos for their Facebook profiles, to enhance their romantic prospects. It is not that simple for young Indian Muslim women.

Much deliberation goes into selecting a modest photo. A bad choice in the wrong hands could have devastating consequences for the woman and her family. It becomes even more difficult when social expectations are in conflict. In 2013 two Indian Muslim clerics issued a fatwa against young Muslim women uploading their photographs on social networking sites such as Facebook. Shortly after that, however, another cleric declared that this fatwa was un-Islamic, positing that as long as it brought about good communal bonding, sharing was indeed caring.[6]

It is no wonder that many women in developing countries stay away from social networking sites. In 2013 Intel released a groundbreaking report, *Women and the Web*, which revealed that in developing countries, nearly 25 percent fewer women than men accessed the internet.[7] This gender gap increased to nearly 45 percent in regions such as sub-Saharan Africa. In India and Egypt, 20 percent of women stated that they did not think it was appropriate for them to be on social networking sites. In our research on digital privacy in Isnapur and Ludhiana, it was difficult to find young women who used Facebook or were willing to talk about what they did on social media sites. In spite of these challenges, a few of the teenage boys did succeed in getting girlfriends through Facebook.

There can be much drama in these digital romances, especially as they seep into their offline lives. For example, Surain, a young male in Isnapur who works part-time at his uncle's mobile shop, loves Facebook. It had transformed his life, he said. However, he admitted that it was intense at times, and that it could have terrible consequences in matters of love. His close friend met a girl on Facebook. They fell in love. They ran away from home and got married. The parents filed a court case when they went missing, and even the police got involved. The couple returned home, however, and showed proof of their marriage. Now he is a driver and she continues to study, but they still have a lot of problems due to their religious backgrounds. Surain became tired of hearing about their plight. "From that day onwards if anyone asks for help, I first ask, is it a love problem? If it is a love problem, I go home. Facebook is cause of lot of bad things . . . but still we like it [he laughs]."[8]

Raj, in Ludhiana, is another young man in search of love. Fed on Bollywood romances since he was a child, he desperately wanted to experience falling in love. He met a girl on Facebook and fell for her immediately. Her online profile hooked him completely. He started sending her private messages, and then it escalated to public Facebook postings of his declaration of love. One day, though, he found out that her family had married her to another man, as they did not approve of this online relationship. He was devastated. He hit his head with a stone and landed up in the hospital.[9]

Unlike many liberal societies in the West where romance is far more open and permissive, love comes at a price in much of the Global South. Young Saudis, for instance, are avid consumers of digital media, but anonymity is an essential part of their digital romances.[10] Raqad Alabdali, a twenty-two-year-old in a suburb of Riyadh, began her romance online when she shared her melancholy posts on Twitter through an anonymous account. A young man responded to cheer her up. That led to a thriving romance through compulsive messaging. They exchanged phone numbers, and shortly after that she sent an unveiled photo of herself in a short-sleeved dress. This gesture meant a lot, as Raqad was putting herself at risk by placing such trust in a relative stranger. He reciprocated appropriately by asking to marry her. Their families arranged to meet. When asked how she could trust a man she had not yet met, she said that she had no doubt since her older brother and his wife had met on Facebook and were still together.[11]

Facebook is a popular platform for romance among young Saudis. However, they recognize that this open space puts them in danger, and many of them therefore hold multiple accounts. Their first account is to communicate with their family and friends. The top reasons for their second and third accounts are to conceal romantic relationships and to enjoy some freedom to state their opinions publicly.

More females than males stated that they use their second account primarily for playing games. Entertainment is a forbidden fruit for females more than for the males, reminding us how the leisure divide is also a gender divide. Part of this is because gaming partners are mostly male. This mixing online is anathema in Saudi life. Most public spaces in Saudi Arabia have strict gender codes, including separate dining spaces for women and men (unless they are married), separate travel compartments, and separate prayer rooms. The Committee for the Promotion of Virtue and the Prevention of Vice, the Saudi Arabian agency that monitors public space, seems always around the corner. Facebook apparently can provide an escape from this surveillance.

Anonymity, particularly for women in the Middle East, is often not a personal choice. Traditional communities in Jordan do not permit women to display their individual identities in public space.[12] It is dishonorable for the family if a young woman becomes visible to society. Even the exposure of their printed name—for example, on a wedding invitation or announcement to friends and relatives—is considered improper. Instead, they are referred to as the daughter of their father. They are an extension of the male honor. Surrounded by such strict norms of behavior, internet cafés have become a refuge and a site for individual expression for women.

In spite of the high risks, young women look for love online. The internet has fostered a culture of dating in the highly gender-segregated community of Irbid in Jordan.[13] The young people there see chatting on the internet as less morally problematic than any form of public face-to-face meeting, however casual. In the spectrum of un-Islamic acts, this is one of the least offensive, as it is merely written words. Young women have made online flirting into an art form, tailoring it to their cultural codes.

They conceal their identities through nicknames but make it easy for their dedicated suitors to find them as they earn their trust. The magic words to start this unpacking should begin with an "I love you" from the boy. He needs to utter these words first in his online chat if he wants to proceed. Nothing less than this can justify their ongoing contact. However, online flirting allows a way to create a buildup, to get to know one another after such a declaration of love. Male suitors fill their courtship with romantic e-cards, scanned photos of love, and poems to serenade the young women.[14]

The Youth IGF Project by Childnet International conducted a survey in 2013 of 1,300 youths from sixty-eight countries about their views on digital anonymity.[15] They found that almost two-thirds of the young people across diverse cultures, from Afghanistan to Saudi Arabia to Finland, reported that they had interacted online without revealing their identities. Key reasons for this preference for anonymity were to freely make comments online and express themselves openly, to protect their personal information, and to be able to discuss taboo or sensitive topics without exposure to their friends and family. While this shows a common bond among the young people across the spectrum, what counts as taboo is what differentiates a young girl in Finland, for instance, from someone like Raqad in Saudi Arabia.

For teens it can be more terrifying to be surveilled by the family than by state agencies. Adolescence is filled with tension between traditional family values and expectations and the teen's developing personhood. Our conversations with the young Brazilian women in favelas were peppered with stories of being stalked online, often by their mothers. Yet they are sympathetic toward their mothers. Raquel in Belo Horizonte explained that even though her mother is a "stalker," she acted from a motivation of care and protection. Still, Raquel struggled to rationalize her mother's actions:

> I owe her gratitude, she is my mother. But it's a lack of privacy you know. Imagine if you are with your boyfriend somewhere and then she knows where you are. Although this is not that important, it is still your privacy. Sometimes I feel that it is a lack of respect and confidence towards me. But it is also a question of safety. I feel bad that she stalks me, but sometimes I don't care. It can be good in case something happens.[16]

The mother seems to have a special place in the lives of Brazilians. Milana in Rio, a young mother herself, finds her mother's monitoring acceptable and would do the same with her own daughter when she grows up:

What I like to do on my cell phone is my business and no one else's. But when my mom wants to look at my cell phone, I give it to her and she goes through it. . . . I don't hide anything from her, because she also doesn't hide anything from me. I have to be with my mother the same as she is with me, an open book. Because friends always want to put you in a tough situation, but with her, she will always be by my side, whenever I need.[17]

These close mother–daughter relationships can be explained partly by the smaller age gap due to the high rates of teenage pregnancy prevalent in favelas.[18] Young single mothers are their children's friends. Rather than lose their childhood completely, the young mothers continue their social experiences with their daughters. As is common in regions of deep poverty and the precariousness that deprivation brings, motherhood is at times a desirable, stable status for young girls.

Brazilian mothers have a small army of helpers in their neighbors. Surveillance in the favelas is a neighborhood exercise that often extends to online. Pablo, in Belo Horizonte, shared his experience:

It's not like out there [the formal city] where you go out, see a neighbor and don't even know their name even when working beside them. Here, people know each other a lot, whether they like it or not. Then there's that thing, where you date someone and another one comes along and you "hook up" with them, and post it on Facebook. Then your neighbors on Facebook will tell one person and the other and then many things come up on your wall that never needed to be there, like swear words and things like this.[19]

Surveillance and romance are tethered to one another. To discover more about young people's views on digital privacy, romance is a critical lens. It is impressive how the young, even in the most constrained settings, put everything at risk for the sake of love. In a short period, young women in conservative environments outside the West, such as

Saudi Arabia and Jordan, have learned how to play with social networking sites to attract a suitor and engage in the dating game. In patriarchal societies where the public domain has long been inaccessible to young women, sites like Facebook give new opportunities to create a public persona.

Digital anonymity empowers these young women to discover their personhood, their aspirations, and desires, all in the public limelight. Most astonishing is the fact that strangers have penetrated the digital lives of these young people for the most intimate of needs. This defies a long history of social norms that scorn the outsider. It challenges the age-old practice of family members vetting prospective partners for arranged marriages. The digital realm has given a newfound respectability to the stranger through the innocuous practice of friending.

Fake Love

To friend a stranger is to open oneself to possible deception. Social networking sites carve out new spaces for both pleasure and vulnerability. Since the beginning of the internet, people have feared that its disembodied quality would facilitate manipulation and misrepresentation. A common vision was of people constantly deceiving one another behind the screen of anonymity. When it came to romance, deception was expected to increase; strangers were not to be trusted.

In the last decade, however, we have witnessed the normalizing of online dating with the rise of numerous dating applications like Tinder, Hinge, Catch, Clover, and Tangle. According to a 2016 study on online dating and relationships, more than half of the internet users surveyed supported online dating sites as a way of meeting a prospective suitor.[20] It is no surprise that at a 2018 conference, Mark Zuckerberg announced an upcoming launch of a new mobile app—Facebook Dating.[21]

This increased trust partly derives from the fact that the structure of social networking sites these days compels users to be far more transparent. Users are required to create a profile to establish their online identity. This usually comes with a number of verification demands, including one's phone number. This is not to say that all personal information displayed is trustworthy. In fact, 54 percent of online daters continue to be skeptical about other people's profiles, as they are convinced that some of the information presented in their profiles is false.

They are on to something. Lying is a common practice in the pursuit of a suitable partner.[22] Nine out of ten people lie about something in their personal profile. After all, the mating game can be vicious. Both women and men invest tremendous effort to position themselves as desirable in this highly competitive romance economy. Men lie more frequently about their height, income, and marital status, and women lie more about their age, weight, and physical appearance. Much of this is harmless. However, deception done systematically to scam people with the promise of love can be tremendously destructive emotionally, psychologically, and financially, and particularly devastating for low-income youths.

An especially devious form of online deception is to use love as a bait to extract money from those desperately seeking companionship. This relatively new cybercrime—the internet romance scam—involves scammers setting up fake profiles and friending lonely people on the internet. Once they friend these people, they serenade them with declarations of love and passion until they build trust. Once an emotional bond is formed, the scammers come up with a range of excuses to elicit money from their new online lover. Some scammers plead that they are in an emergency, some claim that they want to send their lover a luxurious gift but it is being withheld by the customs until some payment is sent, or that they want to visit their new love but do not have sufficient money to make that happen. Whatever the reason, the victims tend to fall for these lines and transfer money to these scammers, sometimes multiple times.

The Royal Malaysian Police recorded 846 such cases with a total loss of RM32.09 million (around US$7 million) in just one year, and stated that there are perhaps many more cases that have gone unreported.[23] These scams have caused significant psychological and financial losses to victims who are already at the margins of society. Many victims do not report these swindles due to shame and embarrassment. When they do report them, it is often difficult to track the scammers, because they are spread across the world and use multiple fake identities and bank accounts.

These scams have become so common that specific sites, such as romancescams.org, have been created to educate people on how to protect themselves. They even have surveys for users to help them distinguish fake love from the real. Questions guide users in managing their romance online: "Has someone fallen in love with you quickly?" "Do they immediately want to leave the dating site to use IM or email?" "Do they have no close family or friend or business associates to turn to?" and "Are they coming to visit you soon but an event prevents them from visiting?"[24]

Nigeria has come under particular scrutiny, as many of these frauds have been found to originate there.[25] These are called "Nigerian Romance Scams" by the US Federal Trade Commission. Today Nigerian scam emails have become something of a joke to millions of people worldwide because they encounter them so often. However, it takes just a small percentage of people to fall for them, often those who are the most naive and vulnerable, to earn the scammers millions of dollars. This has become quite a cottage industry in Nigeria, with the police discovering training centers where online scammers learn to develop their social skills online to maximize their romantic persuasiveness. In August 2016, Interpol caught "Mike," one of the most notorious Nigerian romance scammers, uncovering his complex global network and fraud totaling about US$60 million.[26]

Friending strangers on Facebook is another powerful strategy to initiate these scams. According to a study by the security firm Cloudmark, 20 to 40 percent of Facebook profiles could be fake, created by malware writers, spammers, and scammers.[27] In Isnapur, one of our chosen research sites, near Hyderabad, India, internet romance scams have become so common that the police have set up a state website to instruct people on how to detect scams and protect themselves.[28] In our conversations with young people in Isnapur and Ludhiana, we listened to a number of stories about romance frauds. The young men told us how "pretty girls" would friend them and ask them to transfer money via their mobile or to digitally recharge their own mobile so they could continue to be connected to these boys. Some girls would send them revealing photos and claim to be in love with them.[29]

Surain, the young man in Ludhiana who was in search of love, realized over time that these girls' profiles were fake. He learned this the hard way after sending money a few times. "I asked if we can meet," he said, but they would come back with a request for him to recharge their mobile first. When he said he could not, they threatened to unfriend him. When he yielded and sent money to them as well as his phone number for them to call, they never called. He went through a steep learning curve in separating fake from authentic profiles on Facebook. Raj, having recently gone through a major heartbreak, also was wary of online encounters. He explained that it was now easier for him to detect fake profiles: "If you send 'how are you' to fake accounts, their reply will be 'hot' almost all the time. We can tell they are fake immediately."[30]

For the young men who have developed strategies to detect fake love, the learning process does not seem to end. Scammers are constantly developing more creative ways to reach their victims. The love baiting is becoming more sophisticated as social bots are able to assimilate their targets' likes, tweets, and comments to tailor their seduction in impressive new ways. The fake girls start slowly, inquiring about the young man's day, what he had for lunch, and how his friends are. This is a special experience for many of the young males from these slums, who do not get this kind of attention from girls where they live. After a while these bots send links to click, which lead the boys to pornography sites. Raj explained how they provoked him, telling him that he did not have any experience in this domain and that "if you don't get into the mood then you are not a man."[31]

Sometimes, though, the victim becomes the victimizer. Girish, a friend of Surain, was tired of being a victim of such frauds. He decided to do some of the scamming himself. He created a girl's profile and started to chat up other men. "There was a boy on Facebook from a far off place. Very far off," he said. "I told him to get me a recharge. I said that I am at home and want a recharge soon so I can talk to him. He then did it." Right after that, Girish stopped contacting the boy. Girish also uses this fake profile to chat up girls in his neighborhood, knowing they will be more disarmed and more likely to friend a girl than a boy.[32]

Girls are catching up fast in this game. Meghana in Ludhiana says she can tell if someone is a boy or not. She explains her technique. She checks out their pictures with friends and clicks on any other friends commenting on the picture. She then goes to the profile of that friend to see if that profile is original or fake. Some girls just use androgynous nicknames as a strategy so that those with fake profiles hesitate before friending them. The words the people use, the gestures, the inside knowledge, are all telltale signs to distinguish the fake from the real.

Slut-Shaming and Revenge Porn

Another major area of digital vulnerability is revenge porn, the nonconsensual sharing of sexual content posted and distributed online, with the purpose of shaming the person featured.[33] This is the digital extension of an age-old practice of slut-shaming—labeling girls and women as "sluts" to punish them for their sexuality. Men, on the other hand, are rarely held to the same standards, and at times gain social credit among their peers for their virility. While this double standard is pervasive worldwide, it far more frequently results in deadly consequences in patriarchal and marginalized societies in the Global South.

Moreover, with women's virtue tied to family honor in such contexts, it has become a currency to be traded in meting out community justice.

In Africa, for instance, the media are saturated with stories of men publicly humiliating women in the name of promoting "good" social values. In 2014 a video went viral of a woman stripped naked on a bus by a group of men in Nairobi. Her crime was to wear jeans, which the men claimed was offensive and tempting to them. She was a "slut" for wearing this provocative piece of clothing to seduce the men in public. Their job was to discipline her in public and set an example for the other women.[34] In Pakistan, numerous incidents in recent years have gained media attention as girls have been physically humiliated or attacked as a way to shame their families. For instance, a fourteen-year-old girl was forced to walk through her village naked by the Pakistani elders because her brother had an affair.[35] In Multan, another Pakistani village, the local council ordered a sixteen-year-old girl to be raped in front of her family and the council as a punishment to her family for a rape her brother allegedly committed.[36]

In India, Pramod Muthalik, the leader of the Rashtriya Hindu Sena, a conservative right-wing Hindu religious party, became notorious for having led some of his party members into a pub in Mangalore to attack both men and women for disgracing traditional Indian values.[37] He suggested that mobile phones had corrupted young women and made them "sluts," as they were exposing themselves to Western values. Facebook, of course, was held complicit in the devaluing of so-called Indian morality because it is a digital public space that brings people together, allowing new avenues to explore sexuality, romance, and dating, all deemed to be products of Western values.

In our conversations with the young men in Isnapur and Ludhiana, some of them echoed support for restoring the traditional values and forbidding any romantic acts in public. Girish, the young man who set up fake profiles, argued, "We don't need that [Western] culture. We are Indians. We have some standards. If I am an American I would have supported it [intermingling of the sexes]." Surain supported his friend on this matter: "If they want to kiss, why don't they go to their home and kiss there?" Some of the young men continued to struggle about what is appropriate female behavior in public spaces. Girish summed up their concern that women needed to consider the society they lived in and the traditional values that kept Indian society together. Their community had the right to label a woman based on her behavior, and "what people think is also important, whether the girl is good or else she is a slut."[38]

The public domain is often a contentious space for women. In patriarchal societies, public space comes with complex rules of conduct that women are forced to abide by. A woman is in a constant state of vulnerability as she navigates this male-dominated sphere. Strangers are especially threatening, as even an inappropriate male gaze in public can transform a public moment into an intensely private violation of the woman's modesty. This creates a perennial fear of violating the public code under patriarchal surveillance. In traditional remote communities, the woman's morality is synonymous with the man's "honor," thus casting privacy as the protection of female virtue.

Public space is a deeply gendered space. It is no wonder that the young women we talked to in these low-income communities approach Facebook with both excitement and trepidation. Facebook does not come with a specific gender-biased cultural code. It offers these women a chance to experience an open public sphere free from strangulating social rules. However, when a woman is exposed and her modesty compromised in this digital public space, it can cause permanent and possibly deadly consequences for her.

In comparison to Africa and India, Brazil is far more sexually permissive and open. This is not to say that young Brazilians have not had their share of incidents. In 2013, Julia Rebecca, a seventeen-year-old, committed suicide after a video of her having sex with other minors went viral online. She posted her last message to her parents: "I love you, I'm sorry for not being the perfect daughter but I tried, I'm sorry

I'm sorry I love you so much."[39] This created public outrage about the posting of the video, pushing for internet regulation. Shortly after, the National Congress of Brazil passed a bill that outlawed the disclosure of any material containing nudity, sex, or other such acts without the permission of the persons pictured. Anybody violating this law would be sentenced to up to three years in prison and would have to pay a fine.

In 2014 the Brazilian Supreme Court banned an application called Secret that allowed people to anonymously post content online.[40] Apple and Google were given ten days to remove this application from their services. Anonymity was viewed as an enabler of illegal activity such as revenge porn. In the same year, Brazil formulated its first comprehensive Civil Rights Framework for the internet, "Marco Civil," incorporating protections for users, including protection against slut-shaming online. In spite of these developments, when we spoke to the young women in the favelas, some of them felt that the onus of protection lay not so much on the state but on the women themselves.

Raquel in Belo Horizonte believes that women are clearly at fault. They cannot afford to be naive. They should know better when using mobile technologies. "Guilty is the person who let the other person take his or her picture, for sure."[41] She was not alone in holding this opinion. These young women found it highly irresponsible for a girl to send nude photos to a boy in the first place, putting her reputation at risk. For others, however, the perspective was one of shared guilt.

Rodrigues in Rio took a more measured stance: "If I need to say who is to blame, I would say that the person who shares this content and the woman who allows these pics are both wrong." Milana, the teenage mother, emphasized her right to privacy instead of playing the blame game: "I made the video with my boyfriend, we broke up and he posted it. Even though I'm wrong, I'm gonna go after my rights, because my image is there. Everybody has the right, so here nobody is a saint."[42]

Milana hits a nerve. Women are not saints. They are human, after all. For centuries society has held them to a different moral standard than men. They have been straitjacketed with expectations of purity and goodness. They have carried the burden of their nation's values and the family's honor. This deliberate coupling of their personal virtue with that of the state, society, and the family makes their personhood a public property. Times are changing, however.

In 2011 India had its first "SlutWalk," part of a larger transnational movement against the rampant gender discrimination and rape culture pervading societies worldwide. Hundreds of women took to the streets in Delhi, fed up with the constant sexual violence they experience in the public domain. As one of the marchers put it, "On public transportation, going out on the streets, anything that has to do with going out of the house is problematic."[43] One of their goals is to transform public space into a terrain that is respectful of their rights.

The young women in Brazil and India have just as much right to love as any other teens. As they enter the new public space of Facebook, they come with newfound hope for security. They cannot afford to be naive, however. Anonymity and deception are their weapons of protection against familial surveillance and male harassment. Ironically, these very same weapons can turn against them, as we have seen with the fake profiles defrauding eager youths in search of love and the circulating of sexual content without consent through anonymous sites and identities. Internet regulation continues to be a serious challenge. The balkanized national approach to regulating sexuality on the internet is inconsistent with the more globalized approach to privacy as a human right.

Although sex has been one of the prime factors prompting the passage of several internet laws in the Global South, these laws also have commercial and political effects. For example, blocking the Secret application that allowed anonymity and encouraged acts of revenge porn resulted in regulations applied across the digital economy. The regulation of sites such as Facebook that allow the friending of strangers and possible suitors creates profound new dilemmas for the users as they balance the trade-offs of privacy with access to the worlds of digital romance.

Privacy Literacy

When privacy is regarded as a "value," it becomes enculturated as a basic human need. The diversity of privacy practices in the world is often attributed to cultural borders and differences. Privacy as "protection" takes on different meanings when applied to girls in a patriarchal village in Jordan in contrast to girls in a middle-class British suburb. The former concerns the guarding of female virtue and male honor; the latter is about preserving childhood innocence. Moral panic about the loss of virtue and purity drive these beliefs. Privacy as "personal" emphasizes the individual over the community. Even China, where the nation comes before the citizen, is witnessing the rise of individualism. Mass migration from the villages to the cities redefines neighborhood surveillance in low-income communities. The intensity and density of illegal urban settlements enhance these surveillance networks.

Privacy is undoubtedly a luxury. Achieving it can require a constant struggle, as we have witnessed through the narratives of these young people as they go about creating private moments within public domains. Romance, sex, and love are the strongest lens through which we can understand teens' deep desire for privacy. With limited prepaid plans, basic phones, and scarce time at cybercafés, low-income youths pioneer creative ways to stretch a moment, and to go beyond their neighborhood networks to gain pleasure.

Courtship falls within the gray zone where culture dictates how people communicate intimacy, both publicly and privately. Few would fault the young people for harnessing Facebook to explore their sexuality, and some would even celebrate these new media outlets as a much-needed safe zone for their freedom of expression, particularly in patriarchal societies.

Digital social networks like Facebook have enabled low-income youths to break free of traditional social norms to pursue their passions. The internet itself is a fast learner, however, deploying bots to exploit these desires. Popular sites like Facebook create not just a digital commons, but also a vulnerable commons. While poverty persists in unfortunate continuity, privacy practices are in constant flux.

To best understand the dynamism of privacy, we need to immerse in its everyday literacy. "Netiquette," a term that frames how rules of online communication surface and become convention, is dictated by politeness and courtesy.[44] This concept is limiting. The poor have learned to play with the rules to survive, to hide from authority, to seduce, to bond. The stories from the favelas and slums give us an overarching message: When motivated and given an opportunity, the poor learn how to use new digital tools to understand, to enjoy, and to value and protect privacy.

Epilogue

IN 2015 Sheryl Sandberg, the chief operating officer of Facebook, told an audience at the World Economic Forum in Davos that people will soon "walk into phone stores and say 'I want Facebook.'"[1] This is not a mere sales pitch. Facebook has acquired seventy different companies, including WhatsApp, Instagram, and the virtual reality company Oculus.[2] As of 2017 there are about 2 billion active Facebook users worldwide. Out of the top five countries that use Facebook, four (Brazil, Indonesia, India, and Mexico) are in the Global South.[3] By December 2016, Google had acquired 200 companies. There are more than 2 billion active users of its Android devices. Google has more than 90 percent market share in developing countries like Argentina, India, Brazil, Indonesia, and Mexico. Jeff Bezos, the CEO of Amazon, one of the world's largest online retailers, believes that the next hot venue for its operations will be India, describing it as "on track to be our fastest country ever to a billion dollars in gross sales."[4]

The empire building of the likes of Facebook, Google, and Amazon, through the aggressive scaling of their platforms worldwide, suggests neocolonial undertakings. These techno-oligarchs have achieved the monopolization of entire publics through their sweeping data mining. These corporate social media platforms justify their growing expansion in the Global South under the banner of "connecting the unconnected," but the datafication race is on. Data is, after all, the new oil. Because they are targeting areas with weak institutions, few privacy and data protection laws, and vast semiliterate populations, there are few checks and balances in how these conglomerates collect and compute the digital lives of low-income communities in these developing nations.

Nineteenth- and twenty-first-century inequalities have much in common.[5] The late nineteenth century, which Mark Twain called the "Gilded Age," was a period of social turmoil, aggravated by globalization and technological innovation. The prosperity it brought to some, came at the expense of many, well beyond the national borders of the West. Today we live with a system that reproduces and reinforces social and economic divides, designed to keep wealth and power in the hands of the few, a system disturbingly similar to that in the past.

Like the colonizers in the colonial era, the conglomerates have a need to justify their systematic exploitation of new markets and standardization of cultures, and they cannot justify this purely on the basis of economic interest. Legitimizing this process requires an ideology. Exoticism was a key strategy in normalizing European culture against the colonial terrain and establishing an enlightened rationale for the imperialist mission. As we have seen in this book, the state, the technology corporations, and even well-meaning nongovernmental development organizations have exoticized the marginalized majority—the global poor—as they index and archive these emerging digital lives against templates of the "mainstream."

In Search of the Exotic

In the nineteenth century, people called themselves "explorers" as they embarked to discover new worlds to exploit. Their projects were driven not just by commerce but also by the ideal of a civilization that they intended to spread across these new worlds. The exotic was that which was fringe and raw, ready to be molded in the image of the so-called saviors. Entire cultures, however historical and large, were considered peripheral to the dominant culture that prevailed in Europe. Tradition needed modernization. The colonized cultures were authentic in a sense of being unfiltered and unprocessed. In more derogatory terms, they were barbarian and heathen, remnants of the humanity of the past that desperately needed civilizing. At the same time, their contaminating influences needed to be kept at a distance from the protected enclaves of the civilized.

This book makes the case that the current targets of such exoticization are the poor of the Global South and their digital cultures. There is much insight to be gained from the history of the notion of "the exotic" and how that notion was framed, applied, and managed to create a phantom or imaginary colonialized public. The various templates about the global poor today—as blank slates, criminals, deviants, virtuous beings, entrepreneurs, self-organizers, victims, and more—is a testament to the mystification strategies at play in the framing of this vast populace. This deliberate schizophrenic obfuscation allows for the birth of diverse tropes to come forth to justify the continued exploitation of this vast public. Following what I call the "three C principles" of exoticism—to convert, to conserve, or to contain—we confront some of the major challenges in compartmentalizing digital life through the fictionalizing of the global poor.

Exotic Digital Cultures as Fringe

When a vast majority of the global poor are marked as the fringe, we are not talking about representation but about power. Since colonial days, mass media in developing countries have been used to propagandize the ideologies of the privileged as if they should be the values of the mainstream. This sustained inequality. Even after independence from colonial powers, many of these nations were ruled by international media conglomerates, such as Rupert Murdoch's media empire, and there is still heated debate about who has the real power—the nation-state or the international corporation.[6] Either way, the mission to normalize the interests of the elite as the interests of the mainstream has persisted.

Today's digital economy gives fringe groups the power to go mainstream. For many, the first impulse is to celebrate this democratization: at last, the underprivileged can broadcast their voices through social media and participate in the unmaking of the media empires. However, the last few years have also brought the rise of fringe factions that are destructive and polarizing, reminding us of the wide spectrum of voices in the world. When people at the margins gain a foothold at the center, we are tempted to romanticize this as empowerment and activism. That is a valid construct, but it is only one of the multiple manifestations of the decentering of broadcasting. Moralizing fringe groups as having an inherent, suppressed goodness is one of the modern pervasive exoticisms. Another myth is to equate economic marginalization and ideological marginalization. Who and what are considered the fringe is a fluid and dynamic paradigm.

Take Myanmar, for instance. In 2014 fewer than 1 percent of the Myanmar population used the internet; in 2017 that figure was up to 27 percent, so that one in four people there are now using the internet.[7] Many people who had known only military dictatorship for decades are now released into the wild online. When online, they are increasingly encountering "fake news," the spread of false information as facts. This has become increasingly pervasive on Facebook, the dominant platform where young people get their news. Fake news is winning attention while mainstream news media are getting sidelined.

Fake news that gets traction can be as banal as a report that drinking ice-cold water while eating hot food gives one a stomachache, or more sensational falsehoods such as the claim that Angelina Jolie keeps her adopted Burmese baby locked away because the baby has a deformity.

"People don't talk about the normal news they see on Facebook. They talk about the crazy stuff," says Shar Ya Wai, a young girl in Yangon, Myanmar, who recently went online.[8] The news economy appears to have become an entertainment economy.

A radical Buddhist anti-Muslim group, once the fringe in Myanmar, has gained serious traction using Facebook. By spreading false stories through viral posts, memes, and jokes, they have bonded entire publics around a single cause: hatred of Rohingya Muslims. Their online tribe has expanded across the country, gaining a loyal following. They have found affinity with other fringe groups across the world, including the Ku Klux Klan, enabling them to situate their local politics within a larger global solidarity movement. Wirathu, a radical anti-Muslim Buddhist, saw his account shut down by Facebook a number of times, only to come out stronger with more than 190,000 followers in 2016. The victimhood discourse and clear divides between the privileged and the underprivileged start to blur as sympathy sways between the fringe and the mainstream.

These events are not anomalies. Conspiracy theories have been promulgated on the internet since its beginning.[9] When the democratization of data was the prime dictate shaping the algorithmic culture of Google, conspiracy theories ruled its top-ranking pages. A significant segment of society that believed, for instance, that 9 / 11 was an "inside job." Such beliefs are for the most part dismissed as "the poor person's cognitive mapping in the postmodern age," as literature professor Fredric Jameson put it.[10] Nevertheless, when these fringe cultures are debunked as exotic anomalies—as paranoid and ignorant cultures—this misses an opportunity to gain insight into one of the big challenges of our time: the intersecting of trust, belief, capitalism, and the fringe in the digital era.

Fringe cultures see themselves as activist cultures, defying the mainstream. The fact is that circumventing the rules of the game has enabled many of the oppressed to find a way to be heard.[11] How many people who participate in these fringe cultures, though, are economically marginalized? Few works focus on how the global poor use social media to mobilize and get themselves heard. As evidence comes to the fore, we learn that the middle class, even on issues that seemingly concern the downtrodden, drive much of online activism.[12] It is dangerous to assume a shared interest between the middle and the lower classes. High-profile hashtag campaigns like #Bringbackourgirls and #StopKony were usurped by well-meaning NGOs and governments in the West in search of a good cause to bring people together.[13]

Even the antipoverty social media campaign #feesmustfall, the largest student-led protest in postapartheid South Africa, faced questions about the driving forces behind this movement.[14] What started with an incremental rise in tuition fees in one of the universities in South Africa became a call for free and high-quality education. In a country that categorizes half its young population as poor, education is essential to escape poverty. What confronts these young people is not the problem of getting into a university, but staying in it. After all, being a student comes with tremendous financial burden and conflicts with the responsibility of working to support a family.

As one young male put it as he marched with his fellow students, "We are here [at the Union Building] to also shut it down. We will burn it and take pictures for the world to see our anger. Our parents are poor at home and we are their only hope."[15] Women at the university rode on this hashtag wave, making their causes explicit. Many of the young women have had to resort to commercial sex work for "sugar daddies" to pay their fees, as expressed in tweets such as "there aren't enough sugar daddies!"[16]

Although these tweets bring to the surface some of the serious barriers for low-income youths, an analysis of this Twitter campaign revealed a disturbing trend. Only twenty tweets managed to reach more than 1,000 re-tweets and/or favorites. These came from politicians, celebrities, and social media consultants, for the most part. Trevor Noah, a South African–born comedian and now a United States television talk show host, dominated this Twitter campaign. Digital activism is clearly a skill that has been honed by professionals, politicians, and others who are privileged and well versed in online politics. They are able to steer social issues through carefully crafted infotainment that has an appearance of being spontaneous. It is hard to compete with such forces online—and arguably this once again leaves the global poor voiceless.

Exotic Digital Cultures as Authentic

Colonialism served up a moral dilemma to the civilized nations. With the early nineteenth-century upheaval of industrialization and technological disruption, the concept of the noble savage had caught the imagination of the public.[17] A wave of romanticizing the "primitive" as authentic—as inherently true, simple, natural, and far from the manufactured—swept society. However, this script sat uncomfortably with the explorers as they sought to exploit and even decimate entire cultures, for they justified their behavior by describing those cultures as primitive. This required a new paradigm that could continue the narrative and yet justify colonialism to the public.

If colonizers wanted to enter and exit native lands without dealing with the local cultures, then romanticism helped justify the approach of conservation. Cultural relativism came in handy, framing interference as infringement. However, as colonialism partnered with religious organizations to capture not just capital but also souls, paternalism was a better alternative. The native subjects were portrayed as childlike, innocent, yet in need of discipline. Darwin's formulation of evolutionary theory in the mid-nineteenth century was useful. Colonialism could be justified as a matter of nature's design. The superior culture of Europe existed to transform the savages or Orientals by schooling them in the language, customs, and behaviors that befit a civilized society.[18]

This book has highlighted the contemporary divide in perceptions of the poor as authentic—as being naturally entrepreneurial, self-organized, and virtuous—but at the same time as deviant and in need of taming. This notional messiness is convenient. It allows tailored interventions based on the technocratic project at hand. This continued exoticizing is possible as long as the belief persists that the global poor have certain inherent cultural traits.

The revelation of the global poor as sexual beings and major consumers of online pornography falls outside their exoticized profile. In spite of the massive scale of their online activities, few studies delve into their online sexuality. Centuries of infantilization continue to serve as a barrier to investigating the poor's sexual practices, unless related to their health. The poor continue for the most part to be framed as asexual beings, and when their sexuality does surface, those who exoticize the poor tend to experience some moral panic. Clearly it is time to acknowledge the desires and pleasures of the poor as they increasingly spend their time online exploring their sexuality, often at great risk to themselves.

Sexuality does, after all, involve power. It does not lend itself to a simple narrative. In August 2017 a large male gathering disrupted Kochi, a small town in Kerala, India. They had come to see Sunny Leone, a former porn star, who drew a larger crowd than politicians or even the top Bollywood star, Shah Rukh Khan.[19] This is not just an interesting anecdote. It is an invitation to investigate how a state that has the largest pornography industry, and one of the highest crime rates against women, in India is also a state with the highest literacy, digital access, and healthiest sex ratios in the country. Is this open display of adulation for the porn star a sign of a progressive or a patriarchal society? Undoubtedly, pornography sites continue to expand their empires online and remain the most-viewed sites. Given this pervasive phenomenon, it is important to truly engage with questions on how the vast numbers of low-income young people discover their sexuality, often in the only way they know how in deeply conservative societies—through their digital lives.

Venturing into the vortex on colonialism and sexuality can reveal new levels of exoticism mapped onto the digital cultures of the global poor. Anthropologist George Paul Meiu has unpacked some of the politics of intimacy and carnal desire during colonial times.[20] Maintaining sovereignty over groups of people required the pacification of the natives' sexuality. It was not sufficient to control and convert their minds. Their bodies needed to be reined in, too. What was seen as raw sexuality gave moral justification to the agents of empire. Demarcating homosexual acts in East Africa as "sin" gave the Church a moral hold over these colonies as they nudged the natives toward Christianity. French historian and philosopher Michel Foucault analyzed the systems of classification that took the biology of sex and modernized it into the social construct of sexuality, which allowed different institutions to exercise their power of judgment over sexuality.

What intrigues me most is how these legacies of colonial sexual politics influence ongoing processes of indexing, categorizing, tagging, and ranking of the global poor's digital explorations of desire. How are female and male sexualities crafted and consumed online by this vast underprivileged and young demographic in the Global South? In what ways does their hidden digital play influence their behaviors in real life? Do they buy into their own templates of exoticism and perhaps even leverage them to become more visible in their digital lives?

After all, authenticity is a commodity online. Some development-studies scholarship shows that the global poor play their part in being the "global poor."[21] When money is channeled toward using mobile phones for education or health care, the poor can play the game of the virtuous, industrious, and enterprising subject. In the attention economy online, these young people may leverage their "authenticity" script to garner more clicks for their videos. For instance, a young Mexican male may be more likely to circulate a video with gang violence if he learns that the audience on LiveGore would more likely click the video if they believe it comes from a Mexican.

Being "exotic" has currency online. The commercialization and commodification of difference, ethnicity, and culture have long served nations and people in their self-branding missions.[22] Sometimes this can invert the exotic from being that which is oppressive to that which is empowering, depending on who is manipulating the script and for what reasons. As the global poor seek ways to enter the digital economy as producers, it is possible that they might use such kinds of cultural tourism to move ahead in this game.

Exotic Digital Cultures as Safe

For those with privilege, exoticism is safe at a distance. As long as those who are exotic are contained and controlled, like a human zoo, it is not a threat. At times it can even be desirable for those seeking diversity. This book has connected the colonial surveillance apparatus to contemporary ways of monitoring and managing the global poor to keep the privileged society "safe." Leading examples are two of the most ambitious projects in the Global South—namely, the biometric identity project in India, which allows the tracking of the global poor, and China's residence registration system, which aims to contain the villages at a safe distance through the careful orchestration of migrant flows into the cities.

Stretching the paternalism metaphor further, if Facebook is the poor people's playground, then the technology companies and governments are their parents. As we have seen in this book, the global poor play hide-and-seek at times, to escape the surveillance within social media's walled gardens. I have strived to dismantle many of the popular fictions about the global poor—such as the fiction that they do not value privacy. This book has uncovered a rich spectrum of their privacy practices, from trusting their mothers to being deeply antagonistic toward corporate intrusion into their digital life. Clearly, there is a great need for detailed explorations into the digital privacy behaviors among low-income youth outside the West. It is time to discover, in detailed research, how surveillance, security, and privacy play out in these much-neglected contexts.

Around the world there is a rising momentum for data justice. Europe's new privacy rules will soon serve as a "golden standard" for privacy rules worldwide. Digital privacy as an essential human right is gaining traction. In August 2017, India's Supreme Court made a landmark ruling establishing that the right to privacy is protected as an intrinsic part of the right to life and personal liberty.[23] This has immediate implications for the government's biometric identity project as it has gone about indiscriminately collating information about the poor, including their religious beliefs, marital status, and so on. Several cases have surfaced of mobs lynching people based on their social media posts about eating beef (which the ruling Hindu party wishes to ban), their political views on Kashmir, and their sexual preferences. This ruling aims to protect citizens against these violations.

The ruling also targets technology companies that have been harvesting and profiling their users in the absence of personal data protection laws. Now that such laws are in place, how will this ruling will affect India and other countries outside the West as they design their own right-to-privacy laws in today's digital economy? We know little about how these rules will trickle down to the poor communities that are the most likely to be impacted by these changes. Will they be aware of their new rights? Will they change their online behavior accordingly? Will their digital play become less circumventing and more confrontational, with this newfound freedom?

We now have a glimpse into the world of e-commerce and the global poor as budding online consumers. After decades of being excluded from the marketplace, the global poor are gaining fast entry into the world of digital consumption. Much is happening in online retail at the margins that demands far more empirical investigation into these new markets. In September 2017, Alibaba, China's e-commerce giant, partnered with the Mexican government to help circulate products and services from small and midlevel enterprises within Mexico.[24] This is just the start of Alibaba's ambitions in Latin America, as it seeks collaborations in Argentina and Brazil. AliResearch, the research wing of Alibaba, predicts that by 2022 the gross merchandise volume of Alibaba will escalate by 340 percent via online shopping, yielding at least US$3 trillion in business in Brazil, Russia, India, China, and South Africa. Combine this with China's advanced mobile payment systems, and China could become the new oligarch in digital commercial life.

Consider, for instance, how people can pay at a KFC in Hangzhou. There is a smile-and-pay system in which a customer can pay with their mobile by smiling at a digital screen with a 3D camera. The purchaser's identity is authenticated through facial scanning, and payment is then made through their mobile phone. This innovation is the work of Ant Financial, Alibaba's financial subsidiary. Keeping society "safe" today has taken on an Orwellian twist.

Such safety is deeply seductive due to its convenience. Shopping is at the forefront of the leisure economy. Consumption is a key aspiration for the global poor. They hunger to partake in the digital cornucopia, wherein privacy may seem a small price to pay for access to choice. This comes at a time where the Chinese government is assigning financial credit to the disenfranchised based on their digital lives online, including their social media behavior. It does not require much imagination to see that this will cause behavioral changes among the vast underclass, as they desire to enter this so-called promising digital life.

In this book I have often used the notion of play to interrogate the exoticism of the online lives of the global poor. Whether they are considered fringe, authentic, or safe, their playfulness enables the breaking down of these fictions into actual social narratives, filled with aspiration, humor, desire, pleasure, subversion, and self-fulfillment. Their yearnings reveal the poor as multifaceted beings—cosmopolitan, exploitative, deviant, ambitious, private. In other words, human.

Let this be a starting point for building understandings of this world's majority through careful empirical evidence and research rather than preordained notions of the global poor deriving from nineteenth-century colonial politics. Evidence should be the guide in designing digital platforms and practices sensitized to this exponentially growing user group of the internet. There is no good reason to replicate exoticism in the digital sphere. The original ethos of the internet was to be inclusive and open, and perhaps governments and development agencies in the Global South can lead by example concerning what a genuine public space should look like in the twenty-first century.

Democratization of Digital Life

The leisure economy is increasingly democratizing, leading the elites to seek new ways to differentiate themselves from the masses.[25] As markets reform to include the vast underprivileged populations through new credit systems, payment plans, affordable products, and global business models, it has become a challenge to create distance between social groups. The elites have taken to cultural goods instead, shopping for fair-trade coffee, pursuing yoga, investing in learning, and taking on adventure travel. In other words, their reformed lifestyle is their marker of class distinction.

To understand the twenty-first-century leisure economy, it helps to revive the work of the Norwegian-American economist Thorstein Veblen and his concept of "conspicuous consumption"—elites differentiating themselves from the rest through their visible, extravagant consumption. Veblen also highlighted the imitative behaviors of the underclass who aspired to be like the upper class, creating parallel markets that fed that hunger for mobility. Being idle or lacking utility was one salient marker of high status in the past.

How does this resonate in the digital economy as it globalizes and incorporates the vast underclass into its fold? Take, for instance, Facebook, the dominant leisure platform for both the rich and the poor in many emerging economies. The social worlds of the rich and the poor do not collide directly, but they are both influenced by the underlying algorithmic culture of this social networking site.

Many low-income young people, as we have found, see themselves as global citizens and pursue being cosmopolitan in numerous and often ingenious ways. Pirating international movies and games, following Bill Gates on Twitter, or Indian boys friending Brazilian girls with a hope to declare their first "foreign girlfriend" are just a few examples of how imitation manifests in the digital realm. We also found narratives of dignity as youths reclaim and reassert their favelas, their lower-caste status, and other identity markers to reveal their embodied selves online. This opens rich opportunities to pursue how the self-expression of underprivileged youths negotiates between authenticity and aspiration for a consolidated global identity.

Are people defined by what they consume? How are the global poor consuming the lifestyle of the rich online? While a growing segment of the wealthy are investing their capital in culture over goods, there is still plenty of old-fashioned leisure consumption out there. Take, for instance, the "rich kids" of Instagram, an account that encourages children of millionaires and billionaires to boast about their lifestyles to the world. For instance, the "rich kids of Tehran" have attracted much attention and a vast following, much to the dismay of the moral police in Iran.[26]

Take digital idleness as another example. Economist Robert Frank speaks of the growing inequality in leisure and the drop in happiness among the rich as they work extended hours.[27] He argues that we may be witnessing an inversion where the poor are consuming more leisure while the rich are consuming less. As we saw in our discussion of the "leisure divide" in Chapter 1, there is evidence that this trend has extended to the digital world. Low-income users spend far more time online consuming entertainment, socializing, and idling compared to wealthier users. Even so, little research has been done to understand the happiness level of the global poor as they immerse themselves in these new digital worlds of play.

This study is just the beginning of the exploration into digital life among the global poor. As old exoticisms are dismantled by their actual online usage, they should not be replaced with new fictions in the digital economy. It is essential to acknowledge the diverse forms of digital activity engaged in by the poor, as well as the digital architectures within which they perform these acts. New narratives can be written, now that new internet laws, policies, and regulations are coming into place in developing countries, with a promise to push back against the technology titans. Up to this point, technology corporations have stood as the experts on the global poor's online engagements. We need to break this trend. It would be tragic if these corporations were the main filters in this game. If this book can achieve one thing, it would be this—to go beyond the instrumental and attend to the full spectrum of digital life in the humanizing of the global poor.

Notes

PROLOGUE

1. For Nigeria and South Africa, see International Telecommunication Union 2017; for China, see "Statistics and Facts about the Smartphone Market in China," n.d.; for India and Brazil, see Statista 2018.
2. "The Top 500 Sites on the Web," n.d., Alexa, https://www.alexa.com /topsites, accessed November 7, 2017.
3. Pimpare 2008.

1. THE LEISURE DIVIDE

1. *The Namibian* 2012, para 2.
2. "Namibian Schoolboy Invents Cellphone That Doesn't Use Airtime" 2016.
3. Friemel 2016.
4. Sandner 2015.
5. Shihomeka and Arora 2017b.
6. Arora 2014.
7. Shihomeka and Arora 2017a, 11.
8. Ibid., 13.
9. Hilbert 2016.

10. Alozie and Akpan-Obong 2017.
11. Sarkar 2016.
12. Hargittai and Walejko 2008; Van Deursen et al. 2017.
13. Oxfam International 2017.
14. Arora 2012a.
15. "World Internet Project" 2014, 21.
16. Toyama 2015.
17. Kumar et al. 2010.
18. Rennie et al. 2016.
19. Shihomeka and Arora 2017a, 12.
20. Ibid., 13.
21. Chang, Zhen, and Cao 2016.
22. Van Deursen and van Dijk 2013.
23. Nazareth 2010.
24. Arora 2012a.
25. Rosenzweig 1985.
26. Ibid., 265.
27. Chance 2010.
28. Arora 2014, 95.
29. Roberts 2006.
30. Gershuny 2005; Bellezza, Paharia, and Keinan 2017.
31. Buckingham and Willett 2013; Statt 2017.
32. Arora 2016.
33. Doshi 2016.
34. *The Economist* 2013.
35. Nakamura 2009.
36. Vázquez and Consalvo 2013.
37. Dibbell 2007.
38. Nardi and Kow 2010.
39. Tassi 2011.
40. Senior 2011.
41. Kim and Woo 2016.
42. Chen 2014.
43. "PokeWalk," n.d.
44. Kuo 2016.
45. Mamabolo 2017.
46. Sengupta 2017.
47. *The Economist* 2010.

48. Constine 2016.
49. Advox 2017.
50. Solon 2017, para. 6.
51. West 2015.
52. Srinivasan 2017, 5.
53. Pursell 2016.
54. Greene 2016.
55. Toyama 2015.

2. DEVIANT BY DESIGN

1. Arora 2016b, 240.
2. Horst and Miller 2006; Arora and Rangaswamy 2013.
3. Kamga 2012.
4. Donner 2015.
5. Pessoa 2009.
6. Lemos and Martini 2010, 33.
7. Feifei 2016.
8. Fullerton 2015.
9. Ibid., para 5.
10. Cohen 2011.
11. Ravindran 2010; Schwittay 2011.
12. Rangaswamy and Arora 2015, 10.
13. Arora and Scheiber 2017, 413.
14. Arora and Rangaswamy 2015.
15. Ibid., 73.
16. Kumar 2014.
17. Wyche, Forte, and Schoenebeck 2013.
18. Ibid.
19. N. Haynes 2016, 35.
20. Degim, Johnson, and Fu 2015.
21. Ibid.
22. Wyche, Forte, and Schoenebeck 2013.
23. BBC News 2016d.
24. Frohlich et al. 2012.
25. Grimley 2016.
26. Ibid.
27. Krasnova et al. 2013.

28. Ganesh 2010.
29. BBC News 2016a.
30. Patel 2014.
31. Iyer 2016.
32. Patel 2014.
33. BBC News 2016b.
34. Ibid., para 6.

3. MEDIA BANDITS

1. Clark 2016, para. 4.
2. Loughlan 2006, 214.
3. Treverton et al. 2009.
4. "Music Piracy" 2011.
5. Karaganis 2011.
6. Ibid.
7. Gray 2011.
8. Lobato 2012, p. 56.
9. Kabore 1995.
10. Gray 2011.
11. Petrescu, Gironda, and Korgaonkar 2017.
12. Thomas 2013.
13. Foster 1965.
14. Espinosa 2014.
15. Ibid., 318.
16. Kumar and Parikh 2013.
17. Zhao and Keane 2013.
18. Pinheiro-Machado 2017.
19. Pinheiro-Machado 2012, 345.
20. Ibid., 346–347.
21. Taylor 2002.
22. Sanchez 2016, para. 3.
23. Poor 2012.
24. Mendes Moreira de Sa 2015; Frosio 2016.
25. Spangler 2018.
26. Mendes Moreira de Sa 2015, 863.
27. Dillon 2015.
28. Curtin 2017.

29. Ramos, Hayes, and Tarafdar 2016.
30. Arora 2006, 124.
31. Arora 2006.
32. J. Haynes 2016.
33. "The Pirate Party" 2009.
34. "About PPI" 2017.
35. "Manifesto Pirate Party UK" 2012.
36. Dobbin and Zeilinger 2014.
37. Lessig 2004.
38. Vaidhyanathan 2003.
39. "United Nations Documents on Piracy" 2012.
40. Bsumek, Kinkela, and Lawrence 2013, 98.
41. Palmås, Schwarz, and Larsson 2014.

4. THE VIRTUOUS POOR

1. See, for example, current content at #AlwaysBeJugaading on Twitter.
2. Radjou, Prabhu, and Ahuja 2012; Radjou and Prabhu 2015.
3. Eshwar 2016.
4. Vidal 2004.
5. "Mobile for Social Benefit Lab" 2015.
6. Kreiner 2016.
7. Runde 2015.
8. Prahalad and Hart 2010, 1; see also Hart 2010; Prahalad 2010.
9. Bhushan 2016.
10. Nelson 2009.
11. Kanani 2011.
12. Shahani 2015; Asia-Europe Foundation 2016.
13. Urban Design Research Institute, Mumbai, India 2017.
14. "Public Service Innovation Lab" 2017.
15. "Innovation Teams" 2017.
16. Ushahidi 2017.
17. Wu 2016.
18. Goodyear 2013.
19. Chao 2013.
20. Swislow 2014.
21. Bradley 2014, 1.
22. Vaswani 2016.

23. Lindtner 2014.
24. Lindtner 2016.
25. Lindtner 2015, 862.
26. Lee and Hung 2014.
27. Tiwari and Herstatt 2013, 5.
28. Birtchnell 2013.
29. "Global Status Report on Road Safety 2015" 2015.
30. Lamont 2010, 2.
31. Menon 2011, 1.
32. *The Economist* 2016.
33. Tiwari and Herstatt 2013.
34. Kolk, Rivera-Santos, and Rufín 2014.
35. Gunther 2014, 1.
36. Gunther 2014.
37. Simanis 2014, 1.
38. Webb, Ireland, and Ketchen 2014.
39. De Soto 2015.
40. De Soto 2000, 2012.
41. "Forbes 85th Anniversary" 2002.
42. MTST 2017.
43. Williams 2014.
44. Charmes 2012.
45. Rogerson 1996.
46. "The 2016 Conference on Inclusive Capitalism" 2017.
47. Prahalad 2010, xiii.
48. "Inclusive Capitalism" 2015, 13.
49. Ibid., 25.
50. Ibid., 29.
51. Piketty 2014.

5. SLUMDOG INSPIRATION

1. Mitra 2013a.
2. Guinness 2014; Rao 2014; Rieland 2014.
3. "IFC Project Information Portal," n.d.
4. Mitra and Dangwal 2010.
5. Mitra and Crawley 2014.
6. Mitra 2013a.

7. Tiitola-Meskanen 2014, 298.
8. Solman 2015, 1.
9. School in the Cloud, n.d.
10. Mitra and Arora 2010.
11. Mitra and Dangwal 2010, 674.
12. Ibid., 672.
13. Mitra and Dangwal 2010.
14. Arora 2010.
15. Ibid., 693.
16. Arora 2005, 2007.
17. Buncombe 2014, 1.
18. Solman 2015, 1.
19. Mitra and Dangwal 2010, 680.
20. Ibid., 674.
21. "Cultural and Linguistic Diversity," n.d.; Phillipson 1992; Livingstone and Haddon 2009.
22. Pimienta, Prado, and Blanco 2009.
23. Mirani 2014.
24. "Unlocking Relevant Web Content for the next 4 Billion People" 2014.
25. Clark 2013.
26. Warschauer 2003.
27. Mitra 2015.
28. Henriksen and Mishra 2016.
29. Bersin 2004; Henriksen and Mishra 2016.
30. Elgot 2013, 1.
31. Wakefield 2012, 1.
32. Ibid.
33. Cadwalladr 2015, 1.
34. Ibid.
35. *The Economist* 2015.
36. Turner 2015.
37. Rix and McElwee 2016.
38. Basu 2016, 1.
39. Mead 2016.
40. Department of Information Technology et al., n.d. This is a partnership with the Ministry of Culture, the Ministry of Communication and Information Technology, and the Archaeological Survey of India.
41. Mitter 1994, 180.

42. Elgot 2013.
43. Mitra 2013b, 1.
44. Cadwalladr 2015, 1.
45. Arora 2012b, 2014.
46. López 2003; Adams 2005; Sawhney 2007; Raffel 2013.
47. Arora 2014, 21.
48. Stefik 1996.
49. Osenga 2013.
50. Mills 2008.
51. Henneberg 2010, 129.
52. Davidson 2010, 1.
53. "Hole-in-the-Wall—Solution," n.d.
54. Mehta 2007.
55. Ibid.
56. Mitra and Dangwal 2010, 679.
57. Cadwalladr 2015.
58. Ibid., 1.
59. Wilson 2013, 1.
60. Arora 2016c.

6. THE POVERTY LABORATORY

1. Hachman 2011.
2. One Laptop per Child, n.d.
3. Adam, Hassler, and Cruickshank 2016.
4. Cristia et al. 2012.
5. Murphy 2014, 1.
6. Cremin 1978.
7. Oppenheimer 1997; Feenberg 2001; Potter 2012.
8. Vygotsky 1978, 97.
9. Dewey 1897, 80.
10. Rancière 1991.
11. Ibid., 46.
12. Gorham 2005.
13. Ibid., 56.
14. Ibid., 47.
15. Russell 2014, 390.
16. Illich 1971, 4.

17. Ibid., 42.
18. Wagner 1989; Elias 1994.
19. Pallikoodam 2016.
20. Auroville, n.d.
21. Ibid.
22. "Education—Words of Wisdom" 2014.
23. Kumar 2008.
24. Crowell 2015, 1.
25. Rich 2008.
26. "Mobile Learning Week," n.d.
27. Arora 2016c.
28. Andersen 2014.
29. Keller 2016.
30. "Meet the Registered Teams," n.d.
31. "What Is Lara?" 2017.
32. Educativo, n.d.
33. "'And the Winner Is'" 2009, 5.
34. Reckhow and Snyder 2014.
35. Traxler 2011.
36. Wu et al. 2012.
37. Arora 2016c, 14.
38. Archibugi and Filippetti 2016.
39. McGoey 2015, 69.
40. Blok and Lemmens 2015.
41. Collingridge 1980.
42. Arora 2016c, 33.
43. "#EDUCATIONFORALL" 2017.
44. Ibid.
45. Jackman 2014.
46. "Project DEFY" 2017, 1.
47. Robinson 2017.
48. AltSchool 2017, 1.
49. Mead 2016.
50. Satariano 2017.
51. Robinson 2017.
52. Chisholm 2008, 1.
53. Allis 2014, 1.
54. Keller 2016.

55. Satariano 2017, para 3.
56. Ibid., para 10.
57. Arora 2014.
58. Barbrook and Cameron 1996.
59. Guinness 2014, 1.

7. PRIVACY, PAUCITY, AND PROFIT

1. Arora and Scheiber 2017, 412.
2. Arora, personal interview, 2016, 4.
3. Ibid., 14.
4. Gao and Madden 2015.
5. Khan 2013.
6. Dwyer 2015, 12.
7. Arora 2015.
8. Cole 2002.
9. Ibid., 203.
10. Cole 2002.
11. Gates 2011.
12. Emsley 2009.
13. McMullan 1998a, 109.
14. Ibid., 102.
15. Eubanks 2014.
16. Gelman, Fagan, and Kiss 2007.
17. Gilliom 2001.
18. Arora 2016a, 1684.
19. Toness 2014, 1.
20. Hatton 2015.
21. Lam 2016, 1.
22. Kristof 1992.
23. Markey 2016.
24. Young 2013.
25. "Marco Civil English Version" 2014.
26. Nissenbaum 2009, 105.
27. "Up for Slum Dwellers" 2016.
28. "Rio Favela Facts" 2015.
29. Cano and Ribeiro 2016.
30. Dowdney 2003.

31. Statista 2018. The United States was ranked second.
32. Arora, personal interview, 2016, 15.
33. Ibid.
34. Rui and Stefanone 2013.
35. Arora, personal interview, 2016, 11.
36. Wilson, Gosling, and Graham 2012.
37. Arora, personal interview, 2016, 16.
38. Ibid., 14.
39. Arora 2015.
40. Arora, personal interview, 2016, 16.
41. Ibid., 17.
42. Author interview notes, 2015. These interviews were taken in four low-income communities and transcribed by local assistants in Brazil and India in 2015 and 2016 (Rio de Janeiro and Belo Horizonte in Brazil, and Ludhiana and Isnapur in India). For the Brazil fieldwork, I wish to thank Laura Scheiber, Lucas Dutra, and Rogerio Rodrigues for their excellent assistance with data collection, as well as Roldolfo Rocha, Luis Nascimento, and Professor Agnez Saraiva for making the necessary arrangements to conduct interviews. For the India fieldwork, I wish to thank Prem Reddy and Mohit Dagga for their excellent assistance with data collection. Moreover, I am deeply indebted to Dr. Nimmi Rangaswamy for her supervision of the fieldwork in India.
43. Yemi 2016.
44. Author interview notes, 2015.
45. Nicolaci-da-Costa and Matos-Silva 2014.
46. Zickuhr 2013.
47. Author interview notes, 2015.
48. Quotations in this paragraph are from author interview notes, 2015.
49. Author interview notes, 2015.
50. Arora 2005.
51. Zuckerberg 2015.
52. Dahlberg 2015.
53. Tucker 2014.
54. Quotations in this paragraph are from author interview notes, 2015.
55. Author interview notes, 2015.
56. Ibid.
57. Ibid.
58. Ibid.

59. Ibid.
60. Ibid.
61. Ibid.
62. Mari 2018.

8. FORBIDDEN LOVE

1. Richtel 2012.
2. Wiseman 2009.
3. Lenhart et al. 2011.
4. Arora and Rangaswamy 2015.
5. Mishra and Basu 2014.
6. Ibid.
7. *Women and the Web* 2012.
8. Arora, personal interview, 2016.
9. Ibid.
10. Hubbard 2015.
11. Aljasir, Woodcock, and Harrison 2014; Hubbard 2015.
12. Kaya 2009.
13. Ibid.
14. Ibid.
15. "Global Perspectives on Online Anonymity" 2013.
16. Arora, personal interview, 2016.
17. Ibid.
18. Santos 2012.
19. Arora, personal interview, 2016.
20. Smith 2016; Smith and Duggan 2013.
21. Ingram 2018.
22. Toma and Hancock 2012.
23. Koon and Yoong 2013.
24. Romance Scams, n.d.
25. Koop et al. 2015.
26. BBC News 2016b.
27. Xiao, Freeman, and Hwa 2015.
28. "Common Frauds," n.d.
29. Arora and Scheiber 2017, 415.
30. Ibid.
31. Arora, personal interview, 2016.

32. Ibid.
33. Levendowski 2014.
34. "Women Shaming in Africa and the Descent into Barbarism" 2014.
35. Davies 2017.
36. BBC News 2017.
37. "Mangalore Pub Attack" 2009.
38. Arora and Scheiber 2017, 415.
39. Berger 2013.
40. Etherington 2014.
41. Arora and Scheiber 2017, 416.
42. Ibid., 416.
43. Hannon 2011.
44. Scheuermann and Taylor 1997.

EPILOGUE

1. Mirani 2015.
2. Heath 2017.
3. Statista 2017.
4. FirstPost 2014.
5. Piketty 2014.
6. Kellner 2012; Rudd 2016.
7. Kanale 2017, 1.
8. Frenkel 2016, 1.
9. König 2013.
10. Jameson 1988, 355.
11. Playful tactics online like the manufacturing of fake news can further one group's interest at the expense of many. Dealing with this theme is beyond the scope of this book. I decided against including the digital activism dimension in this book because I faced the hurdle of finding studies that focused specifically on marginalized communities. Much available scholarship did not differentiate groups, and in those that did, the digital activism participants were middle-class.
12. Chen and Suen 2015.
13. Maxfield 2016; Kligler-Vilenchik and Thorson 2016.
14. Ngidi et al. 2016.
15. Ibid., 9.
16. Ibid.

17. Ellingson 2001.
18. Said 1978.
19. Menacherry 2017.
20. Meiu 2015.
21. Henman and Chambers 2001; Kaner 2014.
22. Comaroff and Comaroff 1999.
23. Biswas 2017.
24. Lee 2017.
25. Currid-Halkett 2017.
26. Dangerfield 2015.
27. Frank 2013.

References

"About PPI." 2017. Pirate Parties International. https://pp-international.net /about-ppi/.

Adam, T., B. Hassler, and H. Cruickshank. 2016. "One Laptop per Child Rwanda: Enabling Factors and Barriers." In *Empowering the 21st Century Learner*, 184–195. Pretoria: African Academic Research Forum.

Adams, Paul C. 2005. *The Boundless Self: Communication in Physical and Virtual Spaces*. Syracuse, NY: Syracuse University Press.

Advox. 2017. "Can Facebook Connect the Next Billion?" Global Voices Online, July 27. https://advox.globalvoices.org/2017/07/27/can-facebook -connect-the-next-billion/.

Aljasir, Shuaa, Andree Woodcock, and Sandra Harrison. 2014. "Usage of Social Network Sites amongst Saudis: Why Do Saudi University Students Have Multiple Facebook Accounts?" *International Journal of Social Science and Humanity* 4, no. 4: 293–297. https://dx.doi.org/10.7763/IJSSH.2014 .V4.366.

Allis, Ryan. 2014. "The Reimagination of Everything." The Startup Guide— Creating a Better World through Entrepreneurship. http://startupguide .com/world/reimagination-of-everything/.

Alozie, Nicholas O., and Patience Akpan-Obong. 2017. "The Digital Gender Divide: Confronting Obstacles to Women's Development in Africa." *Development Policy Review* 35, no. 2: 137–160.

AltSchool. 2017. https://www.altschool.com/.

Andersen, Ross. 2014. "Elon Musk Puts His Case for a Multi-Planet Civilisation." *Aeon,* September 30. https://aeon.co/essays/elon-musk-puts-his -case-for-a-multi-planet-civilisation.

"'And the Winner Is . . .': Philanthropists and Governments Make Prizes Count." 2009. McKinsey & Company. http://mckinseyonsociety.com /capturing-the-promise-of-philanthropic-prizes/.

Archibugi, Daniele, and Andrea Filippetti. 2016. "The Retreat of Public Research and Its Adverse Consequences on Innovation." SSRN Scholarly Paper ID 2837736. Rochester, NY: Social Science Research Network. https://ssrn.com/abstract=2837736.

Arora, Payal. 2005. "Profiting from Empowerment? Investigating Dissemination Avenues for Educational Technology Content within an Emerging Market Solutions Project." *International Journal of Education and Development Using ICT* 1, no. 4. http://ijedict.dec.uwi.edu/printarticle.php?id =74&layout=html.

———. 2006. "Karaoke for Social and Cultural Change." *Journal of Information, Communication and Ethics in Society* 4, no. 3: 121–130.

———. 2007. "The ICT Laboratory: An Analysis of Computers in Public High Schools in Rural India." *AACE Journal* 15, no. 1: 57–72.

———. 2010. "Hope-in-the-Wall? A Digital Promise for Free Learning." *British Journal of Educational Technology* 41, no. 5: 689–702. https://doi.org/10.1111 /j.1467-8535.2010.01078.x.

———. 2012a. "The Leisure Divide: Can the 'Third World' Come Out to Play?" *Information Development* 28, no. 2: 93–101. https://doi.org/10.1177 /0266666911433607.

———. 2012b. "Typology of Web 2.0 Spheres: Understanding the Cultural Dimensions of Social Media Spaces." *Current Sociology* 60, no. 5: 599–618. https://doi.org/10.1177/0011392112440439.

———. 2014. *The Leisure Commons: A Spatial History of Web 2.0.* New York: Routledge.

———. 2015. "Facebook and the Digital Romance Economy: Courtship, Scams, and Internet Regulation in the Global South." *London School of Economics Impact Blog,* October 27. http://blogs.lse.ac.uk/impactof socialsciences/2015/10/27/facebook-and-the-digital-romance-economy/.

———. 2016a. "The Bottom of the Data Pyramid: Big Data and the Global South." *International Journal of Communication* 10 (January): 1681–1699. https://doi.org/1932-8036/20160005.

———. 2016b. *Dot Com Mantra: Social Computing in the Central Himalayas.* London: Routledge.

———. 2016c. "Prizes for Innovation: Impact Analysis in the ICT for Education Sector." Paris: UNESCO. https://www.researchgate.net/publication /308372025_Prizes_for_Innovation_Impact_analysis_in_the_ICT_for _education_sector.

Arora, Payal, and Nimmi Rangaswamy. 2013. "Digital Leisure for Development: Reframing New Media Practice in the Global South." *Media, Culture & Society* 35, no. 7: 898–905.

———. 2015. "Digital Romance in the Indian City." In *The City and South Asia*, 73–77. Cambridge, MA: Harvard South Asia Institute.

Arora, Payal, and Laura Scheiber. 2017. "Slumdog Romance: Facebook Love and Digital Privacy at the Margins." *Media, Culture & Society* 39, no. 3: 408–422.

Asia-Europe Foundation. 2016. "Cities: Living Labs for Culture? Case Studies from Asia and Europe." Singapore: Asia-Europe Foundation. http://asef.org/images/docs/asef-living-labs-for-culture.pdf.

Auroville. n.d. http://www.auroville.org.

Barbrook, Richard, and Andy Cameron. 1996. "The Californian Ideology." *Science as Culture* 6, no. 1: 44–72. https://doi.org/10.1080/095054396095 26455.

Basu, Indrani. 2016. "Indian Teacher Gives Kids Real World Problems to Solve. The Answers Will Surprise You." *Huffington Post India*, April 25. http://www.huffingtonpost.in/2016/04/25/indian-teacher-gives-kids-real -world-problems-to-solve-the-answ/.

BBC News. 2016a. "The Indian Actress Who Hit Back after Being Photoshopped into Porn," *BBC News*, March 21, sec. BBC Trending. http://www .bbc.com/news/blogs-trending-35846278.

———. 2016b. "Iran Arrests Eight for 'Un-Islamic' Instagram Modelling," *BBC News*, May 16, sec. Middle East. http://www.bbc.com/news/world-middle -east-36302405.

———. 2016c. "Online Fraud: Top Nigerian Scammer Arrested," *BBC News*, August 1, sec. Africa. http://www.bbc.com/news/world-africa-36939751.

———. 2016d. "Saudis on Social: Faith, Freedom and Fun," *BBC News*, March 2, sec. BBC Trending #SaudisOnSocial: A Special Series. http:// www.bbc.com/news/blogs-trending-35664637.

———. 2017. "Pakistan Village Council Orders 'Revenge Rape' of Girl," *BBC News*, July 26, sec. Asia. http://www.bbc.com/news/world-asia-india-40731035.

Bellezza, Silvia, Neeru Paharia, and Anat Keinan. 2017. "Conspicuous Consumption of Time: When Busyness and Lack of Leisure Time Become a Status Symbol." *Journal of Consumer Research* 44, no. 1: 118–138. https://doi.org/10.1093/jcr/ucw076.

Berger, Miriam. 2013. "Brazilian 17-Year-Old Commits Suicide after Revenge Porn Posted Online." *BuzzFeed,* November 21. http://www.buzzfeed.com /miriamberger/brazilian-17-year-old-commits-suicide-after-revenge-porn -pos.

Bersin, Josh. 2004. "Chapter One: How Did We Get Here? The History of Blended Learning." In *Blended Learning Book: Best Practices, Proven Methodologies, and Lessons Learned.* San Francisco: Pfeiffer.

Bhushan, Kul. 2016. "Ringing Bells Freedom 251: Hands-On with the World's Cheapest Smartphone." *BGR India,* August 9. http://www.bgr.in /news/ringing-bells-freedom-251-hands-on-with-the-worlds-cheapest -smartphone/.

Birtchnell, T. 2013. *Indovation: Innovation and a Global Knowledge Economy in India.* Critical Studies of the Asia-Pacific. Basingstoke, UK: Palgrave Macmillan.

Biswas, Soutik. 2017. "How Significant Is India's Landmark Privacy Judgement?" *BBC News,* August 24, 2017. http://www.bbc.com/news/world -asia-india-41037992.

Blok, V., and P. Lemmens. 2015. "The Emerging Concept of Responsible Innovation: Three Reasons Why It Is Questionable and Calls for a Radical Transformation of the Concept of Innovation." In *Responsible Innovation 2: Concepts, Approaches, and Applications,* edited by B.-J. Koops, I. Oosterlaken, H. Romijn, T. Swierstra, and J. Van den Hoven, 19–35. New York: Springer.

Bradley, Theresa. 2014. "El Hacker Cívico: Civic-Minded Techies Gain Sway with Government in Mexico and Beyond." *Huffington Post,* January 25. http://www.huffingtonpost.com/theresa-bradley/el-hacker-civico-how -civi_b_4334088.html.

Bruno, Fernanda Glória, Liliane da Costa Nascimento, Rodrigo Jose Firmino, Marta M. Kanashiro, and Rafael Evangelista. 2013. "Human Traces on the Internet: Privacy and Online Tracking in Popular Websites in Brazil." Special English edition 2012–2013 annual selection of articles. Privacy and New Technologies. Laxenburg, Austria: International Federation for Information Processing. http://www2.ati.es/novatica /2013/ASA/NvS2013-Digital.pdf#page=39.

Bsumek, Erika Marie, David Kinkela, and Mark Atwood Lawrence. 2013. *Nation-States and the Global Environment: New Approaches to International Environmental History*. New York: Oxford University Press.

Buckingham, David, and Rebekah Willett, eds. 2006. *Digital Generations: Children, Young People, and the New Media*. London: Routledge.

Buncombe, Andrew. 2014. "This 'School in the Clouds' Teaches Us a Valuable Lesson about Learning. Letter from Asia: Can Children Learn with No Supervision?" *The Independent*, September 2. http://www.inde pendent.co.uk/voices/comment/this-school-in-the-clouds-teaches-us-a -valuable-lesson-about-learning-9707162.html.

Cadwalladr, Carole. 2015. "The 'Granny Cloud': The Network of Volunteers Helping Poorer Children Learn." *The Guardian*, August 2, sec. Education. https://www.theguardian.com/education/2015/aug/02/sugata-mitra -school-in-the-cloud.

Cano, Ignacio, and Eduardo Ribeiro. 2016. "Old Strategies and New Approaches towards Policing Drug Markets in Rio de Janeiro." *Police Practice and Research* 17, no. 4: 364–375. https://doi.org/10.1080 /15614263.2016.1175709.

Chance, Helena. 2010. "'The Factory in a Garden': Corporate Recreational Landscapes in England and the United States, 1880–1939." DPhil, University of Oxford. https://ora.ox.ac.uk/objects/uuid%3A98e6efda -ea51-4bbd-834d-a606fcd5eec7.

Chang, Enyu, Feng Zhen, and Yang Cao. 2016. "Empirical Analysis of the Digital Divide from the Perspective of Internet Usage Patterns: A Case Study of Nanjing." *International Review for Spatial Planning and Sustainable Development* 4, no. 1: 49–63.

Chao, Loretta. 2013. "Brazil: The Social Media Capital of the Universe." *Wall Street Journal*, February 4, sec. Tech. https://www.wsj.com/articles/SB1000 142412788732330110457825795085789 1898.

Charmes, Jacques. 2012. "The Informal Economy Worldwide: Trends and Characteristics." *Margin: The Journal of Applied Economic Research* 6, no. 2: 103–132. https://doi.org/10.1177/097380101200600202.

Chen, Adrian. 2014. "The Laborers Who Keep Dick Pics and Beheadings Out of Your Facebook Feed." *Wired*, October 23. https://www.wired.com/2014 /10/content-moderation/.

Chen, Heng, and Wing Suen. 2015. "Aspiring for Change: A Theory of Middle Class Activism." *Economic Journal* (October 29). https://doi.org/10 .1111/ecoj.12346.

Chisholm, Sir John. 2008. "Innovation Age: Where Will It Take the Human Race?" *SPIE Professional,* April. https://spie.org/membership/spie-profes sional-magazine/spie-professional-archives-and-special-content/april-2008 /innovation-age-where-will-it-take-the-human-race.

Clark, Bryan. 2016. "Piracy in the UK Could Earn You a Decade in Jail." *The Next Web,* September 15. https://thenextweb.com/insider/2016/09/15 /piracy-in-the-uk-could-earn-you-a-decade-in-jail/.

Clark, Donald. 2013. "Sugata Mitra: Slum Chic? 7 Reasons for Doubt." Donald Clark Plan B, March 4. http://donaldclarkplanb.blogspot.hk /2013/03/sugata-mitra-slum-chic-7-reasons-for.html.

Cleaver, Frances. 1999. "Paradoxes of Participation: Questioning Participatory Approaches to Development." *Journal of International Development* 11, no. 4: 597.

Cohen, Stanley. 2011. *Folk Devils and Moral Panics: The Creation of the Mods and Rockers.* New York: Routledge.

Cole, Simon A. 2002. *Suspect Identities: A History of Fingerprinting and Criminal Identification.* Cambridge, MA: Harvard University Press.

Collingridge, David. 1980. *The Social Control of Technology.* New York: St. Martin's Press.

Comaroff, Jean, and John L. Comaroff. 1999. "Occult Economies and the Violence of Abstraction: Notes from the South African Postcolony." *American Ethnologist* 26, no. 2: 279–303.

"Common Frauds." n.d. Official Website of Hyderabad City Police. http:// www.hyderabadpolice.gov.in/CommonFrauds.html.

Constine, Josh. 2016. "Facebook Has Connected 40M People with Internet .org." *TechCrunch,* November 2. https://techcrunch.com/2016/11/02 /omnipresent/.

Cremin, Lawrence. 1978. "The Free School Movement: A Perspective." In *Alternative Schools: Ideologies, Realities, Guidelines,* edited by Terrence E. Deal and Robert R. Nolan, 203–210. Chicago: Nelson-Hall.

Cristia, Julian, Santiago Cueto, Pablo Ibarraran, Ana Santiago, and Eugenio Severin. 2012. "Technology and Child Development: Evidence from the One Laptop per Child Program." Inter-American Development Bank. http://www.iadb.org/en/research-and-data/publication-details,3169 .html?pub_id=IDB-WP-304.

Crowell, Maddy. 2015. "Trouble in Utopia." *Slate,* July 24. http://www.slate .com/articles/news_and_politics/roads/2015/07/auroville_india_s

_famed_utopian_community_struggles_with_crime_and_corruption
.html.

"Cultural and Linguistic Diversity." n.d. UNESCO. http://www.unesco.org
/new/en/indigenous-peoples/cultural-and-linguistic-diversity/.

Currid-Halkett, Elizabeth. 2017. *The Sum of Small Things: A Theory of the
Aspirational Class.* Princeton, NJ: Princeton University Press.

Curtin, Michael. 2017. "Between State and Capital: Asia's Media Revolution
in the Age of Neo-Liberal Globalization." *International Journal of Communication* 11: 1378–1396.

Dahlberg, Lincoln. 2015. "Expanding Digital Divides Research: A Critical
Political Economy of Social Media." *Communication Review* 18, no. 4:
271–293. https://doi.org/10.1080/10714421.2015.1085777.

Dangerfield, Micha Barban. 2015. "What the Rich Kids of Tehran Instagram
Tells Us about Iranian Youth Culture." Vice, June 3. https://www.vice
.com/en_ca/article/yvxdb7/meet-the-rich-kids-of-tehran.

Davidson, Max. 2010. "Teaching: Inspiring British Children, Slumdog Style."
Telegraph, April 14, sec. Education. http://www.telegraph.co.uk/education
/7585505/Teaching-Inspiring-British-children-Slumdog-style.html.

Davies, Gareth. 2017. "Girl, 14, Is Forced to Parade through Her Village
Naked by Pakistani Elders because Her Brother Had an Affair." *Daily
Mail,* November 2. http://www.dailymail.co.uk/news/article-5041939
/Girl-14-forced-parade-village-NAKED.html.

Degim, Aliv, James Johnson, and Tao Fu. 2015. *Online Courtship: Interpersonal
Interactions across Borders.* Amsterdam: Institute of Network Cultures.

Department of Information Technology, Ministry of Communication and
Information Technology, and Archaeological Survey of India, Government of India. n.d. "National Databank on Indian Art and Culture: A
Pilot Project." http://ignca.nic.in/ndb_0001.htm.

De Soto, Hernando. 2000. *The Mystery of Capital: Why Capitalism Triumphs in
the West and Fails Everywhere Else.* London: Bantam Press.

——. 2012. "Alleviating Poverty through Data." *Global Dialogue* 14, no. 1:
46–51.

——. 2015. "Why Thomas Piketty Is Wrong about Capital in the 21st Century." *The Independent,* May 15. http://www.independent.co.uk/news
/business/comment/why-thomas-piketty-is-wrong-about-capital-in-the
-21st-century-10251801.html.

Dewey, John. 1897. "My Pedagogic Creed." *School Journal* 54, no. 3: 77–80.

Dibbell, Julian. 2007. "The Life of the Chinese Gold Farmer." *New York Times Magazine*, June 17. http://www.nytimes.com/2007/06/17/magazine/17 lootfarmers-t.html.

Dillon, Kaylin. 2015. "Hollywood in China: The Chinese Reception of *Titanic* as a Case Study." PhD diss., University of Kansas.

Dobbin, Lisa, and Martin J. Zeilinger. 2014. "Treasuring IP: Free Culture, Media Piracy and the International Pirate Party Movement." In *The SAGE Handbook of Intellectual Property*, edited by Matthew David and Deborah Halbert, 370–386. London: Sage.

Donner, Jonathan. 2015. *After Access: Inclusion, Development, and a More Mobile Internet*. Cambridge, MA: MIT Press.

Doshi, Vidhi. 2016. "Cash for Queues: People Paid to Stand in Line amid India's Bank Note Crisis." *The Guardian*, November 28.

Dowdney, Luke. 2003. *Children of the Drug Trade: A Case Study of Children in Organised Armed Violence in Rio de Janeiro*. Rio de Janeiro: 7Letras. https:// resourcecentre.savethechildren.net/sites/default/files/documents/3261 .pdf.

Dwyer, Tim. 2015. *Convergent Media and Privacy*. Houndmills, UK: Palgrave Macmillan.

The Economist. 2010. "Nearer My God to Thee: India's Telecoms Operators Promote Devotional Uses for Mobile Phones." May 26. https://www .economist.com/blogs/babbage/2010/05/religion_and_mobile_phones _india.

———. 2013. "Generation Jobless." April 27. https://www.economist.com /news/international/21576657-around-world-almost-300m-15-24-year -olds-are-not-working-what-has-caused.

———. 2015. "Why Girls Do Better at School than Boys." March 6. http://www .economist.com/blogs/economist-explains/2015/03/economist-explains-3.

———. 2016. "Way, José: A Guide to Cutting Corners." May 28. http://www .economist.com/news/americas/21699494-guide-cutting-corners-way-jos.

"Education—Words of Wisdom." 2014. Auroville, October 21. http://www .auroville.org/contents/2811.

"#EDUCATIONFORALL." 2017. Hello World. Accessed March 22. http:// projecthelloworld.org/.

Educativo. n.d. http://educativo.eu/.

Elgot, Jessica. 2013. "'Slumdog Millionaire' Professor, Sugata Mitra, Fixing Education by Bringing iPads into Exams." *Huffington Post*, May 18.

http://www.huffingtonpost.co.uk/2013/05/17/professor-sugata-mitra
-ipad-exams-education_n_3292959.html.

Elias, John L. 1994. *Paulo Freire: Pedagogue of Liberation*. Malabar, FL: Krieger.

Ellingson, Ter. 2001. *The Myth of the Noble Savage*. Berkeley: University of
California Press.

Emsley, Clive. 2009. *The Great British Bobby: A History of British Policing from the
18th Century to the Present*. London: Quercus.

Eshwar, Bart. 2016. "UberMOTO Cleverly Sidesteps Bangalore Govt. Ruling
by Calling Itself a Bikepooling Service." *OfficeChai*, March 20. https://
officechai.com/news/ubermoto-bikepooling-no-commission/.

Espinosa, Shirlita Africa. 2014. "Labour, Gender and Ethnicities in the
'Heart of Manila.'" *Journal of Sociology* 52, no. 2: 311–324. https://doi.org
/10.1177/1440783314530528.

Etherington, Darrell. 2014. "Brazil Court Issues Injunction against Secret
and Calls for App to Be Remotely Wiped." *TechCrunch*, August 20. http://
social.techcrunch.com/2014/08/20/brazil-court-issues-injunction
-against-secret-and-calls-for-app-to-be-remotely-wiped/.

Eubanks, Virginia. 2014. "Want to Predict the Future of Surveillance? Ask
Poor Communities." *American Prospect*, January 15. http://prospect.org
/article/want-predict-future-surveillance-ask-poor-communities.

Feenberg, Andrew. 2001. "Whither Educational Technology?" *International
Journal of Technology and Design Education* 11: 83–91.

Feifei, Fan. 2016. "Yesteryear's Internet Cafes Morph into High-Tech Fun
Dens." *China Daily*, March 9. http://www.chinadaily.com.cn/business
/tech/2016-03/09/content_23789709.htm.

FirstPost. 2014. "Billion Dollar Sales: India on Track to be Amazon's
Fastest-Growing Market, Says Jeff Bezos." July 31. https://www.firstpost
.com/corporate/billion-dollar-sales-india-on-track-to-be-amazons-fastest
-growing-market-says-jeff-bezos-1981717.html.

"Forbes 85th Anniversary: A Celebration of Business Innovators and Ideas."
2002. *Forbes*, December 5. https://www.forbes.com/85th.

Foster, George M. 1965. "Peasant Society and the Image of Limited Good."
American Anthropologist 67, no. 2: 293–315.

Frank, Robert. 2013. *Falling Behind: How Rising Inequality Harms the Middle
Class*. Vol. 4. Berkeley: University of California Press.

Frenkel, Sheera. 2016. "This Is What Happens When Millions of People
Suddenly Get the Internet." *Buzzfeed News*, November 20. https://www

.buzzfeed.com/sheerafrenkel/fake-news-spreads-trump-around-the-world?utm_term=.rx7qV47dn#.nuLlNVdgL.

Friemel, Thomas N. 2016. "The Digital Divide Has Grown Old: Determinants of a Digital Divide among Seniors." *New Media & Society* 18, no. 2: 313–331. https://doi.org/10.1177/1461444814538648.

Frohlich, David, Simon Robinson, Kristen Eglinton, Matt Jones, and Elina Vartiainen. 2012. "Creative Cameraphone Use in Rural Developing Regions." In *Proceedings of the 14th International Conference on Human-Computer Interaction with Mobile Devices and Services*, 181–190. San Francisco: ACM Digital Library. https://doi.org/10.1145/2371574.2371603.

Frosio, Giancarlo F. 2016. "Resisting the Resistance: Resisting Copyright and Promoting Alternatives." *Richmond Journal of Law and Technology* 23. http://jolt.richmond.edu/index.php/volume23_issue2_frosio/.

Fullerton, Jamie. 2015. "China Has Had Enough of Its Illegal Internet Cafés." *Motherboard*, December 9. https://motherboard.vice.com/en_us/article/china-has-had-enough-of-its-illegal-internet-cafs.

Ganesh, Indira Maya. 2010. "'Mobile Love Videos Make Me Feel Healthy': Rethinking ICTs for Development." *IDS Working Papers* 2010 (352): 1–43. https://doi.org/10.1111/j.2040-0209.2010.00352_2.x.

Gao, George, and Mary Madden. 2015. "Privacy and Cybersecurity: Key Findings from Pew Research." Pew Research Center, January 16. http://www.pewresearch.org/key-data-points/privacy/.

Gates, Kelly A. 2011. *Our Biometric Future: Facial Recognition Technology and the Culture of Surveillance.* New York: New York University Press.

Gelman, Andrew, Jeffrey Fagan, and Alex Kiss. 2007. "An Analysis of the New York City Police Department's 'Stop-and-Frisk' Policy in the Context of Claims of Racial Bias." *Journal of the American Statistical Association* 102, no. 479: 813–823. https://doi.org/10.1198/016214506000001040.

Gershuny, Jonathan. 2005. "Busyness as the Badge of Honor for the New Superordinate Working Class." *Social Research* 72, no. 2: 287–314.

Gilliom, John. 2001. *Overseers of the Poor: Surveillance, Resistance, and the Limits of Privacy.* Chicago Series in Law and Society. Chicago: University of Chicago Press.

"Global Perspectives on Online Anonymity: Age Trends in the Use of Anonymity Online and Its Impact on Human Behaviour and Freedom of Expression." 2013. Youth IGF Project—Childnet International. http://www.youthigfproject.com/uploads/8/5/3/6/8536818/global_perspectives_on_online_anonymity.pdf.

"Global Status Report on Road Safety 2015." 2015. World Health Organization. http://www.who.int/violence_injury_prevention/road_safety_status/2015/en/.

Goodyear, Sarah. 2013. "In Wake of New Delhi Rape, an App to Protect against Sexual Violence Undergoes Makeover for India." *Next City,* April 4. https://nextcity.org/daily/entry/in-wake-of-new-delhi-rape-an-app-to-protect-against-sexual-violence-undergo.

Gorham, Deborah. 2005. "Dora and Bertrand Russell and Beacon Hill School." *Russell: The Journal of Bertrand Russell Studies* 25, no. 1: 39–76. https://doi.org/10.15173/russell.v25i1.2071.

Gray, Jonathan. 2011. "Mobility through Piracy, or How Steven Seagal Got to Malawi." *Popular Communication* 9, no. 2: 99–113.

Greene, Daniel. 2016. "Discovering the Divide: Technology and Poverty in the New Economy." *International Journal of Communication* 10 (February): 1212–1231.

Grimley, Naomi. 2016. "Identity 2016: 'Global Citizenship' Rising, Poll Suggests." *BBC News,* April 28, sec. World. http://www.bbc.com/news/world-36139904.

Guinness, Molly. 2014. "Sugata Mitra Interview: 'A Reduction in Resources Can Cause Something Nice to Happen.'" *The Spectator,* May 10. https://www.spectator.co.uk/2014/05/sugata-mitra-interview-a-reduction-in-resources-can-cause-something-nice-to-happen/.

Gunther, Marc. 2014. "The Base of the Pyramid: Will Selling to the Poor Pay Off?" *The Guardian,* May 22, sec. Guardian Sustainable Business. https://www.theguardian.com/sustainable-business/prahalad-base-bottom-pyramid-profit-poor.

Hachman, Mark. 2011. "Negroponte: We'll Throw OLPCs out of Helicopters to Teach Kids to Read." *PCMAG,* November 2. http://www.pcmag.com/article2/0,2817,2395763,00.asp.

Hannon, Elliot. 2011. "Indian Women Take SlutWalk to New Delhi's Streets." *Time,* August 1. http://content.time.com/time/world/article/0,8599,2086142,00.html.

Hargittai, Eszter, and Gina Walejko. 2008. "The Participation Divide: Content Creation and Sharing in the Digital Age." *Information, Communication & Society* 11, no. 2: 239–256. https://doi.org/10.1080/13691180801946150.

Hart, S. L. 2010, *Capitalism at the Crossroads : Next Generation Business Strategies for a Post-Crisis World.* 3rd ed. Upper Saddle River, NJ: Wharton School.

Hatton, Celia. 2015. "China 'Social Credit': Beijing Sets Up Huge System." *BBC News,* October 26, sec. China. http://www.bbc.com/news/world-asia -china-34592186.

Haynes, Jonathan. 2016. "Neoliberalism, Nollywood, and Lagos." In *Global Cinematic Cities: New Landscapes of Film and Media,* edited by Johan Andersson and Lawrence Webb, 59–76. New York: Columbia University Press.

Haynes, Nell. 2016. *Social Media in Northern Chile: Posting the Extraordinarily Ordinary.* London: UCL Press.

Heath, Alex. 2017. "Facebook Has Acquired around Seventy Companies Including WhatsApp, Instagram and the Virtual Reality Company Oculus." *Business Insider,* January 19. https://www.businessinsider.nl /mark-zuckerberg-explains-facebooks-acquisition-strategy-2017-1 /?international=true&r=US.

Henman, Vanessa, and Robert Chambers. 2001. "Participatory Rural Appraisal." In *Planning Agricultural Research: A Sourcebook,* edited by Govert Gijsbers et al., 291–299. Wallingford, UK: CAB International.

Henneberg, Sylvia. 2010. "Moms Do Badly, but Grandmas Do Worse: The Nexus of Sexism and Ageism in Children's Classics." *Journal of Aging Studies* 24, no. 2: 125–134. https://doi.org/10.1016/j.jaging.2008.10.003.

Henriksen, D., and P. Mishra. 2016. *Creativity, Technology and Teacher Education.* Waynesville, NC: Association for the Advancement of Computing in Education. http://www.punyamishra.com/2016/06/22/hot-of -the-press-ebook-on-creativity-technology-teacher-education/.

Hilbert, M. 2016. "The Bad News Is That the Digital Access Divide Is Here to Stay: Domestically Installed Bandwidths among 172 Countries for 1986–2014." *Telecommunications Policy* 40, no. 6: 567–581. https://doi.org /https://doi.org/10.1016/j.telpol.2016.01.006.

"Hole-in-the-Wall—Solution." n.d. Hole-in-the-Wall Educational Project. http://www.hole-in-the-wall.com/solution.html.

Horst, Heather A., and Daniel Miller. 2006. *The Cell Phone: An Anthropology of Communication.* New York: Berg.

Hubbard, Ben. 2015. "Young Saudis, Bound by Conservative Strictures, Find Freedom on Their Phones." *New York Times,* May 22. https://www.nytimes .com/2015/05/23/world/middleeast/saudi-arabia-youths-cellphone -apps-freedom.html.

"IFC Project Information Portal." n.d. International Finance Corporation, World Bank Group. https://disclosures.ifc.org/#/landing.

Illich, Ivan. 1971. *Deschooling Society.* New York: Harper and Row.

"Inclusive Capitalism: The Pathway to Action." 2015. London: Coalition for Inclusive Capitalism. http://www.inc-cap.com/wp-content/uploads/2015/07/Book-2.pdf.

Ingram, David. 2018. "Facebook to Play Cupid in Online Dating Debut." Reuters, May 1. https://www.reuters.com/article/us-facebook-f8conference/facebook-to-play-cupid-in-online-dating-debut-idUSKBN1I23YV.

"Innovation Teams." 2017. Bloomberg Philanthropies. https://www.bloomberg.org/program/government-innovation/innovation-teams/.

International Telecommunication Union. 2017. World Telecommunication/ICT Development Report and Database 2017. http://www.itu.int/en/ITU-D/Statistics/Pages/stat/default.aspx.

Iyer, Maitrayee. 2017. "Porn Consumption in India Rises by 75% as Mobile Data Rates Drop: Report." BGR India, June 3. http://www.bgr.in/news/porn-consumption-in-india-rises-by-75-percent-as-mobile-data-rates-drop-report/.

Jackman, Hugh. 2014. "Connecting to Nigeria for Giving Tuesday." *Huffington Post,* last updated December 6, 2017. http://www.huffingtonpost.com/hugh-jackman/connecting-to-nigeria-for_b_6110922.html.

Jameson, Fredric. 1988. "Cognitive Mapping." In *Marxism and the Interpretation of Culture,* edited by Cary Nelson and Lawrence Grossberg, 347–357. Urbana: University of Illinois Press.

Kabore, Gaston. 1995. "The African Cinema in Crisis." *UNESCO Courier,* July–August.

Kamga, Osée. 2012. "Digital Technologies and the Imaginary of Uses in the Developing World: Mobile Phone Inroads in the Côte d'Ivoire's Social Fabric." *Proceedings of M4D 2012 28–29 February 2012 New Delhi, India* 28, no. 29: 377–382.

Kanale, Herbert. 2017. "Myanmar to Reach 28% Internet Penetration and 15 Million Users." *Internet in Myanmar,* October 12. https://www.internetinmyanmar.com/internet-penetration-sept-17/.

Kanani, Rahim. 2011. "Jaipur Foot: One of the Most Technologically-Advanced Social Enterprises in the World." *Forbes,* August 8. http://www.forbes.com/sites/rahimkanani/2011/08/08/jaipur-foot-one-of-the-most-technologically-advanced-social-enterprises-in-the-world/.

Kaner, Sam. 2014. *Facilitator's Guide to Participatory Decision-Making.* San Francisco: Jossey-Bass.

Karaganis, Joe. 2011. "Media Piracy in Emerging Economies." Social Science Research Council. http://www.ssrc.org/publications/view/C4A69B1C -8051-E011-9A1B-001CC477EC84/.

Kaya, Laura Pearl. 2009. "Dating in a Sexually Segregated Society: Embodied Practices of Online Romance in Irbid, Jordan." *Anthropological Quarterly* 82, no. 1: 251–278. https://doi.org/10.1353/anq.0.0043.

Keller, Matt. 2016. "Global Learning XPRIZE." Presented at the UNESCO Mobile Learning Week, Paris, France, March 7. http://www.unesco.org /new/fileadmin/MULTIMEDIA/HQ/ED/pdf/RANKINGS/xprice.pdf.

Kellner, Douglas. 2012. "The Murdoch Media Empire and the Spectacle of Scandal." *International Journal of Communication* 6: 1169–1200.

Khan, Ghazanfar Ali. 2013. "Saudis Share Almost 'Everything' Online." *Arab News,* June 3, sec. Saudi Arabia. http://www.arabnews.com/news/453858.

Kim, Huy Kang, and Jiyoung Woo. 2016. "Detecting and Preventing Online Game Bots in MMORPGs." In Lee Newton, *Encyclopedia of Computer Graphics and Games* (Springer International), June, 1–8. https://link .springer.com/referencework/10.1007/978-3-319-08234-9.

Kligler-Vilenchik, Neta, and Kjerstin Thorson. 2016. "Good Citizenship as a Frame Contest: Kony2012, Memes, and Critiques of the Networked Citizen." *New Media & Society* 18, no. 9: 1993–2011.

Kolk, Ans, Miguel Rivera-Santos, and Carlos Rufín. 2014. "Reviewing a Decade of Research on the 'Base / Bottom of the Pyramid' (BOP) Concept." *Business & Society* 53, no. 3: 338–377. https://doi.org/10.1177 /0007650312474928.

König, René. 2013. "Wikipedia: Between Lay Participation and Elite Knowledge Representation." *Information, Communication & Society* 16, no. 2: 160–177.

Koon, Tan Hooi, and David Yoong. 2013. "Preying on Lonely Hearts: A Systematic Deconstruction of an Internet Romance Scammer's Online Lover Persona." *Journal of Modern Languages* 23: 28–40.

Koop, Christian, Robert Layton, Jim Sillitoe, and Iqbal Gondal. 2015. "The Role of Love Stories in Romance Scams: A Qualitative Analysis of Fraudulent Profiles." *International Journal of Cyber Criminology* 9, no. 2: 205–217.

Krasnova, Hanna, Helena Wenninger, Thomas Widjaja, and Peter Buxmann. 2013. "Envy on Facebook: A Hidden Threat to Users' Life Satisfaction?" Paper presented at 11th International Conference on Wirtschaftsinformatik, February 27–March 1, Leipzig, Germany. http://www.ara.cat /2013/01/28/855594433.pdf?hash=b775840d43f9f93b7a9031449f809 c388f342291.

Kreiner, Thane. 2016. "Hacking Poverty through Mobile Tech and Social Entrepreneurship." *TechCrunch*, July 22. http://social.techcrunch.com /2016/07/22/hacking-poverty-through-mobile-tech-and-social-entrepre neurship/.

Kristof, Nicholas D. 1992. "Beijing Journal; Where Each Worker Is Yoked to a Personal File." *New York Times*, March 16, sec. World. http://www.ny times.com/1992/03/16/world/beijing-journal-where-each-worker-is -yoked-to-a-personal-file.html.

Kumar, Anuj, Anuj Tewari, Geeta Shroff, Deepti Chittamuru, Matthew Kam, and John Canny. 2010. "An Exploratory Study of Unsupervised Mobile Learning in Rural India." In *Proceedings of the SIGCHI Conference on Human Factors in Computing Systems*. Atlanta: ACM. https://doi.org/10.1145 /1753326.1753435.

Kumar, Neha. 2014. "Facebook for Self-Empowerment? A Study of Facebook Adoption in Urban India." *New Media & Society* 16, no. 7: 1122–1237. https://doi.org/10.1177/1461444814543999.

Kumar, Neha, and Tapan S. Parikh. 2013. "Mobiles, Music, and Materiality." In *Proceedings of the SIGCHI Conference on Human Factors in Computing Systems*, 2863–2872. CHI '13. Paris: ACM. https://doi.org/10.1145 /2470654.2481396.

Kumar, P. C. Vinoj. 2008. "The End of a Dream?" *Tehelka*, September 20. http://bestofpcvinojkumar.blogspot.com/2010/02/end-of-dream.html.

Kuo, Lily. 2016. "The Africa Rising Story Isn't Over Yet." *Quartz Africa*, September 23. https://qz.com/788288/the-africa-rising-story-isnt-over-yet/.

Lam, Oiwan. 2016. "'Orwellian Dystopia' or Trustworthy Nation? Get the Facts on China's Social Credit System." *Global Voices Advocacy*, January 8. https://advox.globalvoices.org/2016/01/08/orwellian-dystopia-or -trustworthy-nation-get-the-facts-on-chinas-social-credit-system/.

Lamont, James. 2010. "The Age of 'Indovation' Dawns." *Financial Times*, June 15. https://www.ft.com/content/993f319c-7814-11df-a6b4-00144 feabdc0.

Lee, C. K., and S. C. Hung. 2014. "Institutional Entrepreneurship in the Informal Economy: China's Shan-Zhai Mobile Phones." *Strategic Entrepreneurship Journal* 8, no. 1: 16–36.

Lee, Emma. 2017. "Alibaba Signs E-Commerce Strategic Partnership with Mexico." *Technode,* September 7. http://technode.com/2017/09/07 /alibaba-signs-e-commerce-strategic-partnership-with-mexico/.

Lemos, Ronaldo, and Paula Martini. 2010. "LAN Houses: A New Wave of Digital Inclusion in Brazil." *Information Technologies & International Development* 6 (SE): 31–35.

Lenhart, Amanda, Mary Madden, Aaron Smith, Kristen Purchell, Kathryn Zickuhr, and Lee Raine. 2011. "Part 3: Privacy and Safety Issues." Pew Research Center: Internet, Science & Tech, November 9. http://www .pewinternet.org/2011/11/09/part-3-privacy-and-safety-issues/.

Lessig, Lawrence. 2004. *Free Culture: How Big Media Uses Technology and the Law to Lock Down Culture and Control Creativity.* New York: Penguin.

Levendowski, Amanda. 2014. "Using Copyright to Combat Revenge Porn." *NYU Journal of Intellectual Property and Entertainment Law* 3: 422–446.

Lindtner, Silvia. 2014. "Hackerspaces and the Internet of Things in China: How Makers Are Reinventing Industrial Production, Innovation, and the Self." *China Information* 28, no. 2: 145–167. https://doi.org/10.1177 /0920203X14529881.

———. 2015. "Hacking with Chinese Characteristics: The Promises of the Maker Movement against China's Manufacturing Culture." *Science, Technology, & Human Values* 40, no. 5: 854–879.

———. 2016. "Makerspaces for the People: China's Approach to Cultivating an Entrepreneurial Mindset." *China Policy Institute: Analysis,* May 26. https://cpianalysis.org/2016/05/26/makerspaces-for-the-people-chinas -approach-to-cultivating-an-entrepreneurial-mindset/.

Livingstone, Sonia, and Leslie Haddon. 2009. *Kids Online: Opportunities and Risks for Children.* Bristol, UK: Policy Press.

Lobato, Ramon. 2012. *Shadow Economies of Cinema: Mapping Informal Film Distribution.* London: Palgrave Macmillan.

López, José. 2003. *Society and Its Metaphors: Language, Social Theory and Social Structure.* London: Continuum.

Loughlan, Patricia. 2006. "Pirates, Parasites, Reapers, Sowers, Fruits, Foxes . . . The Metaphors of Intellectual Property." *Sydney Law Review* 28, no. 2: 211–226.

Mamabolo, Matshelane. 2017. "Namibia's MTC Announces N$1,1 Billion Infrastructure Investment." *Web Africa,* August 1, 2017. http://www .itwebafrica.com/more-countries/namibia/239123-namibias-mtc -announces-n11-billion-infrastructure-investment.

"Mangalore Pub Attack: 17 Held, Ram Sena Unapologetic." 2009. *The Economic Times, Times of India,* January 26. http://economictimes .indiatimes.com/news/politics-and-nation/mangalore-pub-attack-17 -held-ram-sena-unapologetic/articleshow/4033613.cms.

"Manifesto Pirate Party UK." 2012. Pirate Party UK. https://www.pirateparty .org.uk/media/uploads/Manifesto2012.pdf.

"Marco Civil English Version." 2014. Public Knowledge, May 27. https://www.publicknowledge.org/documents/marco-civil-english -version.

Mari, Angelica. 2018. "Brazil Moves Forward with Online Data Protection Efforts." ZDNet, July 5. https://www.zdnet.com/article/brazil-moves -forward-with-online-data-protection-efforts/.

Markey, David. 2016. "The Socialist Network: Why China's Proposed Credit Rating System Is Anything but Credible." *Brown Political Review,* March 16. http://www.brownpoliticalreview.org/2016/03/the-socialist -network-why-chinas-proposed-credit-rating-system-is-anything-but -credible/.

Maxfield, Mary. 2016. "History Retweeting Itself: Imperial Feminist Appro- priations of 'Bring Back Our Girls.'" *Feminist Media Studies* 16, no. 5: 886–900.

McGoey, L., 2015. *No Such Thing as a Free Gift: The Gates Foundation and the Price of Philanthropy.* London: Verso.

McMullan, John L. 1998a. "The arresting eye: Discourse, surveillance and disciplinary administration in early English police thinking." *Social & Legal Studies* 7, no. 1: 97–128.

Mead, Rebecca. 2016. "Learn Different: Silicon Valley Disrupts Education." *New Yorker,* March 7. http://www.newyorker.com/magazine/2016/03/07 /altschools-disrupted-education.

"Meet the Registered Teams." n.d. Global Learning XPRIZE. http://learning .xprize.org/teams.

Mehta, Lyla. 2007. "Whose Scarcity? Whose Property? The Case of Water in Western India." *Land Use Policy* 24, no. 4: 654–663. https://doi.org/10 .1016/j.landusepol.2006.05.009.

Meiu, George Paul. 2015. "Colonialism and Sexuality." *The International Encyclopedia of Human Sexuality.* https://doi.org/10.1002/9781118896877.

Menacherry, Miriam Chandy. 2017. "Why the Sea of Humanity That Greeted Sunny Leone in Kochi Isn't a Sign of Growing Girl Power." *News Minute,* August 27. https://www.thenewsminute.com/article/why-sea

-humanity-greeted-sunny-leone-kochi-isn-t-sign-growing-girl-power
-67451.

Mendes Moreira de Sa, Vanessa. 2015. "From Orkut to Facebook: How
Brazilian Pirate Audiences Utilize Social Media to Create Sharing
Subcultures." *International Journal of Communication* 9, no. 1: 852–869.

Menon, Nikhil. 2011. "Indovation or Indian Jugaad Goes Abroad." *Economic
Times,* November 26. http://economictimes.indiatimes.com/magazines
/corporate-dossier/indovation-or-indian-jugaad-goes-abroad/articleshow
/10859404.cms.

Mills, Sara. 2008. *Language and Sexism.* Cambridge: Cambridge University
Press.

Mirani, Leo. 2014. "Why You Probably Won't Understand the Web of the
Future." *Quartz,* November 6. https://qz.com/292364/why-you-probably
-wont-understand-the-web-of-the-future/.

———. 2015. "On African Mobile Phones There's Social Networking, and
Then There's Everything Else." *Quartz,* February 19. https://qz.com
/1156957/this-year-the-world-woke-up-to-the-society-shifting-power-of
-artificial-intelligence/.

Mishra, Smeeta, and Surhita Basu. 2014. "Family Honor, Cultural Norms
and Social Networking: Strategic Choices in the Visual Self-Presentation
of Young Indian Muslim Women." *Cyberpsychology: Journal of Psychosocial
Research on Cyberspace* 8, no. 2: article 3. https://doi.org/10.5817/CP2014
-2-3.

Mitra, Sugata. 2013a. "Build a School in the Cloud." TED. https://www.ted
.com/talks/sugata_mitra_build_a_school_in_the_cloud.

———. 2013b. "The Internet Can Harm, but Can Also Be a Child's Best Tool
for Learning." *The Guardian,* November 3, sec. Opinion. https://www
.theguardian.com/commentisfree/2013/nov/03/child-safety-internet
-web-access.

———. 2015. "SOLE Toolkit: How to Bring Self-Organised Learning Environments to Your Community." School in the Cloud. https://s3-eu-west-1
.amazonaws.com/school-in-the-cloud-production-assets/toolkit/SOLE
_Toolkit_Web_2.6.pdf.

Mitra, Sugata, and Payal Arora. 2010. "Afterthoughts." *British Journal of
Educational Technology* 41, no. 5: 703–705. https://doi.org/10.1111/j.1467
-8535.2010.01079.x.

Mitra, Sugata, and Emma Crawley. 2014. "Effectiveness of Self-Organised
Learning by Children: Gateshead Experiments." *Journal of Education and*

Human Development 3, no. 3: 79–88. https://doi.org/10.15640/jehd
.v3n3a6.

Mitra, Sugata, and Ritu Dangwal. 2010. "Limits to Self-Organising Systems
of Learning: The Kalikuppam Experiment." *British Journal of Educational
Technology* 41, no. 5: 672–688.

Mitter, Partha. 1994. *Art and Nationalism in Colonial India, 1850–1922:
Occidental Orientations.* Cambridge: Cambridge University Press.

"Mobile for Social Benefit Lab." 2015. Frugal Innovation Hub, Santa Clara
University School of Engineering, September 10. https://www.scu.edu
/engineering/labs -- research/labs / frugal-innovation-hub / labs-and
-projects / mobile-for-social-benefit-lab /.

"Mobile Learning Week." n.d. UNESCO ICT in Education. http://www
.unesco.org/new/en/unesco/themes/icts/m4ed/mobile-learning-week
/symposium/.

MTST (Movimento Dos Trabalhadores Sem Teto). 2017. http://www.mtst.org/.

Murphy, Tom. 2014. "Is This the Nail in the One Laptop per Child Coffin?"
Humanosphere, September 30. http://www.humanosphere.org/social
-business/2014/09/nail-one-laptop-per-child-coffin/.

"Music Piracy: Serious, Violent and Organised Crime." 2011. IFPI. http://
globalinitiative.net/documents/music-piracy-and-organised-crime
-serious-violent-and-organised-crime/.

Nakamura, Lisa. 2009. "Don't Hate the Player, Hate the Game: The Racial-
ization of Labor in World of Warcraft." *Critical Studies in Media Communication* 26, no. 2: 128–144. https://doi.org/10.1080/15295030902860252.

The Namibian. 2012. "Namibia Has More Cellphones than People." October
11, sec. Front page. http://www.namibian.com.na/index.php?page
=archive-read&id=101003.

"Namibian Schoolboy Invents Cellphone That Doesn't Use Airtime." 2016.
News24, July 29. http://www.news24.com/Africa/News/namibian
-schoolboy-invents-cellphone-that-doesnt-use-airtime-20160729.

Nardi, Bonnie, and Yong Ming Kow. 2010. "Digital Imaginaries: How We
Know What We (Think We) Know about Chinese Gold Farming." *First
Monday* 15, no. 6. https://doi.org/10.5210/fm.v15i6.3035.

Nazareth, Linda. 2010. *The Leisure Economy: How Changing Demographics,
Economics, and Generational Attitudes Will Reshape Our Lives and Our
Industries.* Mississauga, ON: John Wiley.

Nelson, Dean. 2009. "Tata Nano, World's Cheapest Car, Launched in India."
The Telegraph, March 23, sec. World. http://www.telegraph.co.uk/news

/worldnews/asia/india/5039397/Tata-Nano-worlds-cheapest-car
-launched-in-India.html.

Ngidi, Ndumiso Daluxolo, Chumani Mtshixa, Kathleen Diga, Nduta
Mbarathi, and Julian May. 2016. "'Asijiki'and the Capacity to Aspire
through Social Media: The #Feesmustfall Movement as Anti-Poverty
Activism in South Africa." In *Proceedings of the Eighth International Confer-
ence on Information & Communication Technologies and Development
(ICTD2016).* https://doi.org/10.1145/2909609.2909654.

Nicolaci-da-Costa, Ana Maria, and Mariana Santiago de Matos-Silva. 2014.
"Smartphones and Location Awareness in Brazil: Users' Reactions."
Paidéia (Ribeirão Preto) 24, no. 57: 115–123. https://doi.org/10.1590/1982
-43272457201414.

Nissenbaum, Helen. 2009. *Privacy in Context: Technology, Policy, and the Integrity
of Social Life.* Stanford, CA: Stanford University Press.

One Laptop per Child. n.d. http://one.laptop.org/map.

Oppenheimer, Todd. 1997. "The Computer Delusion." *The Atlantic,* July.
https://www.theatlantic.com/magazine/archive/1997/07/the-computer
-delusion/376899/.

Osenga, Kristen Jakobsen. 2013. "The Internet Is Not a Super Highway:
Using Metaphors to Communicate Information and Communications
Policy." *Journal of Information Policy* 3 (January): 30–54.

Oxfam International. 2017. "Why the Majority of the World's Poor Are
Women." https://www.oxfam.org/en/even-it/why-majority-worlds-poor
-are-women.

Pallikoodam. 2016. http://www.pallikoodam.org/main/aboutus.asp.

Palmås, Karl, Jonas Andersson Schwarz, and Stefan Larsson. 2014. "The
Liability of Politicalness: Legitimacy and Legality in Piracy-Proximate
Entrepreneurship." *International Journal of Entrepreneurship and Small
Business* 22, no. 4: 408–425. https://doi.org/10.1504/IJESB.2014.064269.

Patel, Atish. 2014. "Everything You Wanted to Know about How India
Watches Porn in One Map and Five Charts." *Quartz India,* November 21.
https://qz.com/india/300478/everything-you-wanted-to-know-about
-how-india-watches-porn-in-one-map-and-five-charts/.

Pessoa, João. 2009. "Inclusion: The LAN House Revolution." *Paraíba Paradise.*
http://paraibaparadise.com/index.php/bureaucracy/politics-2/socio
-digital-inclusion-through-the-lan-house-revolution/.

Petrescu, Maria, John Gironda, and Pradeep Korgaonkar. 2017. "Online
Piracy versus Policy and Cultural Influencers." *International Journal of*

Marketing and Social Policy 1, no. 1: 3–13. https://doi.org/10.17501/23621044.2017.1102.

Phillipson, Robert. 1992. *Linguistic Imperialism.* Oxford: Oxford University Press.

Piketty, Thomas. 2014. *Capital in the Twenty-First Century.* Translated by Arthur Goldhammer. Cambridge, MA: Belknap Press of Harvard University Press.

Pimienta, Daniel, Daniel Prado, and Álvaro Blanco. 2009. "Twelve Years of Measuring Linguistic Diversity in the Internet: Balance and Perspectives." UNESCO Publications for the World Summit on the Information Society. http://unesdoc.unesco.org/images/0018/001870/187016e.pdf.

Pimpare, Stephen. 2008. *A People's History of Poverty in America.* New York: New Press.

Pinheiro-Machado, Rosana. 2012. "Copied Goods and the Informal Economy in Brazil and China: Outlining a Comparison of Development Models." *Vibrant: Virtual Brazilian Anthropology* 9, no. 1: 333–359.

———. 2017. *Counterfeit Itineraries in the Global South: The Human Consequences of Piracy in China and Brazil.* Abingdon, UK: Routledge.

"The Pirate Party." 2009. *Piratpartiet,* April 17. https://web.archive.org/web/20090417001447/http://www.piratpartiet.se/international/english.

"PokeWalk." n.d. https://www.pokewalk.com.

Poor, Nathaniel. 2012. "When Firms Encourage Copying: Cultural Borrowing as Standard Practice in Game Spaces." *International Journal of Communication* 6: 689–709.

Potter, Simon J. 2012. *Broadcasting Empire: The BBC and the British World, 1922–1970.* Oxford: Oxford University Press.

Prahalad, C. K. 2010. *The Fortune at the Bottom of the Pyramid: Eradicating Poverty through Profits.* 5th anniversary ed. Upper Saddle River, NJ: Wharton School.

Prahalad, C. K., and S. L. Hart. 2002. "The Fortune at the Bottom of the Pyramid." *Strategy + Business,* issue 26.

"Project DEFY." 2017. Hackaday.io. http://hackaday.io/project/11223-project-defy.

"Public Service Innovation Lab." 2017. United Nations Development Programme. http://www.undp.org/content/undp/en/home/ourwork/global-policy-centres/publicservice/PSI-Lab.html.

Pursell, Caroll. 2016. "Technology and Social Inequality." *Spontaneous Generations: A Journal for the History and Philosophy of Science* 8, no. 1: 22–26. https://doi.org/10.4245/sponge.v8i1.22610.

Radjou, Navi, and Jaideep Prabhu. 2015. *Frugal Innovation: How to Do More with Less*. London: The Economist / Profile Books.

Radjou, Navi, Jaideep Prabhu, and Simone Ahuja. 2012. *Jugaad Innovation: Think Frugal, Be Flexible, Generate Breakthrough Growth*. San Francisco: Jossey-Bass.

Raffel, Stanley. 2013. *The Method of Metaphor*. Bristol, UK: Intellect.

Ramos, R. R., Niall Hayes, and Monideepa Tarafdar. 2016. "Valuation Assemblages within Informal Markets in the Global South: The Case of Urban Piracy in Recife, Brazil." Paper presented at 6th Latin American and European Meeting on Organization Studies, April, Viña del Mar, Chile.

Rancière, Jacques. 1991. *The Ignorant Schoolmaster: Five Lessons in Intellectual Emancipation*. Translated by Kristin Ross. Stanford, CA: Stanford University Press.

Rangaswamy, Nimmi, and Payal Arora. 2015. "The Mobile Internet in the Wild and Every Day: Digital Leisure in the Slums of Urban India." *International Journal of Cultural Studies* 19, no. 6: 1–16. http://payalarora .com/Images/IJCS%20Final%20Paper-Rangaswamy-Arora%202015.pdf.

Rao, Rajiv. 2014. "How Semi-Literate Children in a Remote Indian Village Taught Themselves Molecular Biology." *ZDNet*, May 15. http://www .zdnet.com/article/how-semi-literate-children-in-a-remote-indian-village -taught-themselves-molecular-biology/.

Ravindran, Gopalan. 2010. "Mobile Phone Intimacies and Moral Panics in India." *Plaridel* 7, no. 2: 59–81.

Reckhow, Sarah, and Jeffrey W. Snyder. 2014. "The Expanding Role of Philanthropy in Education Politics." *Educational Researcher* 43, no. 4: 186–195. https://doi.org/10.3102/0013189X14536607.

Rennie, Ellie, Eleanor Hogan, Robin Gregory, Andrew Crouch, Alyson Wright, and Julian Thomas. 2016. *Internet on the Outstation: The Digital Divide and Remote Aboriginal Communities*. Edited by Miriam Rasch. Amsterdam: Institute of Network Cultures. http://networkcultures.org /wp-content/uploads/2016/06/TOD19-Internet-on-the-Outstation-INC .pdf.

Rich, Loic. 2008. "My Bizarre Childhood in Auroville." *The Week*, May 23. http://www.theweek.co.uk/26909/my-bizarre-childhood-auroville.

Richtel, Matt. 2012. "Young, in Love and Sharing Everything, Including a Password." *New York Times*, January 17. http://www.nytimes.com/2012 /01/18/us/teenagers-sharing-passwords-as-show-of-affection.html.

Rieland, Randy. 2014. "How Do Kids Learn Where There Are No Teachers? It May Take a Village . . . Computer." *Smithsonian,* December 9. http://www .smithsonianmag.com/innovation/how-do-kids-learn-where-there-are-no -teachers-it-may-take-village-computer-180953552/.

"Rio Favela Facts." 2015. CatComm.org. http://catcomm.org/favela-facts/.

Rix, Sally, and Stefan McElwee. 2016. "What Happens if Students Are Asked to Learn Geography Content, Specifically Population, through SOLE?" *Other Education: The Journal of Educational Alternatives* 5, no. 1: 30–54.

Roberts, Kenneth. 2006. *Leisure in Contemporary Society.* 2nd ed. Oxfordshire, UK: CABI.

Robinson, Melia. 2017. "Tech Billionaires Spent $170 Million on a New Kind of School—Now Classrooms Are Shrinking and Some Parents Say Their Kids Are 'Guinea Pigs.'" *Business Insider Nederland,* November 21. https:// www.businessinsider.nl/altschool-why-parents-leaving-2017-11/?inter national=true&r=US.

Rogerson, Christian M. 1996. "Urban Poverty and the Informal Economy in South Africa's Economic Heartland." *Environment & Urbanization* 8, no. 1: 167–179. https://doi.org/10.1177/095624789600800115.

Romance Scams: The Official Romance Scams Website. n.d. http://romance scams.org.

Rosenzweig, Roy. 1985. *Eight Hours for What We Will: Workers and Leisure in an Industrial City, 1870–1920.* Cambridge: Cambridge University Press.

Rudd, Chris. 2016. "Political Economy of the Media." In *Politics and the Media,* 2nd ed., edited by Geoff Kemp, Babak Bahador, Kate McMillan, and Chris Rudd, 38–54. Auckland: University of Auckland Press.

Rui, Jian, and Michael A. Stefanone. 2013. "Strategic Self-Presentation Online: A Cross-Cultural Study." *Computers in Human Behavior* 29, no. 1: 110–118. https://doi.org/10.1016/j.chb.2012.07.022.

Runde, Daniel. 2015. "M-Pesa and the Rise of the Global Mobile Money Market." *Forbes,* August 12. http://www.forbes.com/sites/danielrunde /2015/08/12/m-pesa-and-the-rise-of-the-global-mobile-money-market/.

Russell, B., 2014. *The Autobiography of Bertrand Russell.* New York: Routledge.

Said, Edward. 1978. *Orientalism.* New York: Vintage.

Sanchez, Daniel Adrian. 2016. "Disney Executive: 'I'm Going to Put It Out There. I Love Piracy' . . ." *Digital Music News,* September 20. http://www .digitalmusicnews.com/2016/09/20/samir-bangara-piracy-discovery/.

Sandner, Philipp. 2015. "Namibia Celebrates 25 Years of Independence and Democracy." *DW.COM,* March 20, sec. Africa. http://www.dw.com/en

/namibia-celebrates-25-years-of-independence-and-democracy/a
-18330787.

Santos, Karine Alves. 2012. "Teenage Pregnancy Contextualized: Understanding Reproductive Intentions in a Brazilian Shantytown." *Cadernos de Saúde Pública* 28, no. 4: 655–664. https://doi.org/10.1590/S0102
-311X2012000400005.

Sarkar, Sreela. 2016. "Beyond the 'Digital Divide': The 'Computer Girls' of Seelampur." *Feminist Media Studies* 16, no. 6: 968–983. https://doi.org/10
.1080/14680777.2016.1169207.

Satariano, Adam. 2017. "Silicon Valley Tried to Reinvent Schools. Now It's Rebooting." *Bloomberg Technology,* November 1. https://www.bloomberg
.com/news/articles/2017-11-01/silicon-valley-tried-to-reinvent-schools
-now-it-s-rebooting.

Sawhney, Harmeet. 2007. "Strategies for Increasing the Conceptual Yield of New Technologies Research." *Communication Monographs* 74, no. 3: 395–401. https://doi.org/10.1080/03637750701543527.

Scheuermann, Larry, and Gary Taylor. 1997. "Netiquette." *Internet Research* 7, no. 4: 269–273. https://doi.org/10.1108/10662249710187268.

School in the Cloud. n.d. https://www.theschoolinthecloud.org.

Schwittay, Anke. 2011. "New Media Practices in India: Bridging Past and Future, Markets and Development." *International Journal of Communication* 5 (February): 349–379.

Sengupta, Ramarko. 2017. "Jio Phone Will Be Available for an Effective Price of Rs 0: Ambani." *Times of India,* July 21. https://timesofindia.indiatimes
.com/business/india-business/ril-agm-jio-launches-affordable-4g-phone
/articleshow/59694582.cms.

Senior, Tom. 2011. "North Korea Deploys Squad of MMO Gold Farmers to Fund Regime." *PC Gamer,* August 8. http://www.pcgamer.com/north
-korea-deploys-squad-of-mmo-gold-farmers-to-fund-regime/.

Shahani, Parmesh. 2015. "Mumbai, the Ultimate Jugaad City." *The Hindu,* December 2. http://www.thehindu.com/opinion/op-ed/mumbai-the
-ultimate-jugaad-city/article7937636.ece.

Shihomeka, S., and Payal Arora. 2017a. "Mobile Phones and the Digital Divide: An Ethnographic Analysis of Youth Participation in Politics in the Ohangwena Region, Namibia." Paper presented at ETMAAL 2017 conference, 26–27 January, Tilburg, the Netherlands.

———. 2017b. "Mobile Social Media and Digital Literacy in Namibia's Regional Politics." Paper presented at Social Media in Africa: Beyond the

Hashtag workshop, 26–27 April, Centre of African Studies, University of Edinburgh.

Simanis, Erik. 2014. "Getting Base-of-the-Pyramid Projects Back to Business Fundamentals." Cornell Enterprise. http://eriksimanis.com/wp-content/uploads/2014/06/Simanis-Vantage-Point-Cornell-Enterprise-Spring-2014.pdf.

Smith, Aaron. 2016. "15% of American Adults Have Used Online Dating Sites or Mobile Dating Apps." Pew Research Center. http://www.pewinternet.org/files/2016/02/PI_2016.02.11_Online-Dating_FINAL.pdf.

Smith, Aaron, and Maeve Duggan. 2013. "Online Dating & Relationships." Pew Research Center. http://www.pewinternet.org/2013/10/21/online-dating-relationships/.

Solman, Paul. 2015. "Meet an Education Innovator Who Says Knowledge Is Becoming Obsolete." PBS NewsHour, November 13. http://www.pbs.org/newshour/making-sense/meet-an-education-innovator-who-says-knowledge-is-becoming-obsolete/.

Solon, Olivia. 2017. "'It's Digital Colonialism': How Facebook's Free Internet Service Has Failed Its Users," The Guardian, July 27. https://www.theguardian.com/technology/2017/jul/27/facebook-free-basics-developing-markets.

Spangler, T. 2018. "Global Piracy in 2017: TV and Music Illegal Activity Rose, While Film Declined." Variety, March 21. https://variety.com/2018/digital/news/piracy-global-2017-tv-music-film-illegal-streaming-1202731243/.

Srinivasan, Ramesh. 2017. Whose Global Village? Rethinking How Technology Shapes Our World. New York: New York University Press.

Statista. 2018. "Leading Countries Based on Number of Facebook Users as of May 2016 (in Millions)." https://www.statista.com/statistics/268136/top-15-countries-based-on-number-of-facebook-users/.

"Statistics and Facts about the Smartphone Market in China." n.d. Accessed on November 7, 2017. https://www.statista.com/topics/1416/smartphone-market-in-china/.

Statt, Nick. 2017. "'Sheeple' Is Now in the Dictionary, and Apple Users Are the Example." The Verge, April 28. https://www.theverge.com/tldr/2017/4/28/15473858/apple-merriam-webster-sheeple-definition-iphone-ipad.

Stefik, Mark J. 1996. Internet Dreams: Archetypes, Myths, and Metaphors. Cambridge, MA: MIT Press.

Swislow, Dan. 2014. "A Permanent Hacker Space in the Brazilian Congress." *Opening Parliament,* January 3. http://blog.openingparliament.org/post /72099651071/a-permanent-hacker-space-in-the-brazilian-congress.

Tassi, Paul. 2011. "Chinese Prisoners Forced to Farm World of Warcraft Gold." *Forbes,* June 2. http://www.forbes.com/sites/insertcoin/2011/06 /02/chinese-prisoners-forced-to-farm-world-of-warcraft-gold/.

Taylor, Alan. 2002. *American Colonies: The Settling of North America.* New York: Penguin.

Thomas, Kedron. 2013. "Brand 'Piracy' and Postwar Statecraft in Guatemala." *Cultural Anthropology* 28, no. 1: 140–160.

Tiitola-Meskanen, T. 2014. "A Mobile School in the Digital Era: Learning Environment Ecosystem Strategies for Challenging Locations and Extreme Poverty Contexts." In *Proceedings of the Annual Architectural Research Symposium in Finland,* Oulu, Finland, October, 292–304. https:// journal.fi/atut/article/view/47968.

Tiwari, Rajnish, and Cornelius Herstatt. 2013. "'Too Good' to Succeed? Why Not Just Try 'Good Enough'! Some Deliberations on the Prospects of Frugal Innovations." Working Paper, Technologie- und Innovationsmanagement, Technische Universität Hamburg-Harburg, no. 76. http://hdl .handle.net/10419/85347.

Toma, Catalina L., and Jeffrey T. Hancock. 2012. "What Lies Beneath: The Linguistic Traces of Deception in Online Dating Profiles." *Journal of Communication* 62, no. 1: 78–97. https://doi.org/10.1111/j.1460-2466 .2011.01619.x.

Toness, Bianca Vázquez. 2014. "India Building Database to Unite Records for 1.2 Billion." *Bloomberg Technology,* December 10. https://www .bloomberg.com/news/articles/2014-12-10/india-building-database-to -unite-records-for-12-billion.

Toyama, Kentaro. 2015. *Geek Heresy: Rescuing Social Change from the Cult of Technology.* New York: PublicAffairs.

Traxler, John. 2011. "Mobile Learning: Starting in the Right Place, Going in the Right Direction?" *International Journal of Mobile and Blended Learning* 3, no. 2: 57–67.

Treverton, Gregory F., Carl F. Matthies, Karla J. Cunningham, Jeremiah Goulka, Greg Ridgeway, and Anny Wong. 2009. "Film Piracy, Organized Crime, and Terrorism." Rand Corporation. http://www.rand.org/pubs /monographs/MG742.html.

Tucker, Catherine E. 2014. "Social Networks, Personalized Advertising, and Privacy Controls." *Journal of Marketing Research* 51, no. 5: 546–562. https://doi.org/10.1509/jmr.10.0355.

Turner, Camilla. 2015. "Girls Do Better than Boys at School, despite Inequality." *The Telegraph,* January 22, sec. Education. http://www.telegraph.co.uk/education/11364130/Girls-do-better-than-boys-at-school-despite-inequality.html.

"The 2016 Conference on Inclusive Capitalism." 2017. Coalition for Inclusive Capitalism. http://www.inc-cap.com/conferences/conference-2016/general/.

"United Nations Documents on Piracy." 2012. United Nations Division for Ocean Affairs and the Law of the Sea. http://www.un.org/depts/los/piracy/piracy_documents.htm.

"Unlocking Relevant Web Content for the Next 4 Billion People." 2014. GSMA and the Mozilla Foundation. http://www.gsma.com/mobilefordevelopment/wp-content/uploads/2016/02/Unlocking-relevant-Web-content-for-the-next-4-billion.pdf.

"Up for Slum Dwellers—Transforming a Billion Lives Campaign Unveiled in Europe." 2016. *UN-Habitat,* July 2. https://unhabitat.org/up-for-slum-dwellers-transforming-a-billion-lives-campaign-unveiled-in-europe/.

Urban Design Research Institute, Mumbai, India. 2017. http://www.udri.org/.

Ushahidi. 2017. https://www.ushahidi.com/.

Vaidhyanathan, Siva. 2003. *Copyrights and Copywrongs: The Rise of Intellectual Property and How It Threatens Creativity.* New York: New York University Press.

Van Deursen, Alexander, Ellen Helsper, Rebecca Eynon, and Jan van Dijk. 2017. "The Compoundness and Sequentiality of Digital Inequality." *International Journal of Communication* 11: 452–473.

Van Deursen, Alexander, and Jan van Dijk. 2013. "The Digital Divide Shifts to Differences in Usage." *New Media & Society* 16, no. 3: 507–526. https://doi.org/10.1177/1461444813487959.

Vaswani, Karishma. 2016. "Designed in China: Can China Innovate?" *BBC News,* June 17, sec. Business. http://www.bbc.com/news/business-36550128.

Vázquez, Irene Serrano, and Mia Consalvo. 2013. "Cheating in Social Network Games." *New Media & Society* 17, no. 6: 829–844. https://doi.org/10.1177/1461444813516835.

Vidal, John. 2004. "Things Grow Better with Coke." *The Guardian,* November 2, sec. World News. https://www.theguardian.com/world/2004/nov/02/india.johnvidal.

Vygotsky, L. S. 1978. *Mind in Society.* Cambridge, MA: Harvard University Press.

Wagner, Daniel A. 1989. "Literacy Campaigns: Past, Present, and Future." *Comparative Education Review* 33, no. 2: 256–260.

Wakefield, Jane. 2012. "Granny Army Helps India's School Children via the Cloud." *BBC News,* April 30, sec. Technology. http://www.bbc.com/news/technology-17114718.

Warschauer, Mark. 2003. *Technology and Social Inclusion: Rethinking the Digital Divide.* Cambridge, MA: MIT Press.

Webb, Justin W., R. Duane Ireland, and David J. Ketchen Jr. 2014. "Toward a Greater Understanding of Entrepreneurship and Strategy in the Informal Economy." *Strategic Entrepreneurship Journal* 8, no. 1: 1–15. https://doi.org/10.1002/sej.1176.

West, Darrell. 2015. *Going Mobile: How Wireless Technology Is Reshaping Our Lives.* Washington, DC: Brookings Institution Press.

"What Is Lara?" 2017. Lara-Learning. http://www.laralearning.org.

Williams, Colin C. 2014. "The Informal Economy and Poverty: Evidence and Policy Review." SSRN Scholarly Paper ID 2404259. York, UK: Joseph Rowntree Foundation. https://papers.ssrn.com/abstract=2404259.

Wilson, Jamia. 2013. "From the Hole in the Wall to Yale: A Q&A with Arun Chavan." *TED Blog,* March 11. http://blog.ted.com/from-the-hole-in-the-wall-to-yale-a-qa-with-arun-chavan/.

Wilson, Robert E., Samuel D. Gosling, and Lindsay T. Graham. 2012. "A Review of Facebook Research in the Social Sciences." *Perspectives on Psychological Science* 7, no. 3: 203–220. https://doi.org/10.1177/174569 1612442904.

Wiseman, Rosalind. 2009. *Queen Bees and Wannabes: Helping Your Daughter Survive Cliques, Gossip, Boyfriends, and the New Realities of Girl World.* New York: Random House.

Women and the Web: Bridging the Internet Gap and Creating New Global Opportunities in Low and Middle-Income Countries. 2012. Intel and Dalberg. http://www.intel.com/content/dam/www/public/us/en/documents/pdf/women-and-the-web.pdf.

"Women Shaming in Africa and the Descent into Barbarism." 2014. Afritorial, November 15. http://afritorial.com/women-shaming-in-africa-and-the-descent-into-barbarism/.

"World Internet Project." 2014. *Oxford Internet Surveys—OxIS,* October 27. http://oxis.oii.ox.ac.uk/research/world-internet-project/.

Wu, Jasmine. 2016. "Hackers Create Apps for Global Development." *Huntington News,* February 18. https://huntnewsnu.com/2016/02/hackers-create -app-for-global-development/.

Wu, Wen-Hsiung, Yen-Chun Jim Wu, Chun-Yu Chen, Hao-Yun Kao, Che-Hung Lin, and Sih-Han Huang. 2012. "Review of Trends from Mobile Learning Studies: A Meta-Analysis." *Computers & Education* 59, no. 2: 817–827.

Wyche, Susan P., Andrea Forte, and Sarita Yardi Schoenebeck. 2013. "Hustling Online: Understanding Consolidated Facebook Use in an Informal Settlement in Nairobi." In *Proceedings of the SIGCHI 2013 Conference on Human Factors in Computing Systems,* 2823–2832, April 27–May 2. Paris: ACM.

Xiao, Cao, David Mandell Freeman, and Theodore Hwa. 2015. "Detecting Clusters of Fake Accounts in Online Social Networks." In *Proceedings of the 8th ACM Workshop on Artificial Intelligence and Security,* 91–101. Denver: ACM. https://doi.org/10.1145/2808769.2808779.

Yemi, Frank. 2016. "Rio 2016 Olympics Problems: Kidnappings, the Disastrous Athletes' Village, Zika Fears, and Crime." *Inquisitr News,* July 28. http://www.inquisitr.com/3357029/rio-2016-olympics-problems -kidnappings-the-disastrous-athletes-village-zika-fears-and-crime/.

Young, Jason. 2013. *China's Hukou System: Markets, Migrants and Institutional Change.* Basingstoke, UK: Palgrave Macmillan.

Zhao, Elaine Jing, and Michael Keane. 2013. "Between Formal and Informal: The Shakeout in China's Online Video Industry." *Media, Culture & Society* 35, no. 6: 724–741. https://doi.org/10.1177/0163443713491301.

Zickuhr, Kathryn. 2013. "Location-Based Services." Pew Research Center: Internet, Science & Tech, September 12. http://www.pewinternet.org /2013/09/12/location-based-services/.

Zuckerberg, Mark. 2015. "We Just Launched Internet.org in India." Facebook, February 10. https://www.facebook.com/zuck/posts/101018992 23817041:0.

Acknowledgments

As with all books, this work was not created in isolation. I am grateful to a number of people and institutions who have aided me over these years. My long-standing collaboration with the anthropologist Nimmi Rangaswamy in the area of mobile phone use in Indian slums has enriched my approach to digital inequality and ingenuity among the poor. My more recent partnerships with the anthropologist Laura Scheiber in low-income communities in Brazil and Sadrag Panduleni Shihomeka on political engagement in rural Namibia helped bring my arguments to life with nuanced narratives from these much-neglected contexts. I am thankful to a number of people for their encouragement regarding the book, including Arjun Appadurai, Radhika Gajjala, Jonathan Gray, Richard Heeks, Marwan Kraidy, Ronaldo Lemos, Punya Mishra, Richard Rogers, Daya Thussu, Padraig Tobin, Sahana Udupa, and Liesbet van Zoonen.

My global policy fellowship at the Institute for Technology & Society (ITS) in Rio de Janeiro provided invaluable exposure to influential private and public actors concerned with internet governance and social justice in Brazil. My research affiliation with Richard Heek's Development Implications of Digital Economies (DIODE) Strategic Research Network broadened my view of how digital technologies are being used beyond the West. My home institution, Erasmus University Rotterdam, gave me the support needed to complete this project.

I would like to offer a special thank-you to my editor, Sharmila Sen, for her tireless work on the manuscript, which undoubtedly improved the quality of the text. She is a reminder of what a true editor looks like, one who really pushes you to the limits because she cares. I am appreciative of the ongoing support of Heather Hughes, associate editor, and the thoughtful feedback from the anonymous reviewers who helped me to further strengthen my argument.

When times got tough, my friends provided me with much-needed respite over good food and wine, and my family, with their tireless championing of my abilities, helped me move forward. When a major health issue hit me during the writing process, my partner, René König, helped me recuperate with his endless patience and support. Thank you, René.

Index